IMAGES
of Sports

HARVARD FOOTBALL

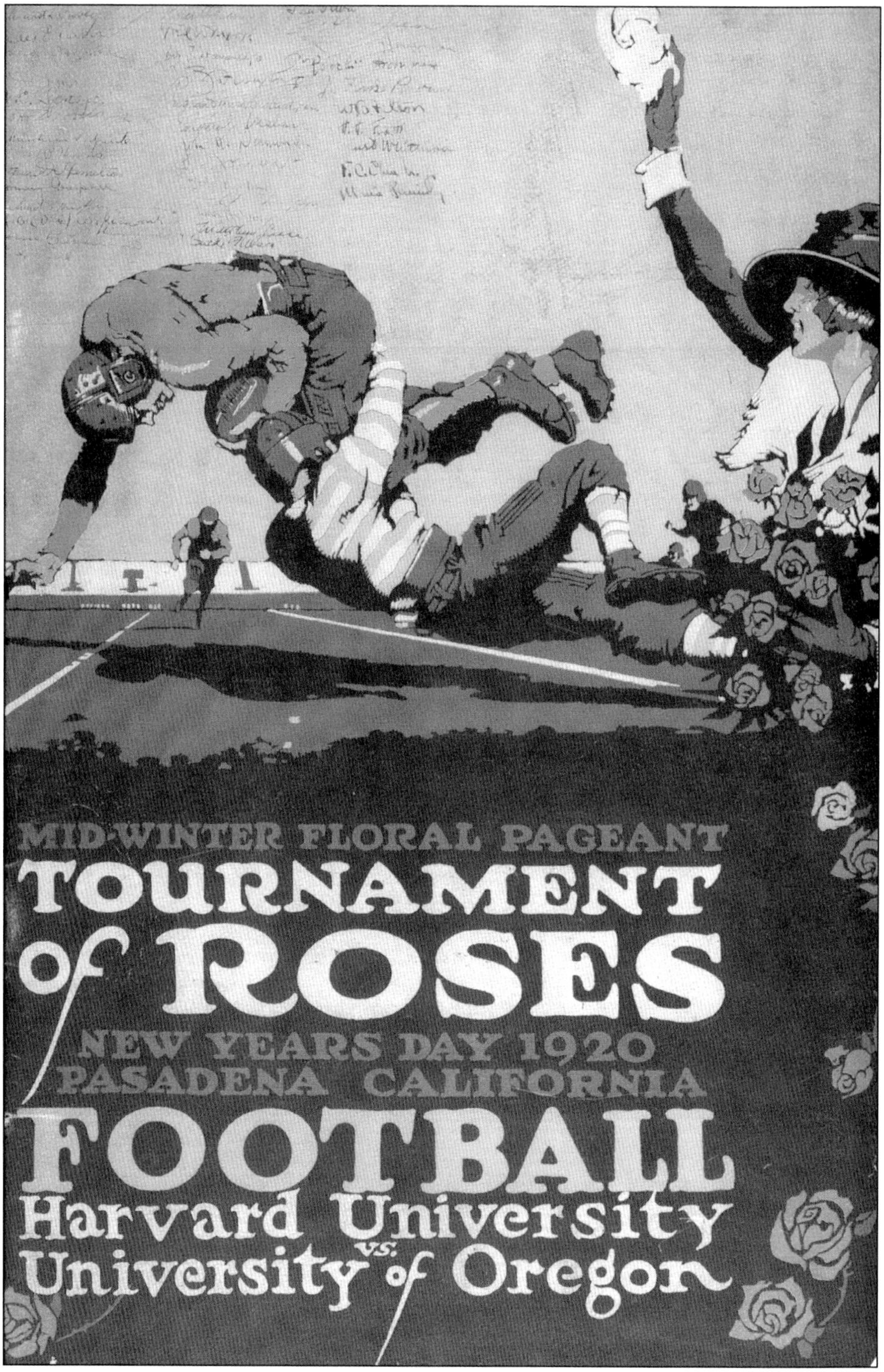

THE 1920 ROSE BOWL PROGRAM COVER. Everything came up roses for the 1919 Crimson football team. The trip to Pasadena was a successful one, as Harvard secured the last of its seven national championships with a 7-6 victory over Oregon. The ornate design pictured is taken from the game's original program cover.

IMAGES
of Sports

HARVARD FOOTBALL

Bernard M. Corbett

ARCADIA
PUBLISHING

ISBN 978-0-7385-1074-3

Published by Arcadia Publishing
Charleston, South Carolina

Printed in the United States of America

Library of Congress Control Number: 2002107357

For all general information, please contact Arcadia Publishing:
Telephone 843-853-2070
Fax 843-853-0044
E-mail sales@arcadiapublishing.com
For customer service and orders:
Toll-Free 1-888-313-2665

Visit us on the Internet at www.arcadiapublishing.com

Contents

Acknowledgments 6

Introduction 7

1. 1874–1918 9
2. 1919–1940 23
3. 1941–1956 39
4. 1957–1967 53
5. 1968–1970 71
6. 1971–1979 81
7. 1980–1989 91
8. 1990–1999 103
9. 2000–2001 125

ACKNOWLEDGMENTS

Sincere thanks go to Harvard University sports information director John Veneziano and Harvard Varsity Club director Bob Glatz for making this project a reality.

Introduction

When Princeton, Rutgers, Yale, and Columbia convened to draw up the first intercollegiate "football" rules in 1873, Harvard declined the invitation to participate.

The men of Harvard had been playing a game more closely resembling what we now know as American football almost a half-century earlier. The rules agreed to by the aforementioned schools formalized competition for a game that most closely resembled soccer: use of the hands in passing, dribbling, or carrying the ball was not allowed.

Although widely criticized at the time, Harvard's decision soon led to the men's first intercollegiate competition playing the more rugbylike game they preferred. Thus, a two-game series with McGill University of Montreal, Quebec, is acknowledged by many as football's true beginning, not the Princeton versus Rutgers match in 1869. The debate continues to the present day.

What cannot be disputed is the fact that 10 days after the first Harvard-Yale football game in 1875, representatives from Princeton and Columbia joined the Crimson and the Eli to form the Intercollegiate Football Association. The Harvard playing rules became the standard.

Since those long bygone days, Harvard football and "first" have continued to be synonymous. In 1881, Harvard hosted Michigan at Boston's South End Grounds in the first East-West intersectional football game. Captain Arthur T. Cumnock led the team in drills on March 14, 1889, conducting the first ever spring practice. On November 22, 1890, Harvard captured its first of seven national championships, defeating Yale. The 1893 Penn game on Thanksgiving Day featured the first use of a football scoreboard, and on November 14, 1903, Harvard Stadium, first cousin to the Roman Coliseum, opened. The magnificent edifice became the first permanent concrete stadium in the country. Nearing its 100th anniversary, the stadium still remains the proud home of Harvard football.

The golden age of Crimson football can be traced back to the legendary Percy Haughton's amazing nine-year tenure (1908–1916) as head coach. Led by numerous All-Americans such as Charlie Brickley '15, Harvard compiled an imposing record of 71-7-5 and won three national titles. The last Crimson national crown was won by virtue of a 7-6 victory over Oregon in the 1920 Rose Bowl.

Harvard has had the good fortune of being led by three worthy heirs to the Haughton legacy of gridiron excellence in Ivy League play. John Yovicisin (1957–1970) led Harvard to its first Ivy League title in 1961. The congenial coach compiled a career record of 78-42-5 (.644) and was on the "winning" side in the most renowned of all the Games (the name adopted for the annual Harvard-Yale gridiron match): the 29-29 tie with Yale in 1968.

The innovative Joe Restic (1971–1993) followed Yovy. His intricate "multiflex" offense produced back-to-back Ivy championships in 1974 and 1975. Restic retired as Harvard's coach with the most all-time wins—117 victories in Cambridge.

Current Crimson coach Tim Murphy (1994–present) has guided the program to lofty heights. He has consistently exhibited a keen awareness of upholding the unique tradition of Harvard football. His (9-1) championship team in 1997 virtually rewrote the Harvard record book for both team and individual achievement.

Through the past eight decades, the Crimson has had its share of heroes. The incomparable Barry Wood '32, an All-American quarterback and three-sport standout, was challenged a generation later by halfback Dick Clasby '52, another nine-letter winner for the title of Harvard's All-Time Greatest Athlete. The All-American honors list has included guard Endicott "Chub" Peabody '42 (who went on to become governor of Massachusetts), and most recently Pat McInally '75, a Super Bowl participant who went on to star for the National Football League's Cincinnati Bengals.

From the time of its formation in 1956, the Ivy League has placed the original ideals of college athletics at its forefront. As a charter member of the league, Harvard has been an annual contender for Ivy honors, finishing in the top three 25 times. Since 1961, 10 seasons have culminated with championship dreams becoming reality.

The 2001 Harvard Ivy League championship football team ascended to a level unattained for some 88 years. The Crimson's 9-0-0 season brought the word "perfect" back into the Harvard football lexicon for the first time since 1913.

An unmatched tradition and legacy of innovation is sustained each autumn when a fledgling squad of Crimson-clad players runs onto the stadium turf. Under the direction of coach Tim Murphy, the third century of Crimson football has auspiciously begun.

One

1874–1918

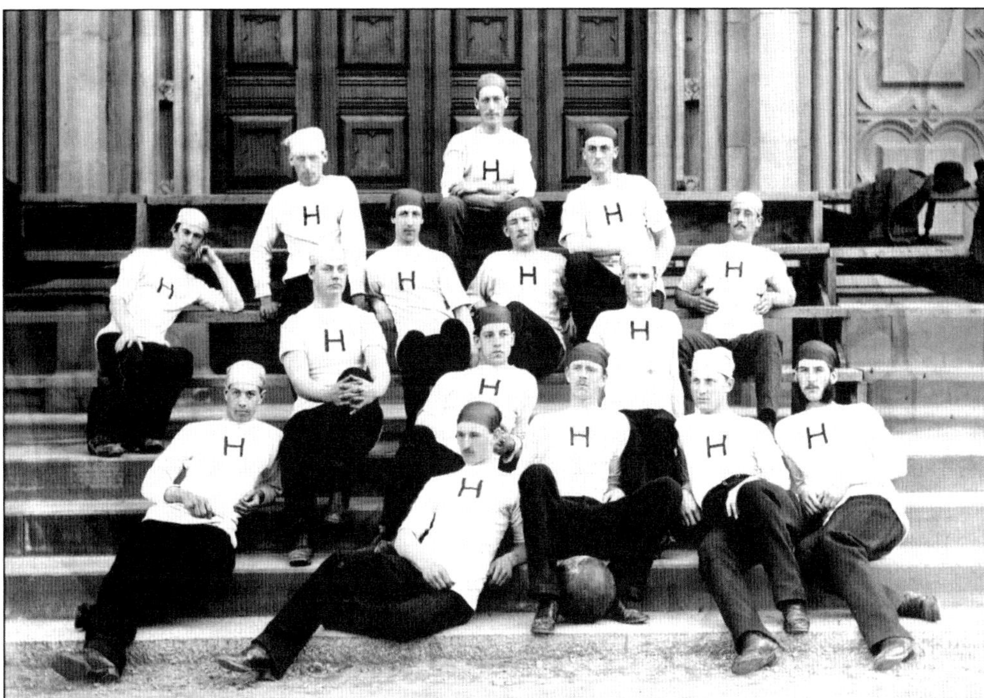

THE 1874 TEAM. Harvard's first intercollegiate football team poses for a portrait. The 1874 club played a return engagement versus McGill in Montreal on October 23, 1874, and won the match by a score of 3-0. The Crimson did not compete again until the following June, losing to Tufts at Jarvis Field.

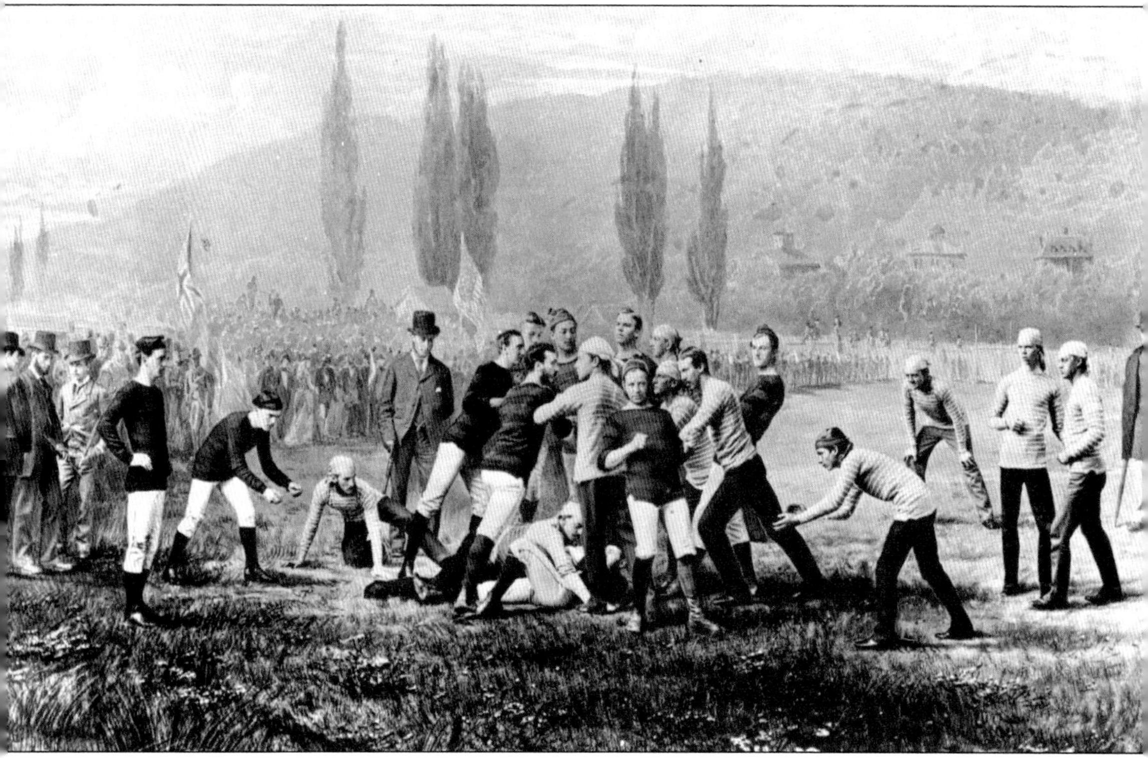

MAY 14 AND 15, 1874. Harvard received a challenge from the football club of McGill University, Montreal, during the winter of 1874. The proposal called for two games to be played—one by the early rules of American football and the other by the rugby rules familiar to the McGill team. The first game was won by Harvard 3-0, and the second ended in a scoreless tie. The games were played on campus at Jarvis Field.

W.A. BROOKS '87. W.A. Brooks captained the 1886 Harvard team, bringing the season to a record of 12-2. The team won all 12 by shutout and only allowed points in losses to Princeton (12-0) and Yale (29-4). Brooks later became the Harvard coach for one season in 1894, guiding the Crimson to an 11-2 record.

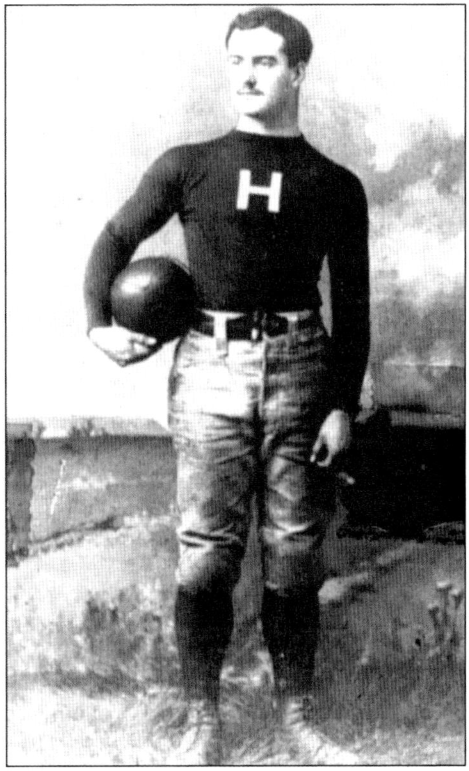

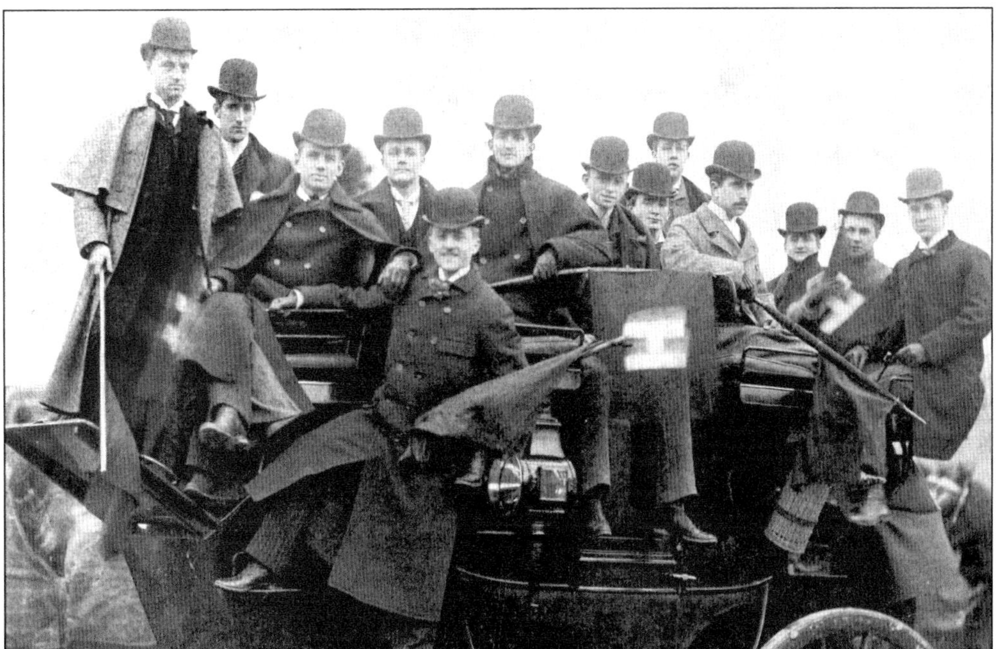

THE 1887 FANS. As long as there has been football, there have been football fans. A group of students armed with umbrellas for inclement weather takes up a perch on a field-side carriage to cheer on the Crimson in an 1887 game.

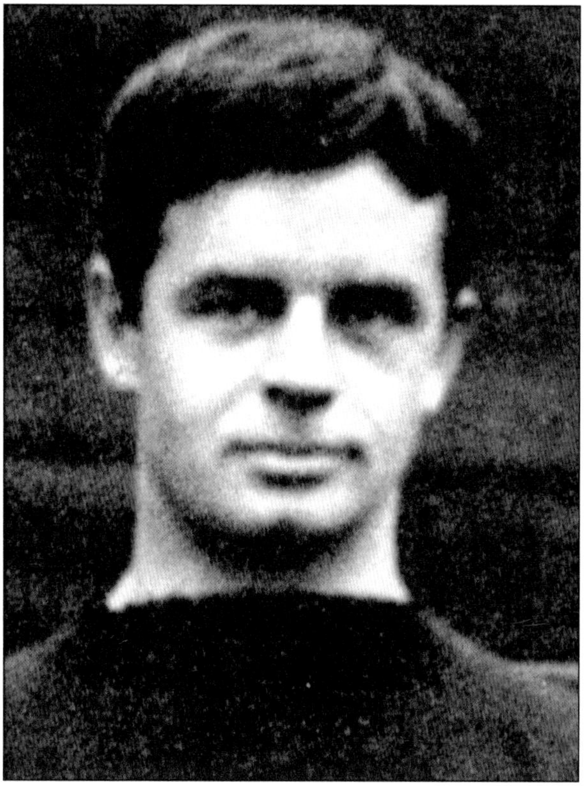

Charles D. Daly '01. Quarterback Charley Daly was a Crimson standout. A Walter Camp All-American for three consecutive years (1898–1900), Daly played on Harvard teams that combined for a record of 31-1-1. The 151-pound Daly captained the 1900 Crimson squad that ended with a record of 10-1, outscoring its opponents 205-44.

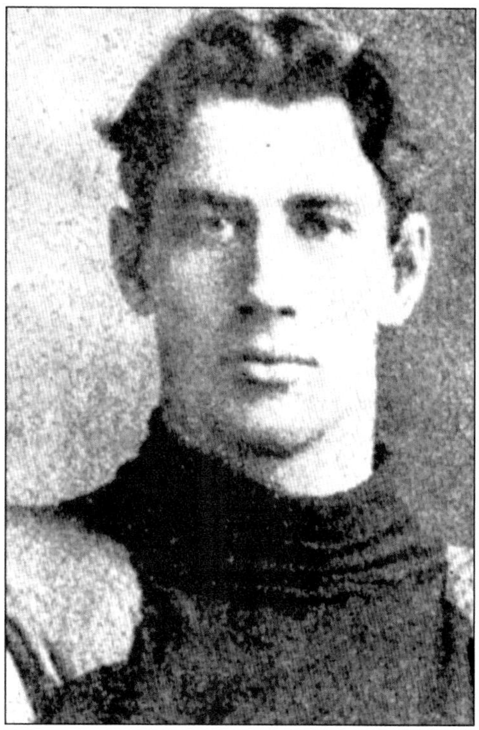

David C. Campbell '02. End David Campbell also attained Walter Camp All-American honors for three consecutive years. The captain of the 1901 team that shut out Yale 22-0 at Soldiers Field, avenging a shutout loss the previous year in New Haven, Campbell and his Crimson teammates triumphed over the Eli without making a single substitution in the game.

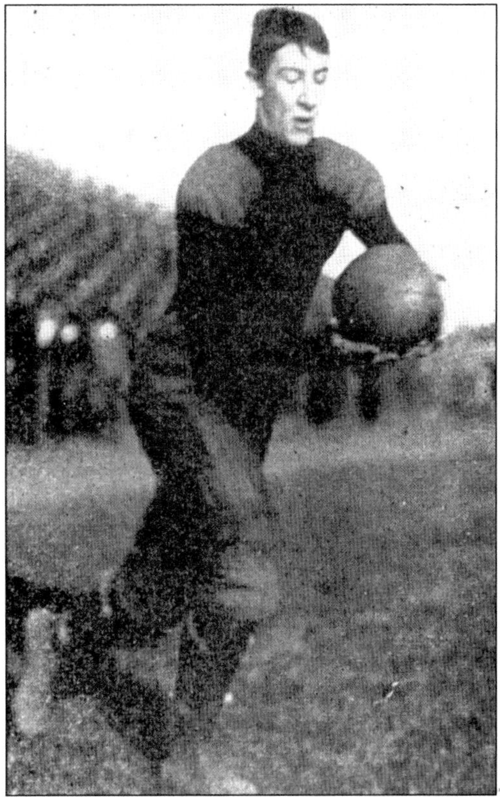

William T. Reid '01. Fullback Bill Reid became the first Harvard player to score two touchdowns against Yale in the 1898 game, a 17-0 Crimson victory. After missing his senior year with a leg injury, Reid became the coach of the 1901 undefeated (12-0) championship team. Reid returned to his native California for three years and then came back to coach Harvard again in 1905 and 1906, combining for an 18-3-1 record. Reid helped prevent Harvard from abolishing football in 1905, when many schools were considering termination of the sport due to rough play. Coach Reid served on the first National Collegiate Athletic Association (NCAA) Rules Committee, along with Walter Camp (Yale) and Amos Alonzo Stagg (University of Chicago), which led to the establishment of the forward pass. Reid rewrote the rule book that was later edited by Camp.

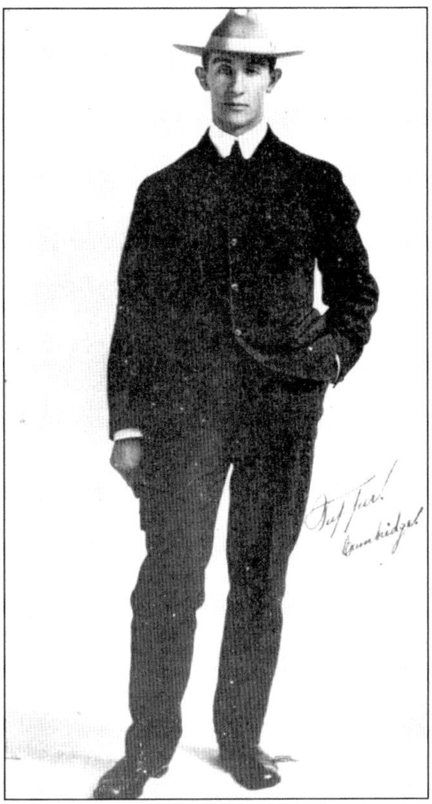

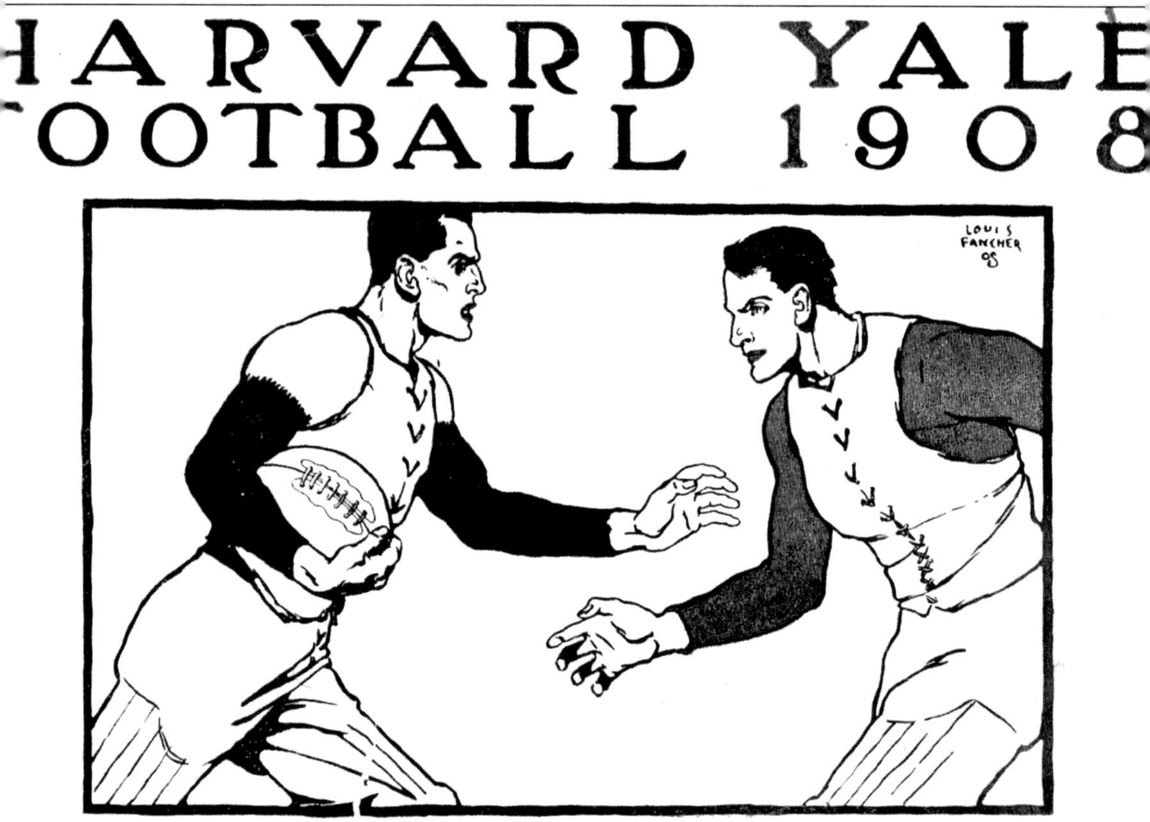

The 1908 Program Cover. Almost 100 years later, it is still about competition and winning the one-on-one battles within the game. The 1908 program cover for the Harvard-Yale game gives an accurate depiction of the far-less-protected look of the players of the day. Harvard defeated Yale 4-0 in New Haven to keep coach Percy Haughton's rookie season perfect.

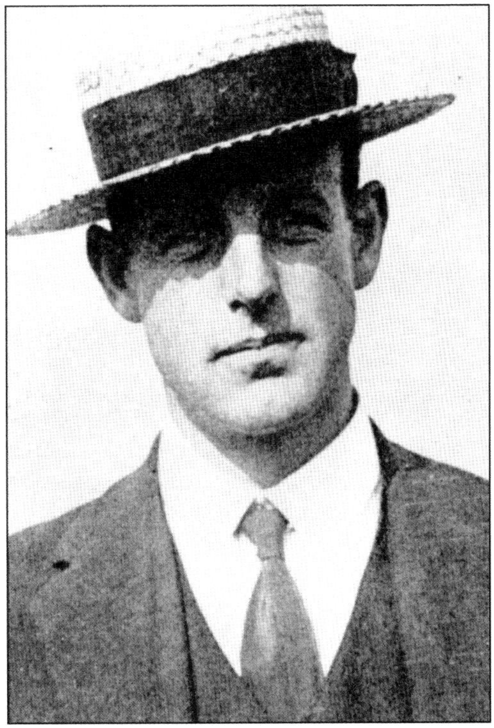

Percy Haughton '99. A second-team All-American tackle and premier punter on the undefeated (11-0) 1898 club, Percy Haughton became head coach of the Crimson in 1908, ushering in the golden era of Harvard football. His teams, noted for their power and cunning, compiled a nine-season record of 71-7-5 (.886). A depiction of Haughton kneeling and observing is among the icons adorning the outer walls of Harvard Stadium.

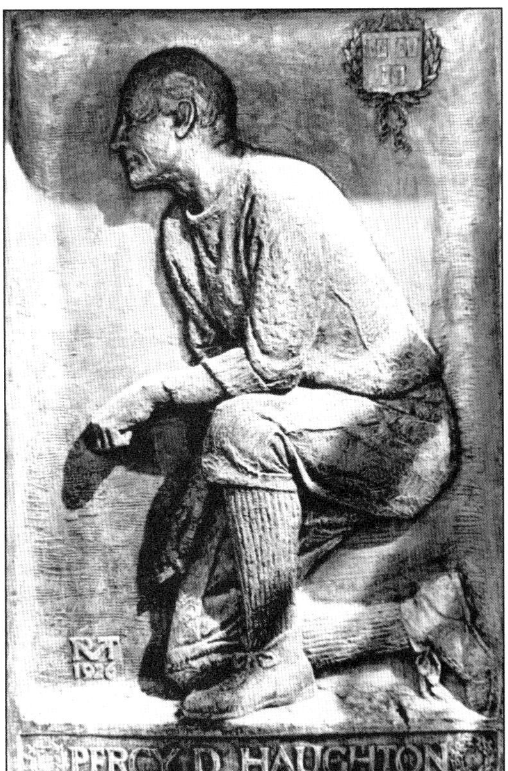

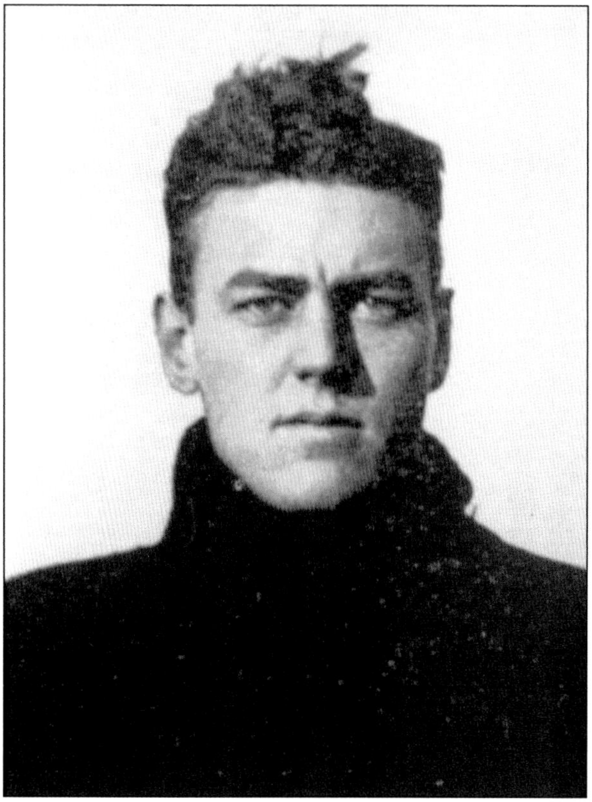

Hamilton Fish '10. A two-time All-American (1908, 1909), Hamilton Fish was an imposing six-foot-four-inch 200-pound tackle. He was one of coach Percy Haughton's first captains, playing on teams that only allowed a combined 25 points during his final two varsity seasons. Fish was later elected to Walter Camp's All-Time All-American Team. A decorated World War I veteran, Fish served as a congressman from New York's Hudson Valley for 24 years. A vigorous man who passed away in January 1995 at the age of 102, Fish attended the Harvard-Princeton game in 1990.

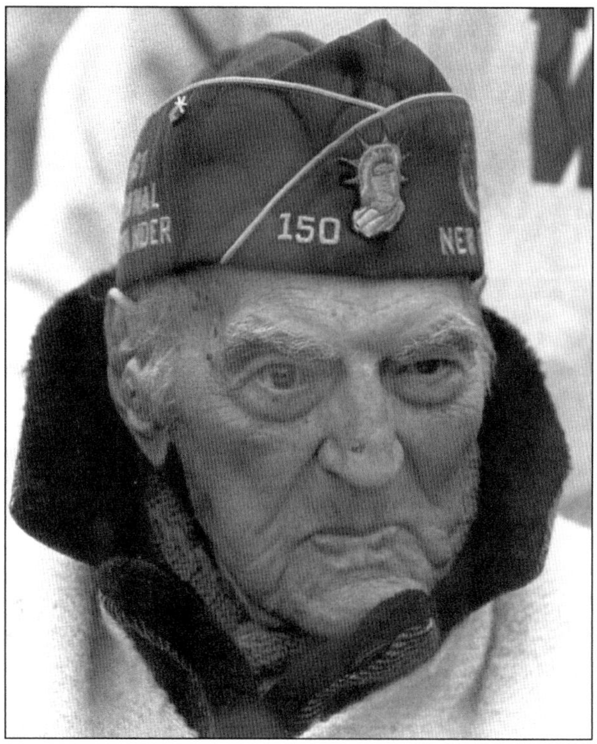

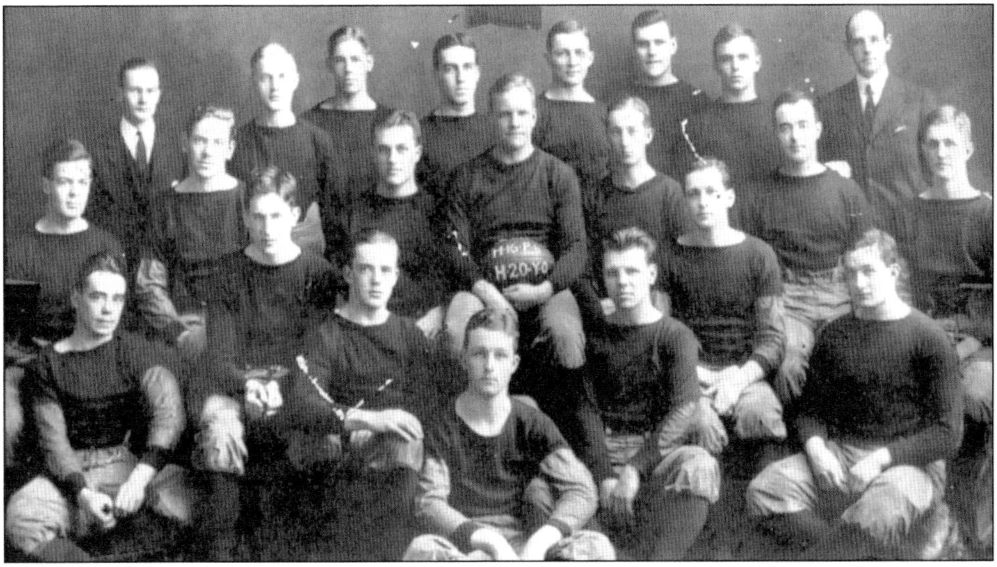

THE 1912 TEAM. The 1912 team posted the first of two consecutive perfect (9-0) seasons. All-American fullback and captain Percy Wendell's team cruised to the Big Three title, with wins over Princeton (16-6) and Yale (20-0), sacrificing just 22 points the entire season. The one intersectional game at Harvard Stadium was a visit from Vanderbilt, which resulted in a 9-3 Harvard victory in the only game ever played between the two schools. Halfback Charlie Brickley, end Sam Felton, center Derrick Parmenter, and guard Stanley Pennock all attained Walter Camp All-American recognition.

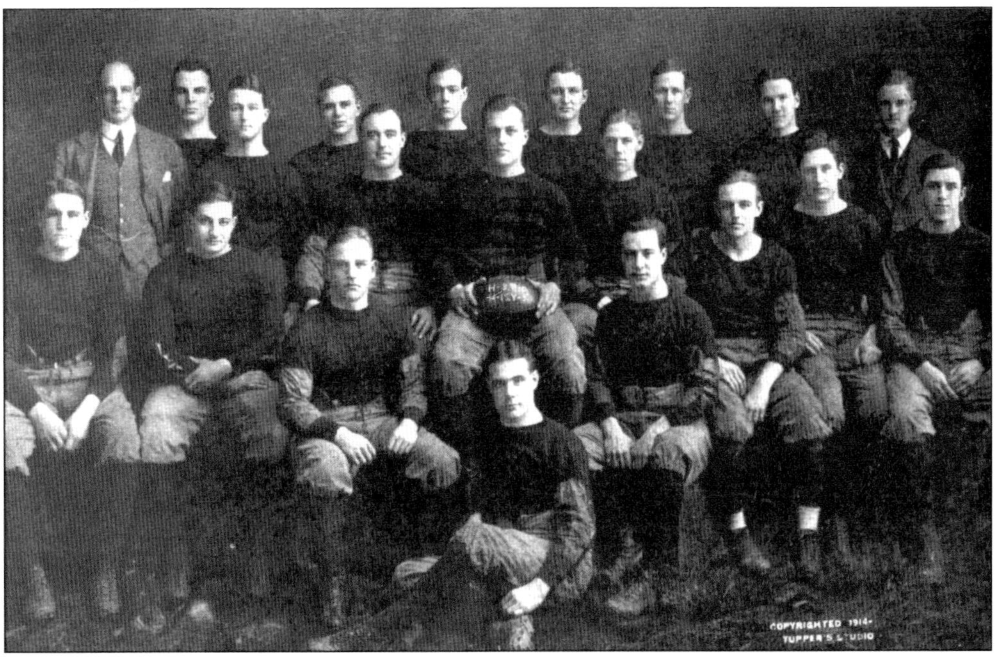

THE 1913 TEAM. The 1913 squad steamrolled opponents en route to a perfect season. Only Cornell and Holy Cross were able to cross the Harvard goal line, as the Crimson outscored opponents by a 225-21 margin. Halfback Eddie Mahan and guard Stan Pennock joined the incomparable Brickley on the Walter Camp All-American team.

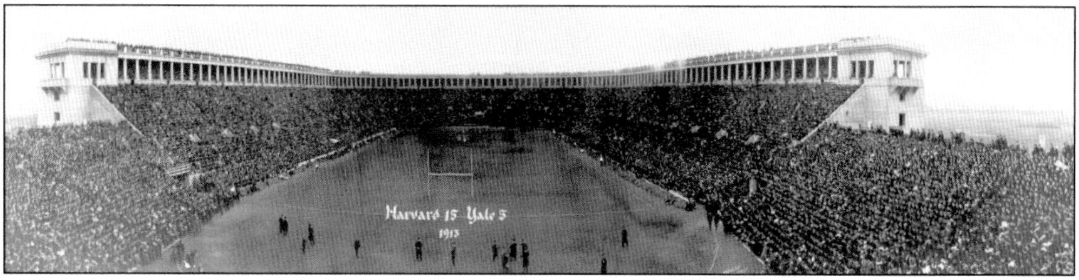

Harvard 15, Yale 5 (1913). Charlie Brickley accounted for all the Crimson points in the 1913 15-5 victory over Yale. Brickley's drop kicks were converted from 35, 38, 32, and 24 yards out. His one successful placement in three attempts came from 40 yards away.

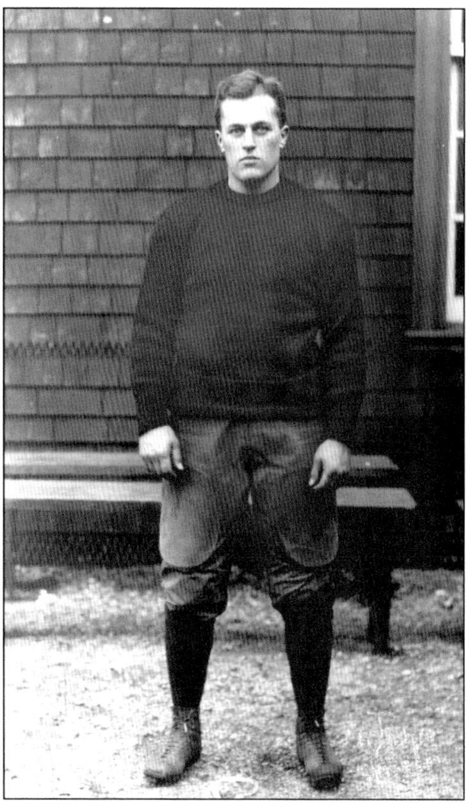

Bob Storer '14. A Walter Camp All-American tackle his senior year, Bob Storer had the distinction of captaining the last undefeated, untied Crimson team (9-0) until the 2001 team matched the feat.

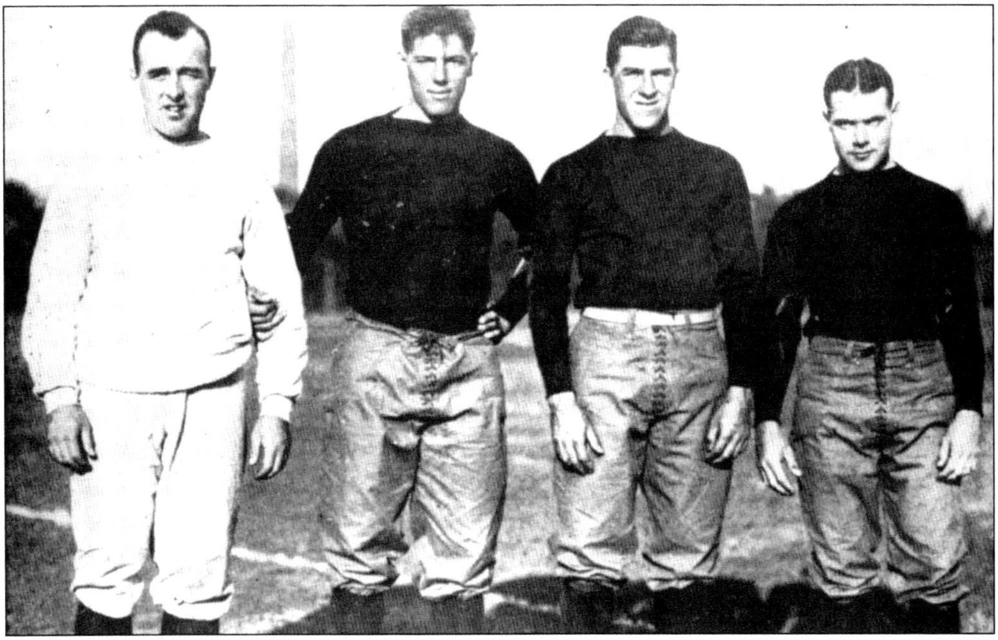

NOVEMBER 21, 1914. Pictured here are Charlie Brickley '15, Tack Hardwick '15, Eddie Mahan '16, and Mal Logan '15. The Crimson, featured here prior to playing the first Harvard-Yale game at the Yale Bowl, handed the Eli its worst ever beating (36-0) on November 21. In the aftermath, the newspapers hailed Haughton's team as "the perfect machine" and "Harvard's greatest 11."

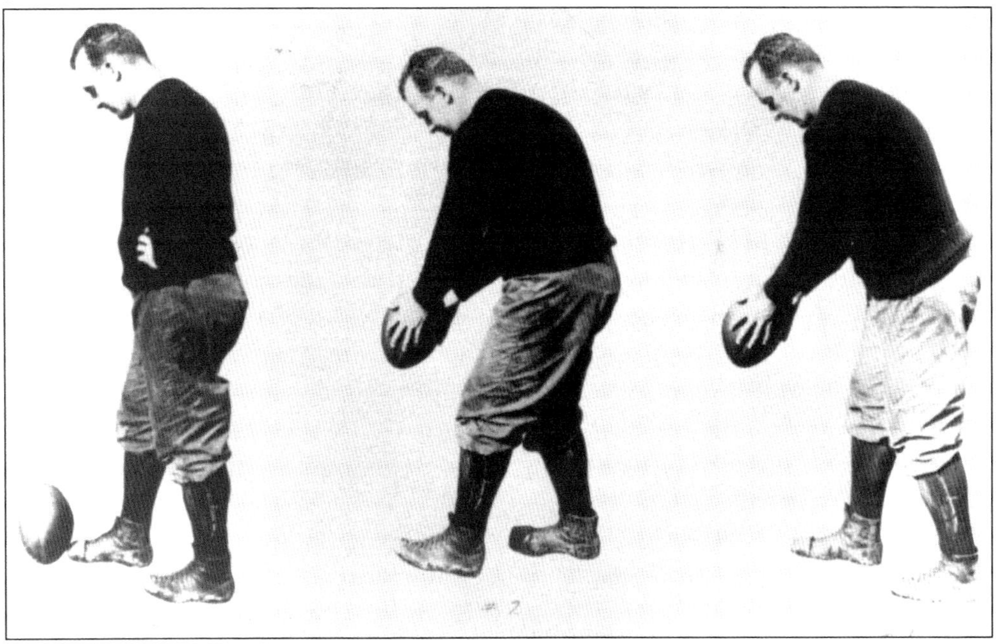

CHARLIE BRICKLEY '15. A two-time (1912, 1913) Walter Camp All-American at the halfback position, local hero (Everett, Massachusetts, High School) Charlie Brickley's mastery of the drop kick became a centerpiece of the Harvard offense. His 13 field goals in 1913 remain the Crimson's all-time one-season mark.

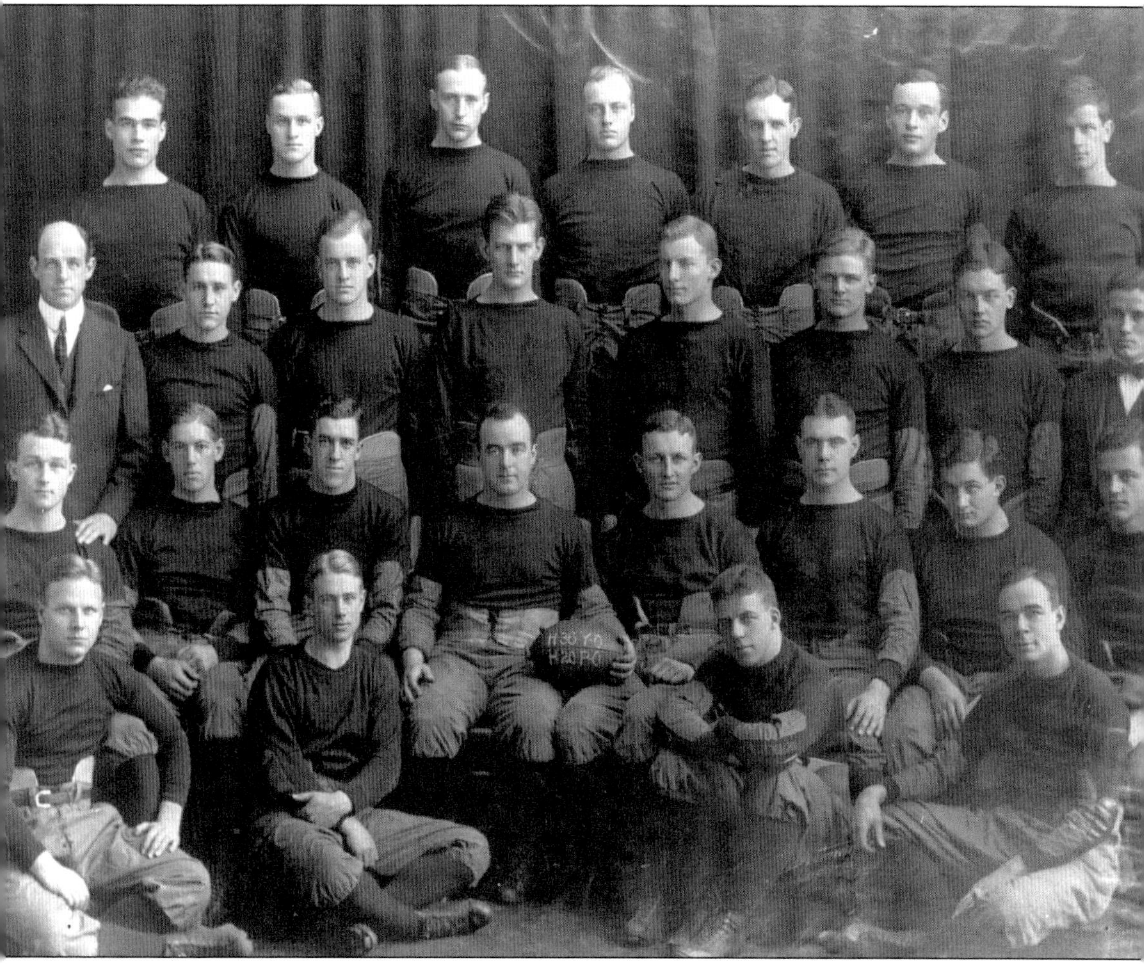

THE 1914 TEAM. The 1914 team rolled to a 7-0-2 record, including a 7-0 victory over Michigan. Penn State (13-13) and Brown (0-0) were able to tie the Crimson. The loss of All-American halfback Charlie Brickley to appendicitis in early October ended his season except for a brief appearance versus Yale. Five Harvard players attained All-American status: guard Stan Pennock (third consecutive year), fullback Eddie Mahan, end Tack Hardwick, tackle Walter Trumbull, and halfback Fred Bradlee.

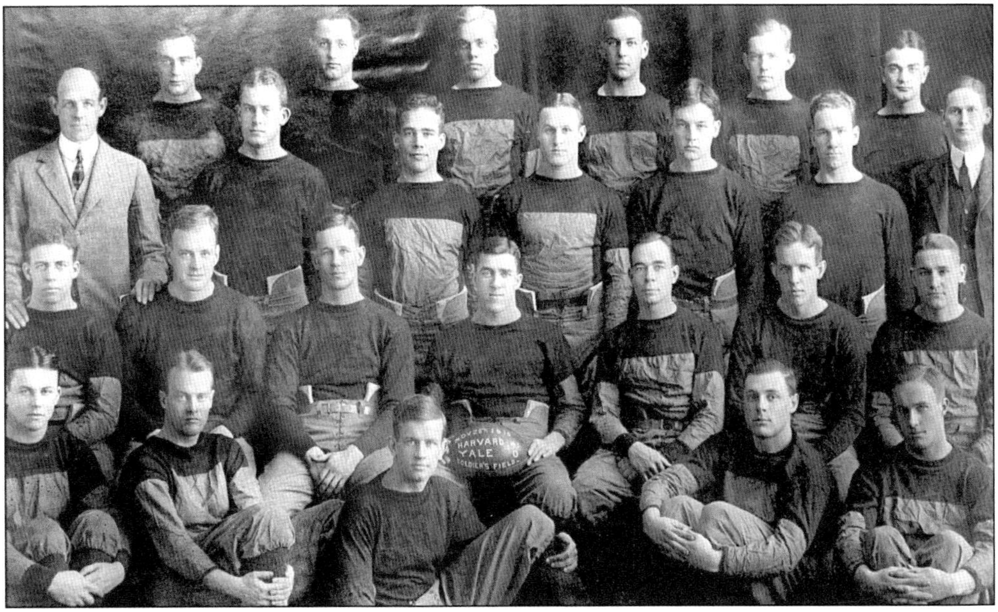

THE 1915 TEAM. Although the 1915 team saw the end of Harvard's 33-game winning streak on October 23 in a 10-0 loss to Cornell (the first ever win by the Big Red), the Crimson went on to compile an 8-1 record. A 41-0 rout of Yale featured a spectacular performance by captain Eddie Mahan, the Harvard quarterback who scored four touchdowns and booted five "goals from touchdowns." Mahan, tackle Joe Gilman, and halfback Dick King were all named to the Walter Camp All-American team.

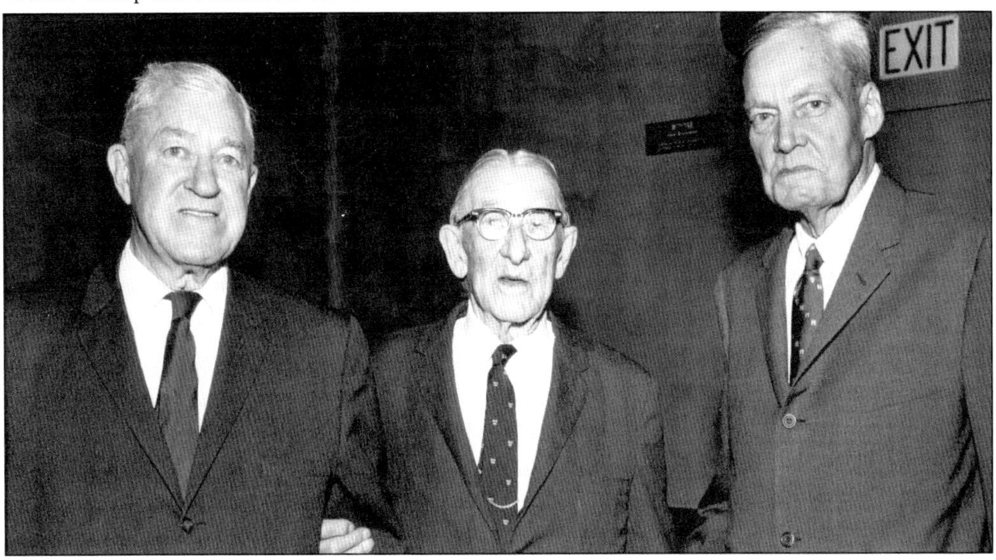

RICHARD HARTE '17, BILL REID '01, AND EDDIE MAHAN '16. This trio of Crimson greats (left to right), is shown at the Harvard Varsity Club Hall of Fame induction of Eddie Mahan and Bill Reid. Richard Harte was a standout end on the 1915 and 1916 teams with Eddie Mahan. Bill Reid played a prominent role in Harvard football as both a player and coach. His diary, later published, has provided significant insight into college football at the beginning of the 20th century. Three-time All-American halfback Eddie Mahan, the captain of the 1915 team, is acknowledged as one of the Crimson's best at his position.

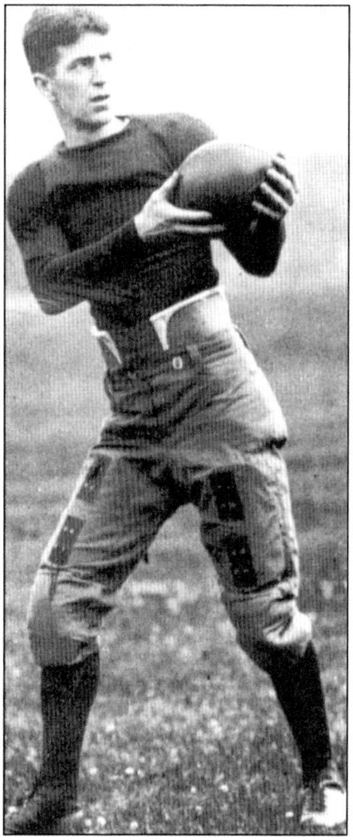

Eddie Casey '19. Eddie Casey had the distinction of earning All-American honors both before and after World War I. A fleet, 161-pound halfback, Casey was the lone Crimson representative on Walter Camp's 1919 All-American first team after being a prewar second-team All-American in 1916. Casey's unique "flying body block" method of tackling opponents was not widely imitated.

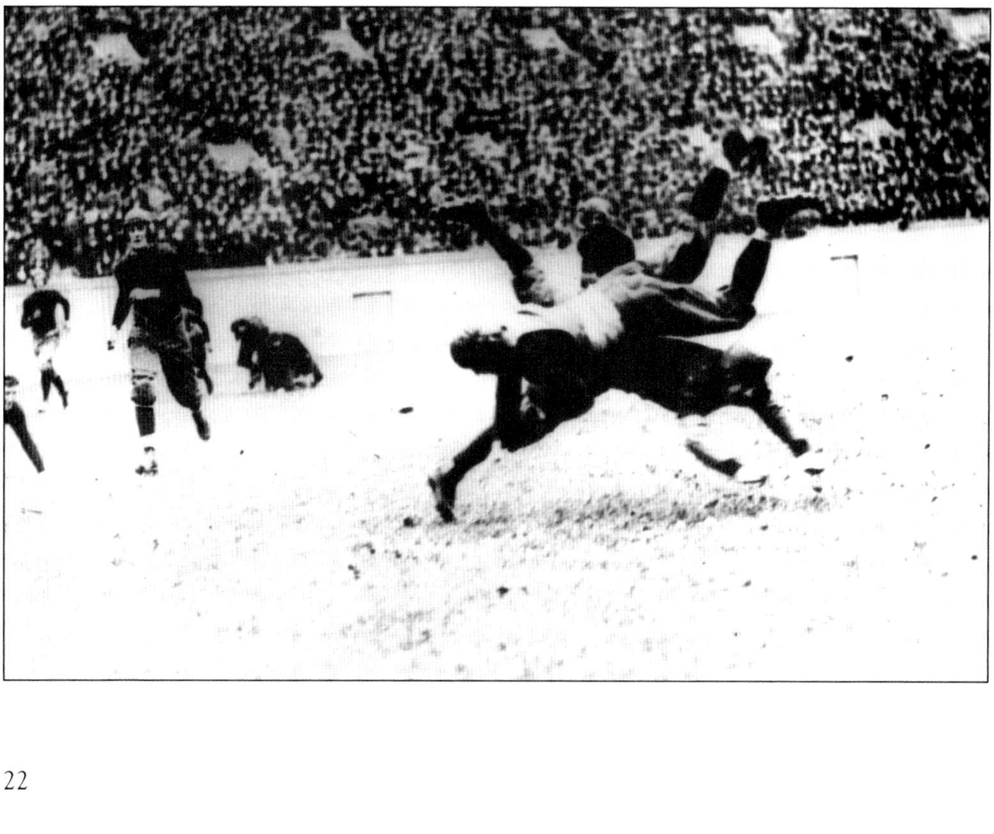

Two

1919–1940

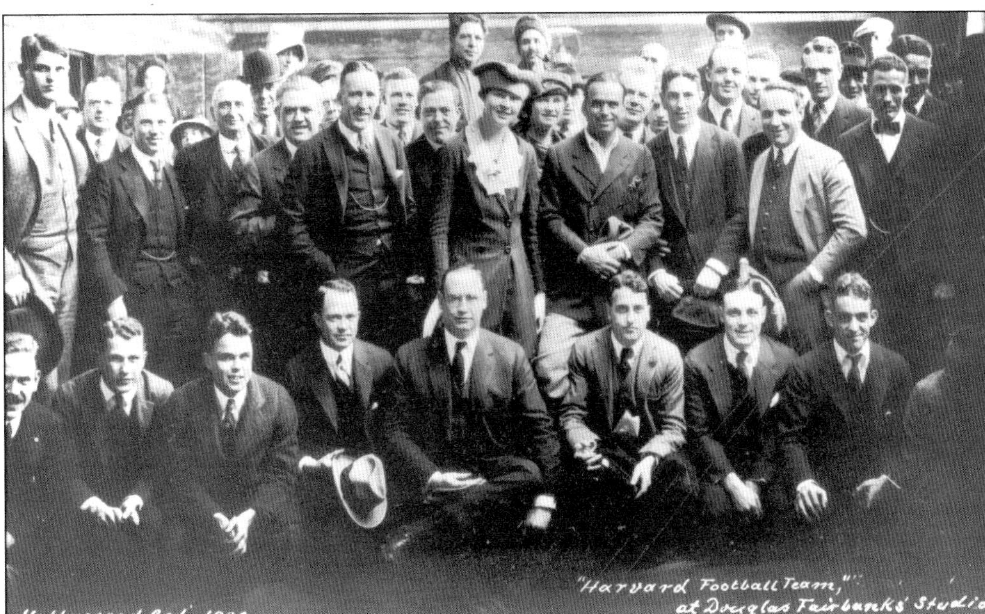

THE 1919 ROSE BOWL TEAM AT THE DOUGLAS FAIRBANKS STUDIO. Some bowl traditions have remained the same. The Rose Bowl is no exception. This Harvard football team publicity picture was taken at the Douglas Fairbanks Studio in Hollywood, California. Shown here is just one of many bowl-week scenes played out during the Crimson's southern California odyssey, which began with the official departure on December 20.

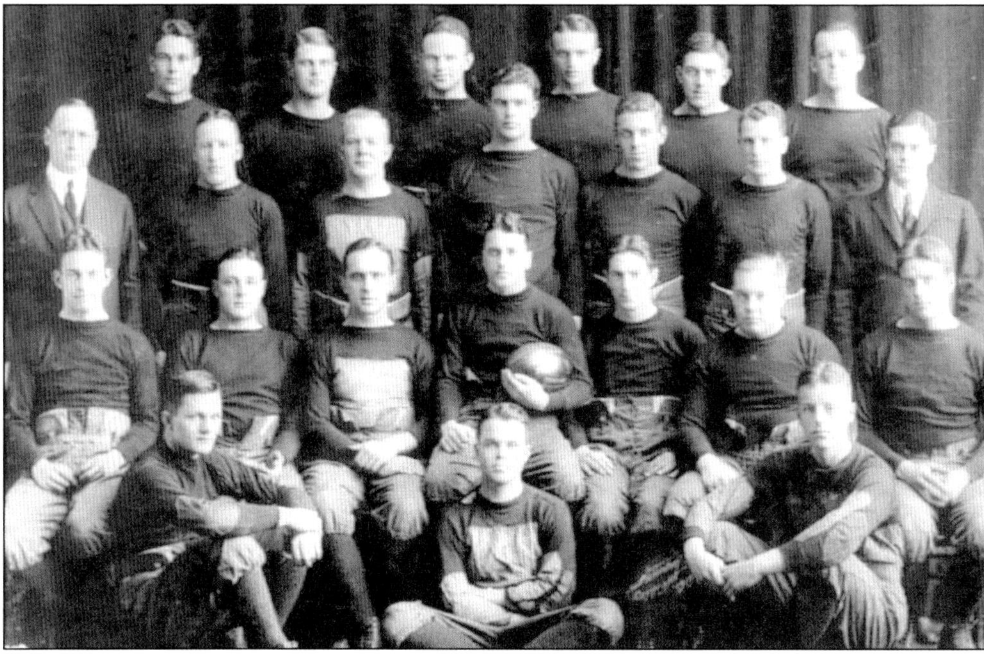

The 1919 Rose Bowl Team. The 1919 team was the only team in Harvard football annals to play in a major bowl game. The team's regular season record of 8-0-1, which included victories over Boston College, Virginia, and Yale, was only blemished by a 10-10 tie at Princeton, a game the Crimson rallied to tie on a late touchdown pass from Babe Felton to Eddie Casey and a conversion by Freddy Church. Church subsequently became the Crimson's Pasadena hero, scoring the game's lone touchdown, followed by Arnold Horween's winning extra point in a 7-6 victory over Oregon.

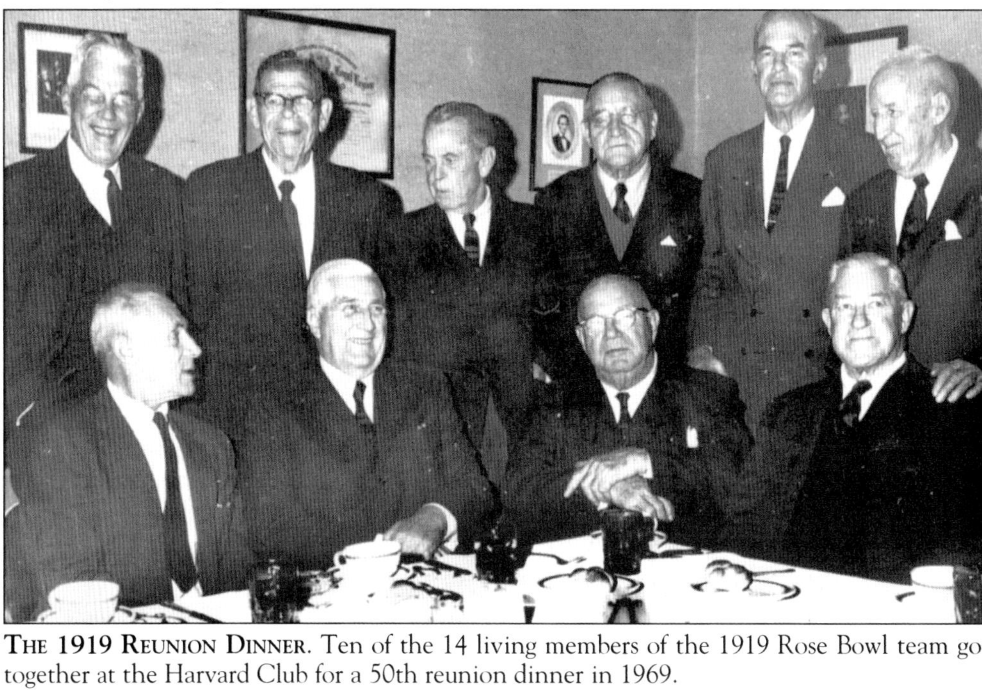

The 1919 Reunion Dinner. Ten of the 14 living members of the 1919 Rose Bowl team got together at the Harvard Club for a 50th reunion dinner in 1969.

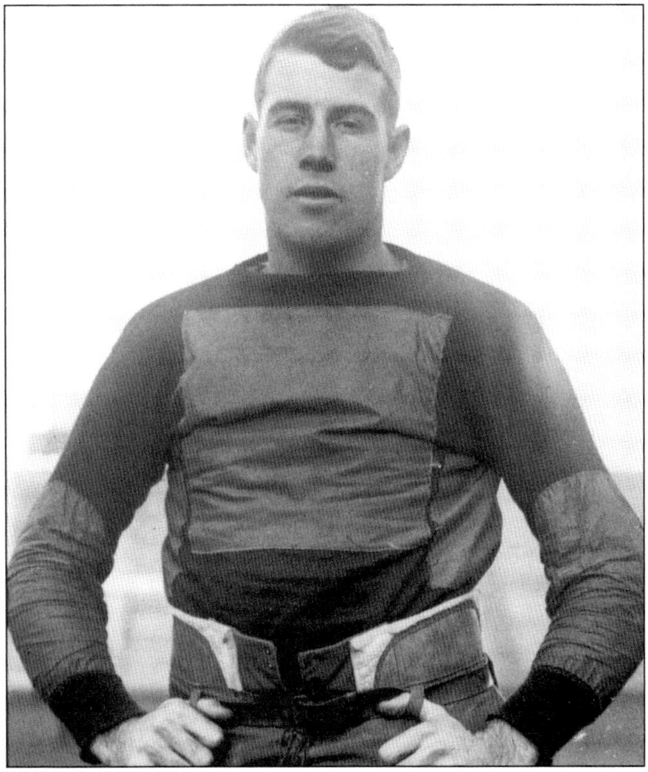

George Owen '23 (Football and Hockey). One of the Crimson's all-time great athletes, George Owen won nine varsity letters in football, hockey, and baseball. A two-time football All-American in 1921 and 1922, he went on to captain the National Hockey League's Boston Bruins.

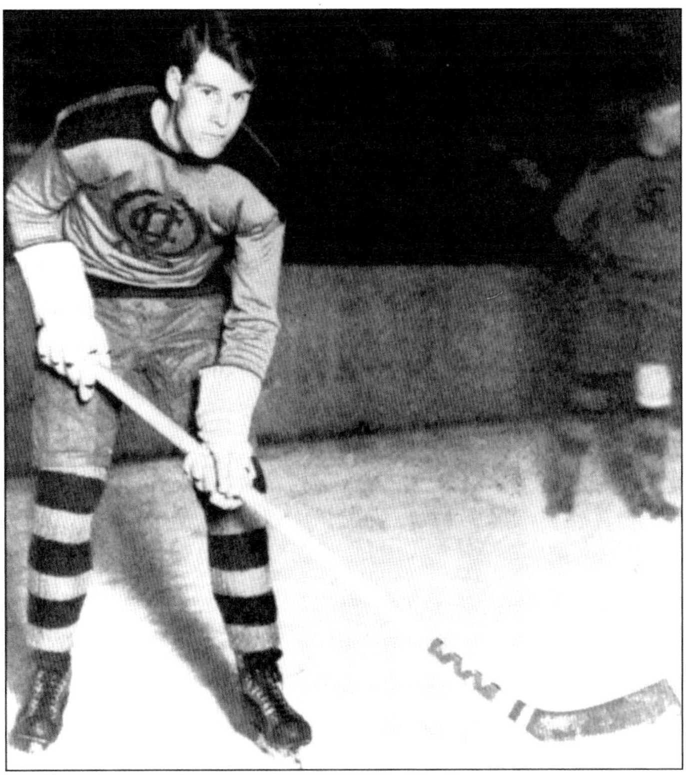

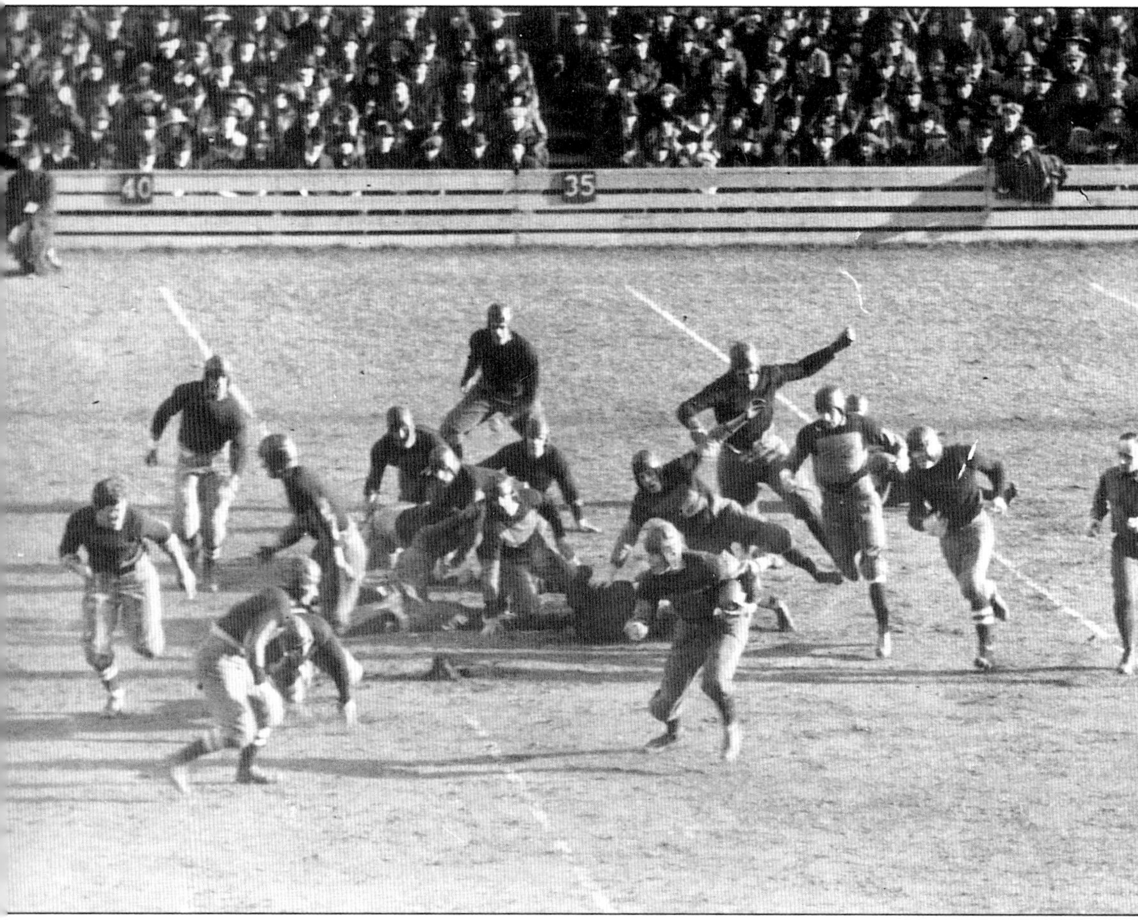

OWEN VERSUS BROWN UNIVERSITY, 1921. A standout halfback on the gridiron, George Owen touts the ball here versus Brown in a game in which the Crimson rallied late for a 9-7 victory over the Bears.

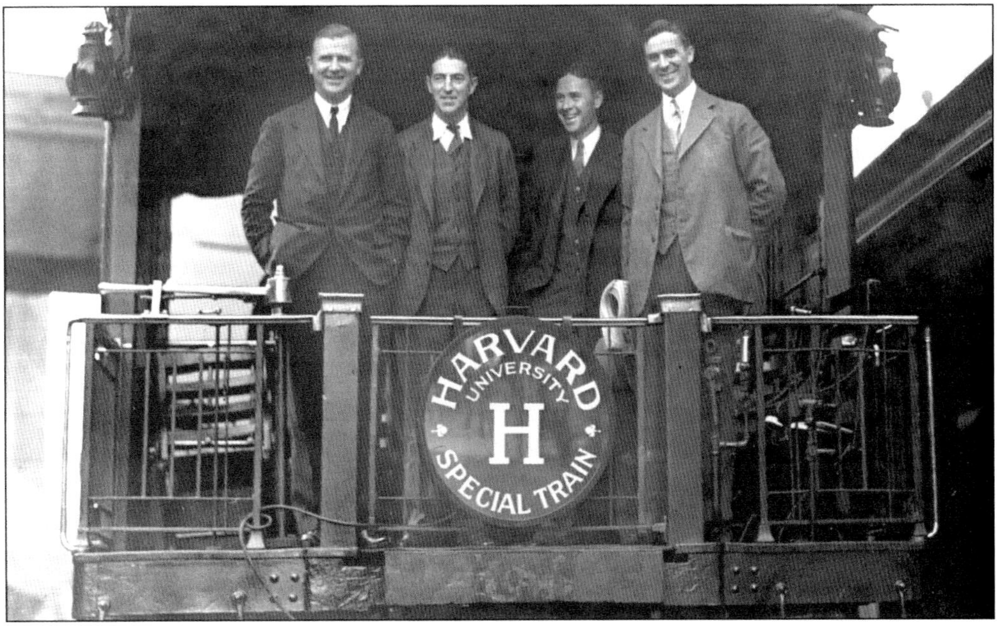

The 1929 Michigan Train. The Crimson embarked on a tough intersectional schedule in 1929 under fourth-year coach Arnold Horween, which included a first-ever trip to the Midwest to take on Michigan in Ann Arbor on November 9. The Crimson dropped a heartbreaking 14-12 decision to the Wolverines before a crowd of 87,000. Athletic director Bill Bingham '16, former star Eddie Casey, Francis Ryan '24, and Dick Hallowell '20 were among the luminaries to make the trek west with the Crimson.

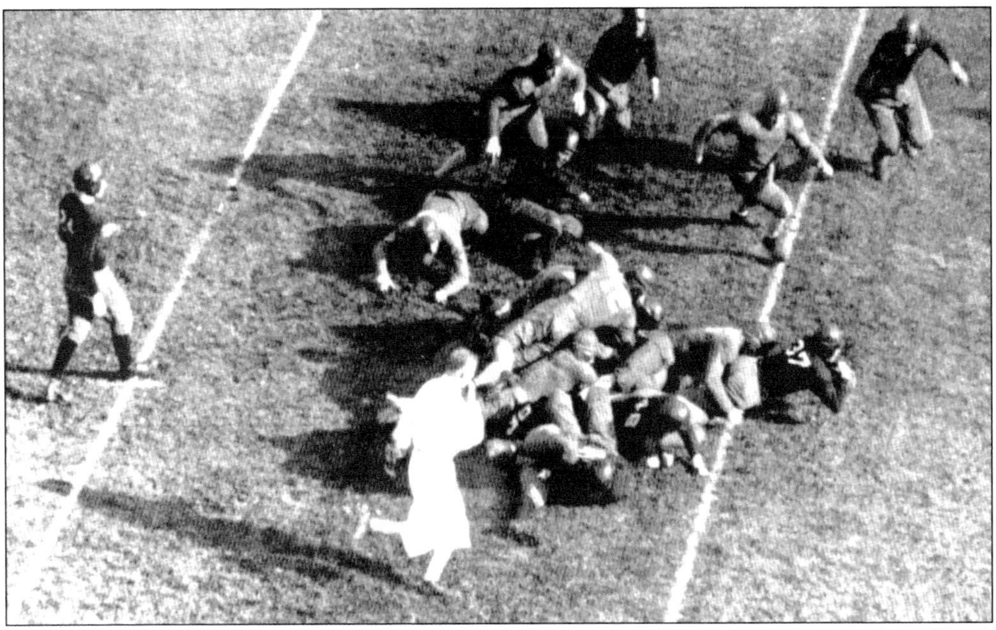

Arnold Horween '21. Arnold Horween joined Casey in the Crimson backfield at the fullback position. A rock-solid 193 pounds, Horween provided the Harvard offense with a strong inside running game. He captained the undefeated 1920 post–Rose Bowl team and later coached the Crimson from 1926 to 1930.

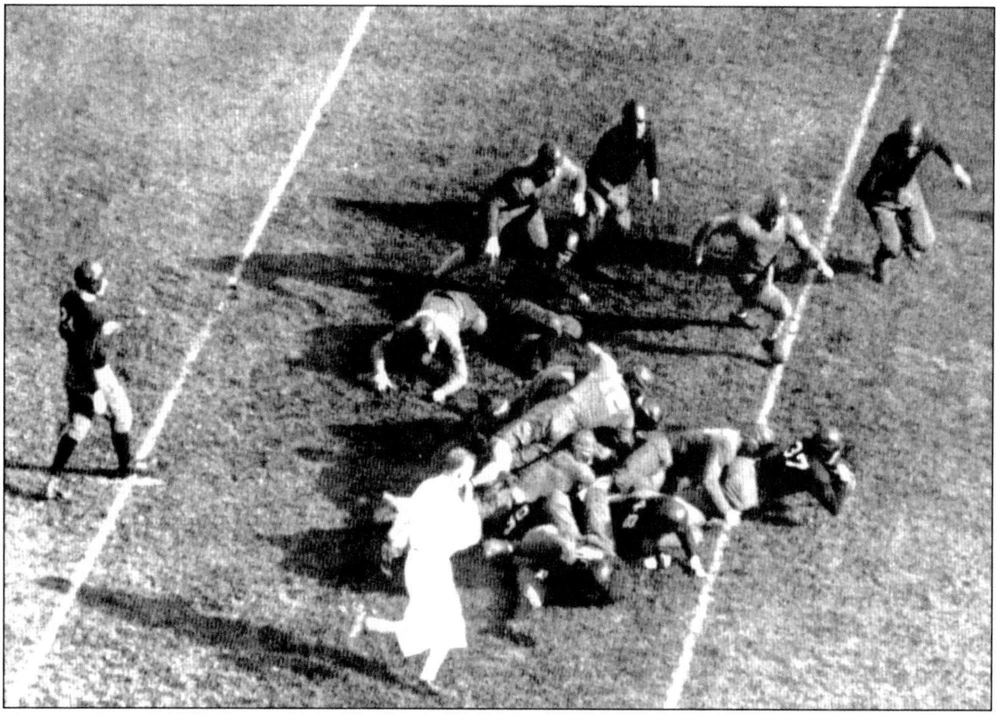

Harper '30 Carries for Harvard against Holy Cross, 1929. Fullback Wallace Harper lunges forward in action versus Holy Cross in a 12-6 victory over the Crusaders at Harvard Stadium. This win occurred the week after the Michigan game and the week prior to the season-ending triumph in the Game (the annual Harvard-Yale match).

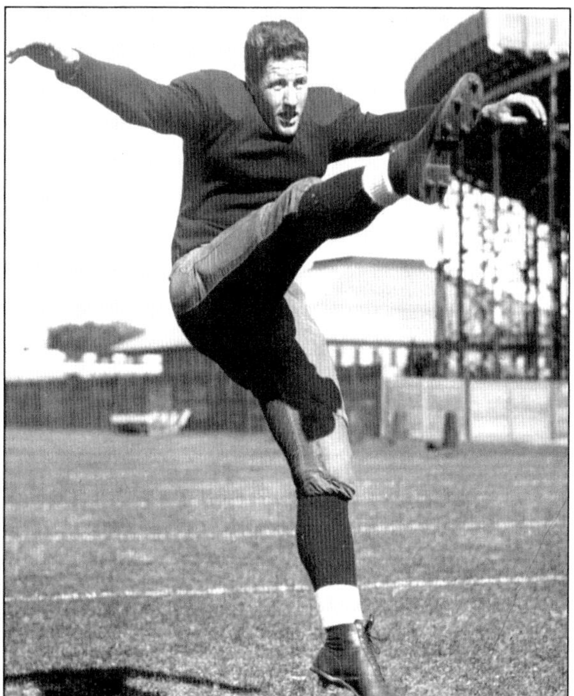

Eugene "Red" Record '32. Eugene "Red" Record, a Harvard halfback and punter, warms up before meeting Yale in New Haven in the 1930 renewal of the Game. The Crimson shut out the Eli 13-0 in Arnold Horween's final game as head coach.

BEN TICKNOR '31. Ben Ticknor was a three-year starter, anchoring the Crimson line at the center position in both 1929 and 1930. Ticknor captained the 1930 team to a 4-4-1 record, highlighted by the season-ending shutout of Yale. A two-time All-American, Ticknor is a member of the Harvard Varsity Club Hall of Fame.

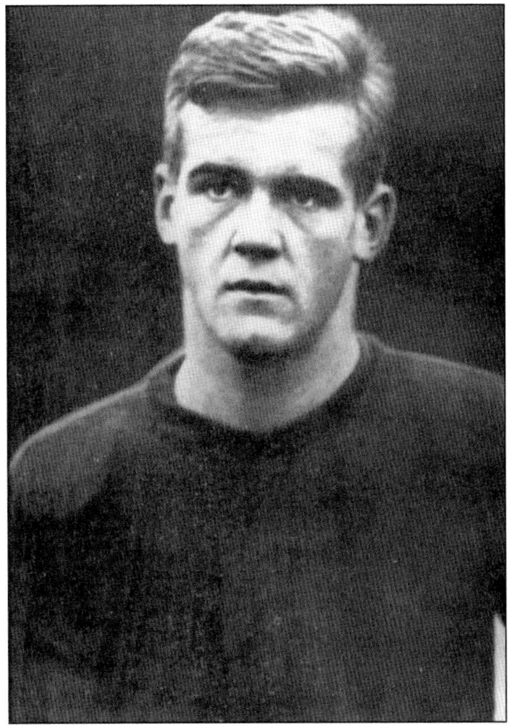

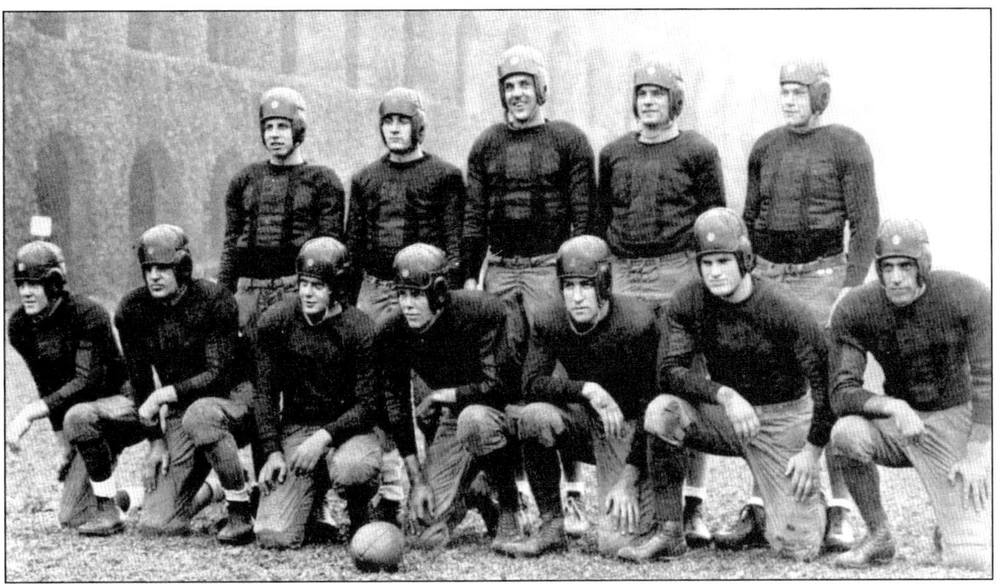

THE 1931 TEAM. Eddie Casey '19, a former All-American back, took over the Crimson program in 1931 and enjoyed immediate success. Led by the incomparable Barry Wood, Harvard rolled to seven straight wins before being upset by Yale in the season finale. Wood's Eli counterpart, the legendary Albie Booth, drop-kicked the winning field goal with time running out, delivering Yale a pulsating 3-0 victory.

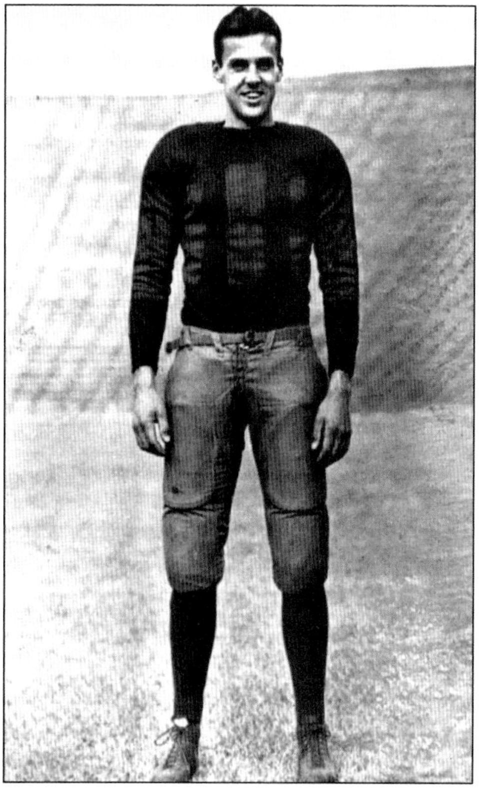

Barry Wood '32. Barry Wood was Harvard's All-American quarterback in 1931, leading the Crimson to a 7-1 record under first-year head coach Eddie Casey. Wood remains one of Harvard's best two-way football players and arguably its all-time greatest athlete, earning 10 letters—three each in football, hockey, and baseball, and one in tennis as a member of the Prentice Cup team (a Harvard-Yale aggregation that competes against an Oxford-Cambridge team from England).

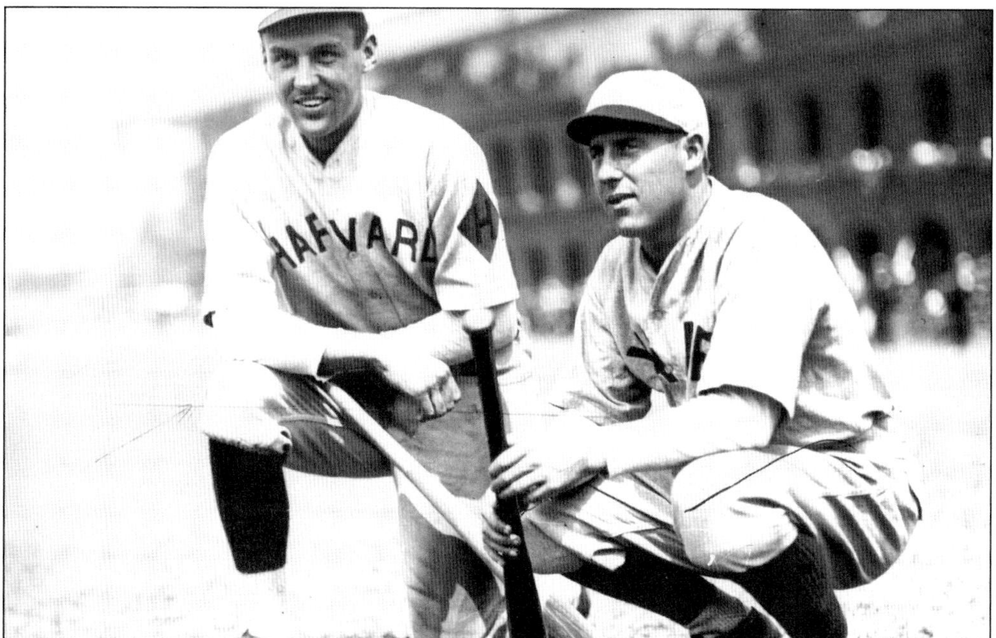

Barry Wood and Albie Booth. The two legends of the gridiron, Barry Wood and Yale's Albie Booth, also competed against each other on the diamond. The duo appears to be relaxed before this June 1932 Harvard-Yale baseball contest.

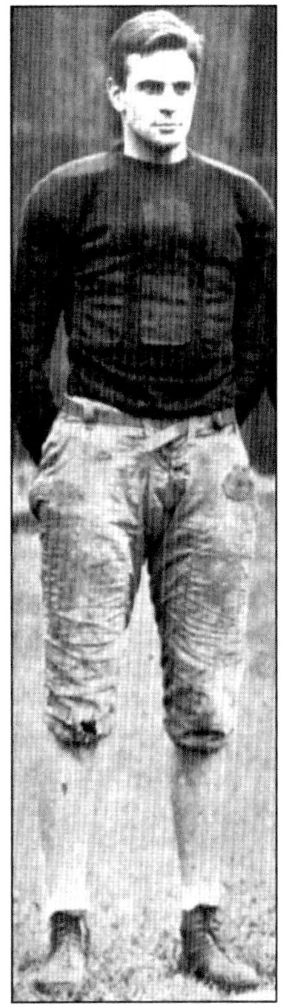

CHARLIE DEVENS '32 (FOOTBALL, BASEBALL). Charlie Devens played football for the Crimson but was better known for his exploits in baseball. After throwing for Harvard, Devens went on to pitch for the New York Yankees in the 1930s. He is the last living teammate of Babe Ruth.

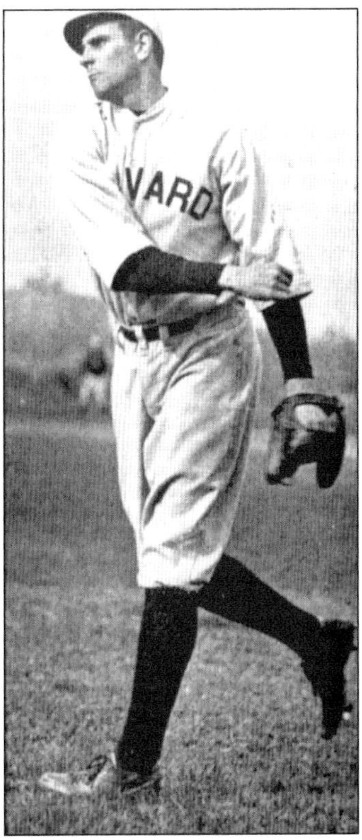

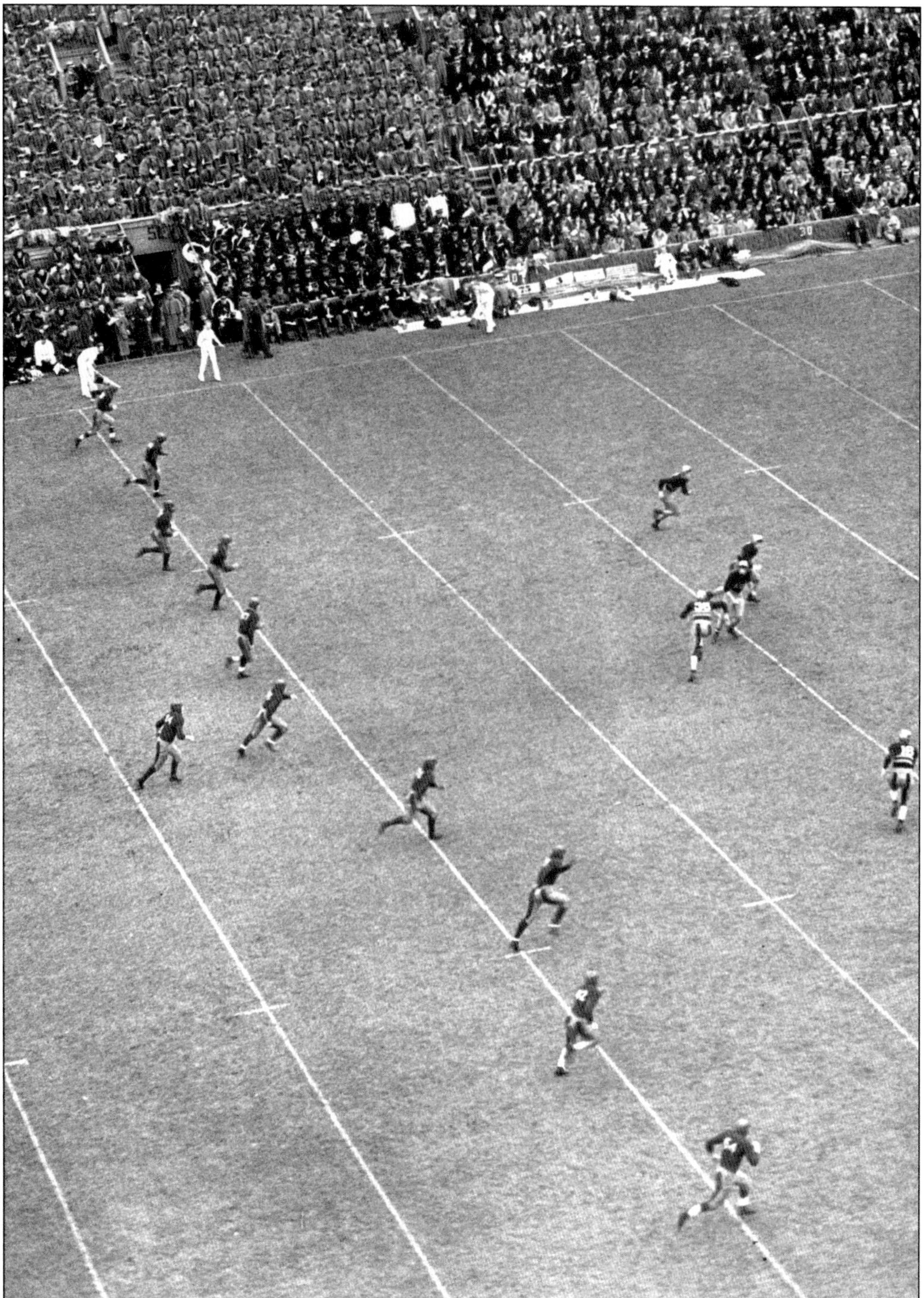

The 1932 Army Game. The Crimson kicks off to Army in November 1932 action at Harvard Stadium. The Cadets trounced Harvard 46-0, the worst defeat in Harvard history since the 1884 Yale game (48-0). Harvard had to wait seven years to gain a measure of revenge with a 15-0 victory over Army at Harvard Stadium in 1939.

John Dean '34. John Dean captained Eddie Casey's 1933 team to a 5-2-1 mark that included a 19-6 victory over Yale. Dean played fullback and handled kicking duties for the Crimson.

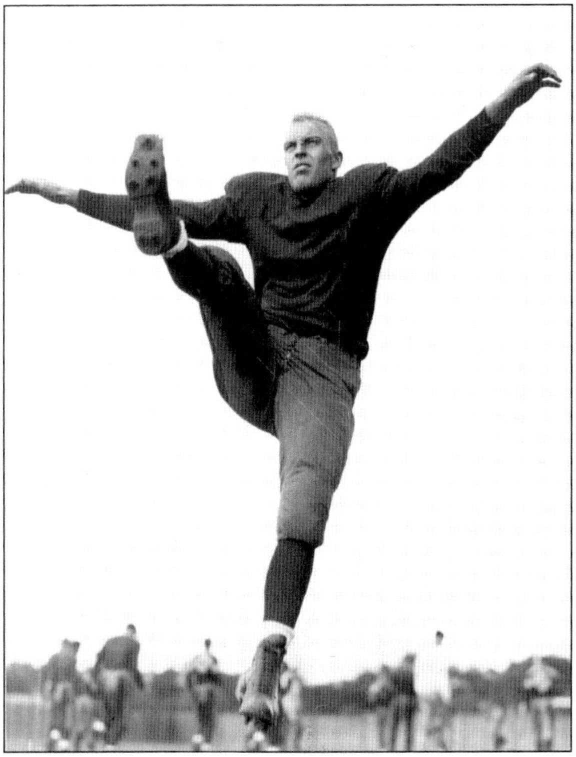

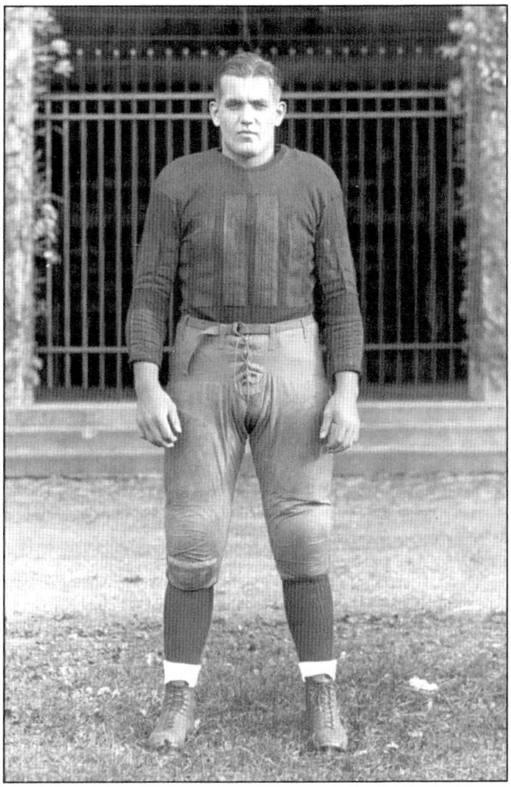

Herman Gundlach '35 (Captain, 1934). Herman Gundlach was the captain of Eddie Casey's final team in 1934. A three-year starter at right guard, Gundlach's career varsity record was 13-10-1.

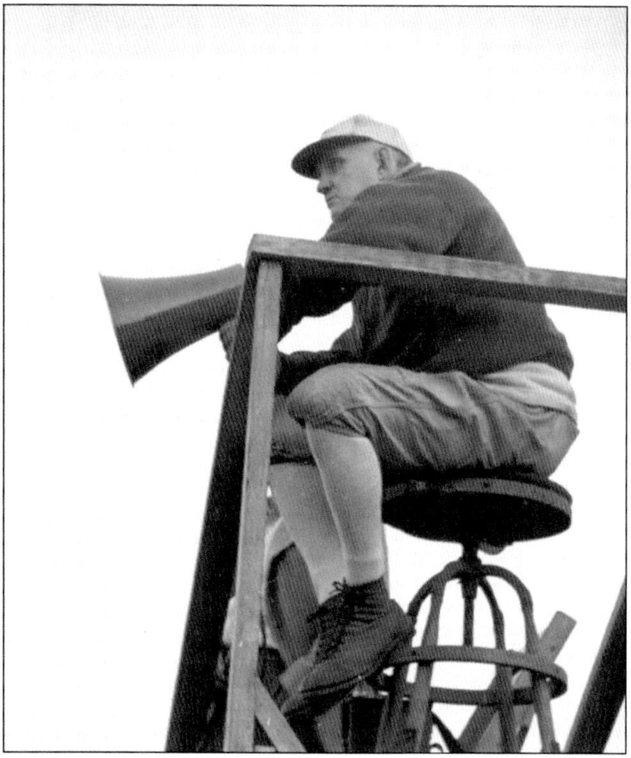

Coach Dick Harlow Addresses the Team. The first non-Harvard man to coach the Crimson, Dick Harlow took over the program in 1935. Arriving from Western Maryland, Harlow lectures this group of players at his first spring practice. Harlow's 11-year tenure (interrupted by World War II) was the longest in the first 90 years of Harvard football. A collector of rare bird eggs, Harlow was appointed as a curator of Harvard's Museum of Comparative Zoology. His career coaching record was 45-39-7 (.533).

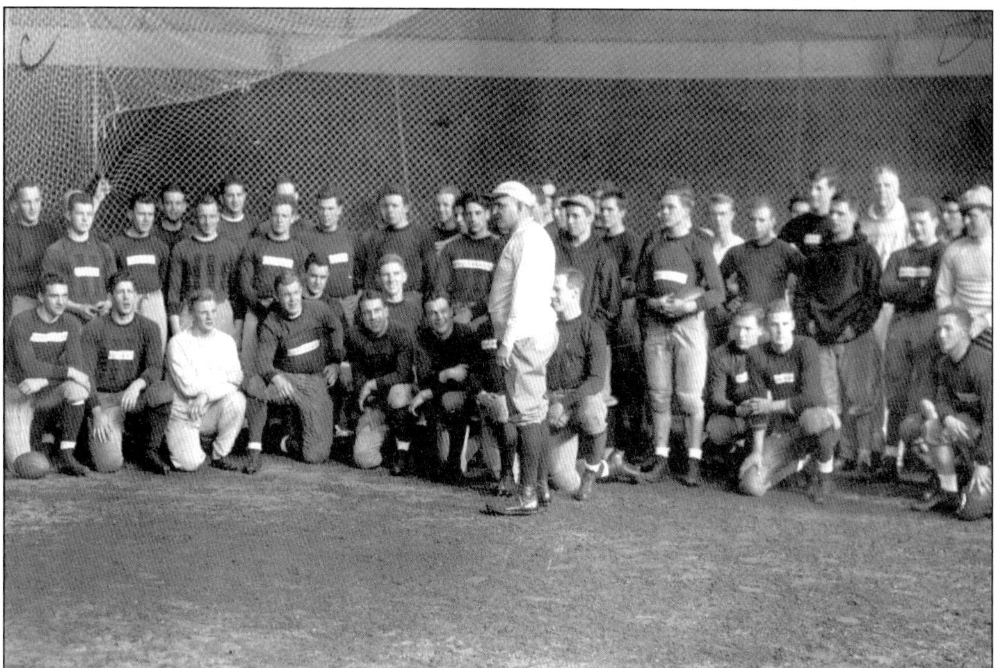

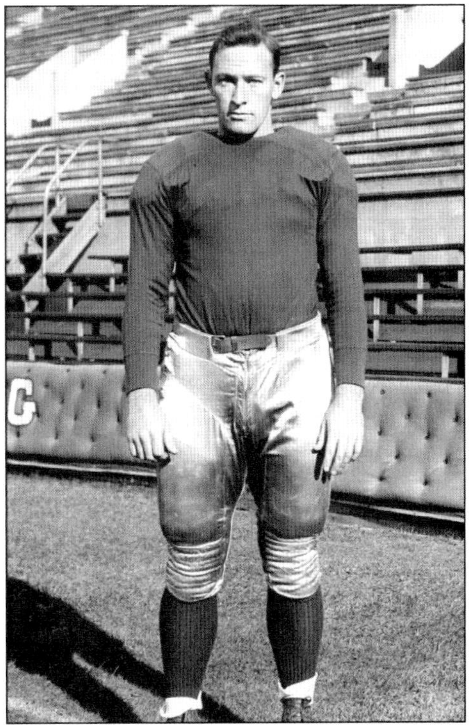

JAMES GAFFNEY '37. James Gaffney started as right guard for coach Dick Harlow's first team in 1935. He shifted to left guard and captained the 1936 team to a 3-4-1 season. The Crimson almost pulled a major upset in Gaffney's final game, losing to the Larry Kelley (Heisman Trophy winner) and Clint Frank–led Yale team by a single point (14-13).

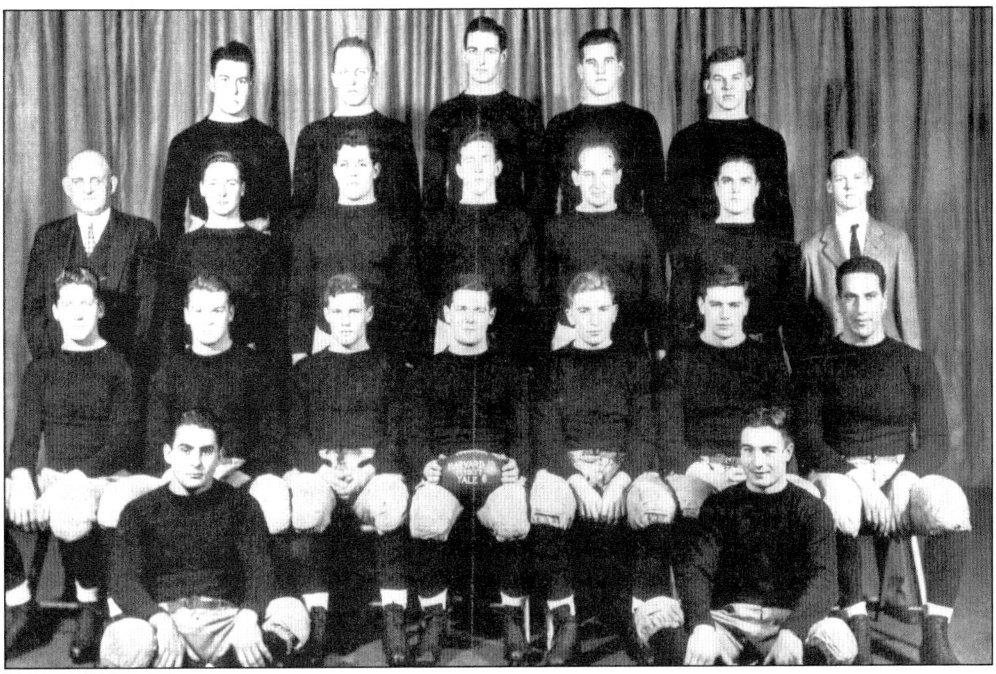

THE 1937 TEAM. Dick Harlow's third season as head coach was a memorable one. The Crimson finished above .500 (5-2-1) and defeated Yale for the first time in four years. The 1937 team dominated Princeton (34-6), played Navy to a scoreless tie, and lost to Yale by a single point (7-6). The victory over Princeton at the Tigers' Palmer Stadium was Harvard's first since 1923.

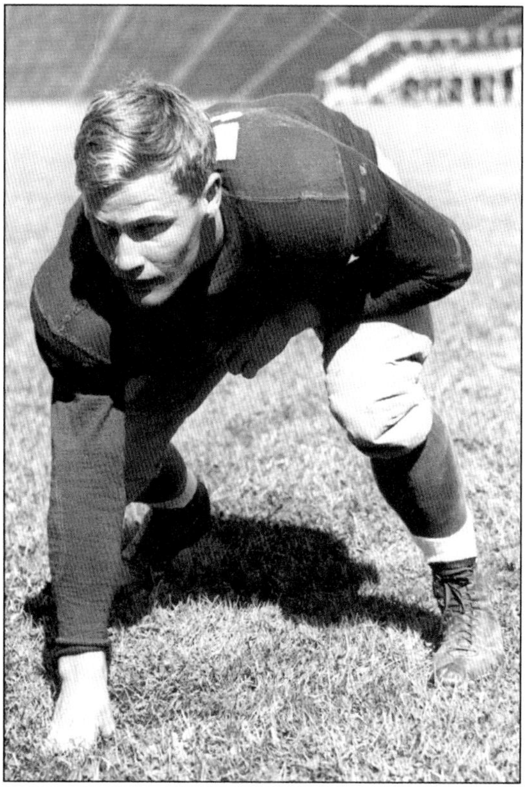

ROBERT GREEN '39 (CAPTAIN, 1938). Robert Green captained a 1938 team that embarked on the ultimate roller-coaster ride. After dropping its first four games to Brown, Cornell, Army, and Dartmouth, the Crimson rallied for four consecutive victories, closing the season by defeating Princeton, Chicago, Virginia, and Yale. The 7-0 victory over Yale in the rain at the Yale Bowl secured a second consecutive Big Three (Harvard, Yale, Princeton) title.

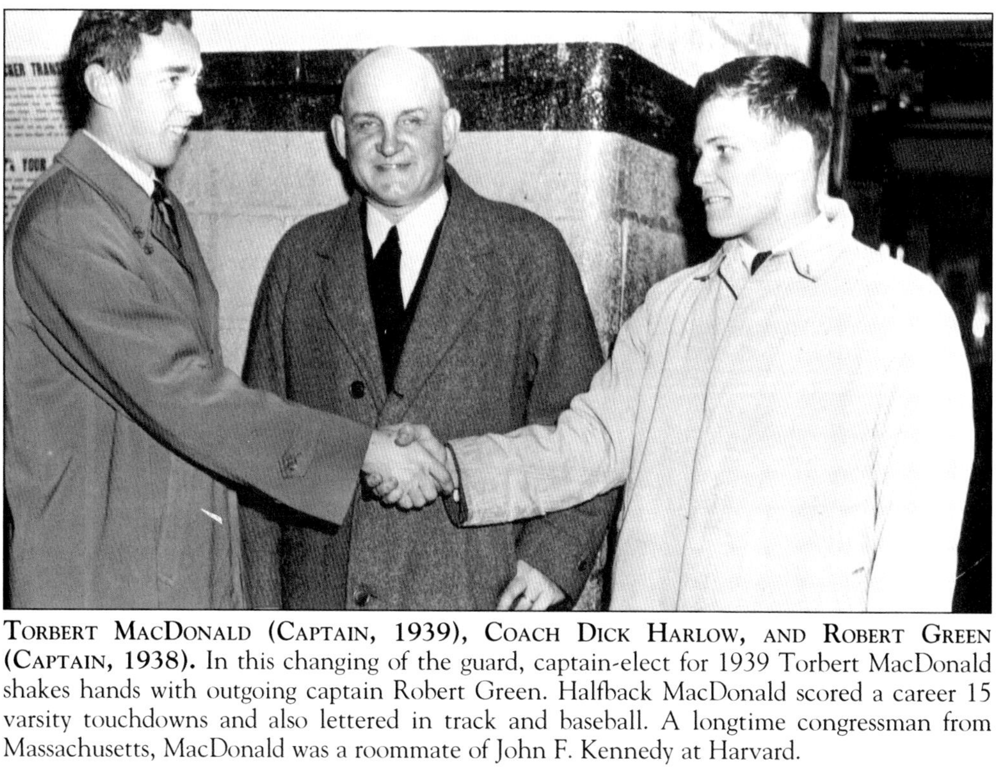

TORBERT MACDONALD (CAPTAIN, 1939), COACH DICK HARLOW, AND ROBERT GREEN (CAPTAIN, 1938). In this changing of the guard, captain-elect for 1939 Torbert MacDonald shakes hands with outgoing captain Robert Green. Halfback MacDonald scored a career 15 varsity touchdowns and also lettered in track and baseball. A longtime congressman from Massachusetts, MacDonald was a roommate of John F. Kennedy at Harvard.

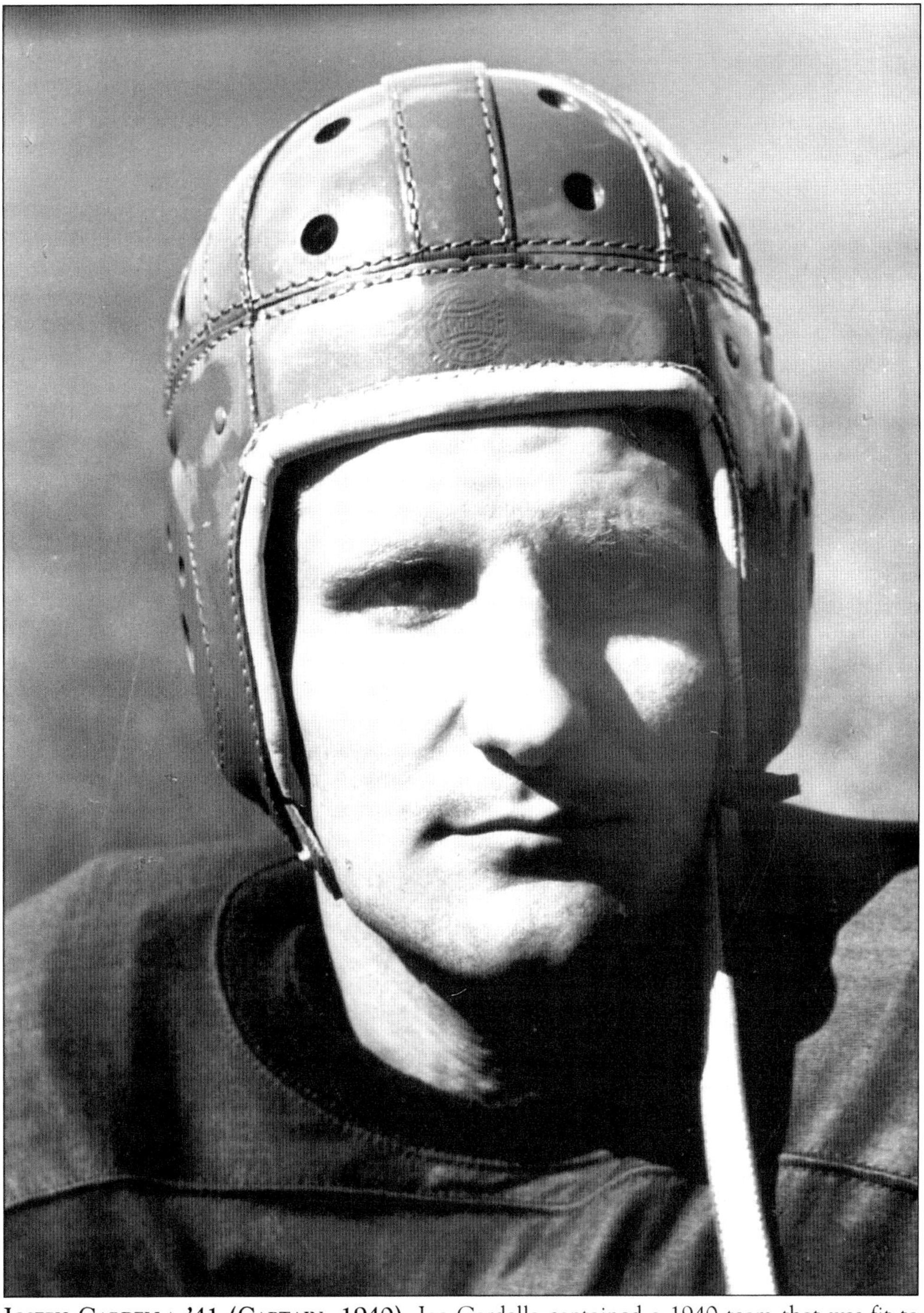

Joseph Gardella '41 (Captain, 1940). Joe Gardella captained a 1940 team that was fit to be tied. The Crimson ended deadlocked with Army (6-6), Princeton (0-0), and Pennsylvania (10-10) en route to a 3-2-3 season. Gardella bounced back from the injured list to score two of Harvard's four touchdowns in a 28-0 thrashing of Yale at the Yale Bowl. Dr. Joseph Gardella went on to become the associate dean of the faculty of Medicine for student affairs at Harvard.

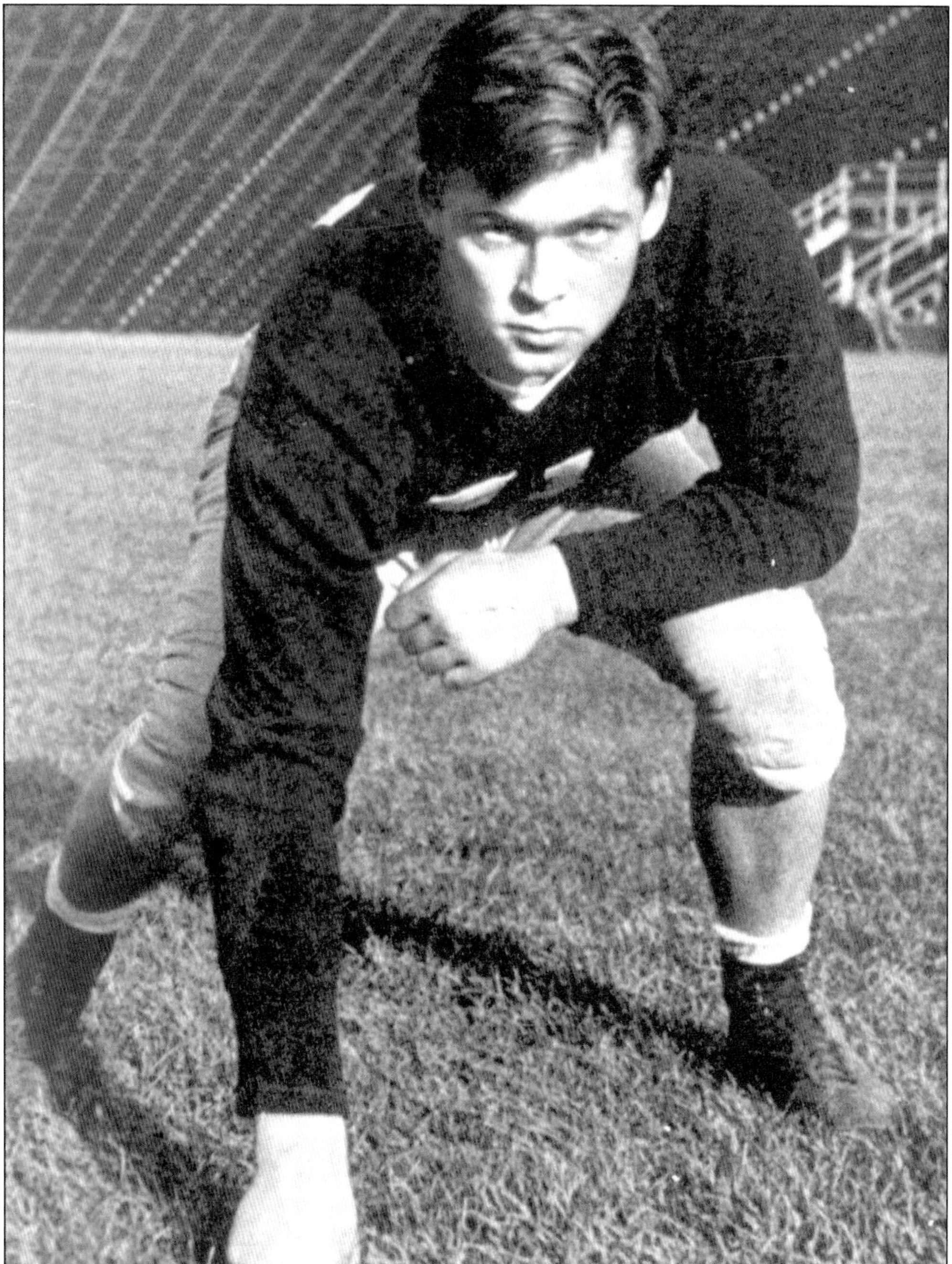

Endicott "Chub" Peabody '42. Known as the "Baby-Faced Assassin" during his playing days, Endicott "Chub" Peabody attained first-team All-American honors as a guard for the Crimson in 1941. Peabody was a three-year standout for coach Dick Harlow; perhaps the most memorable of Peabody's signature jarring tackles was used on Navy's All-American back Bill Busik in a 1941 game at Harvard Stadium. Peabody separated Busik from the ball with a spectacular hit and made the fumble recovery to preserve a scoreless tie. Peabody was elected governor of Massachusetts in 1962.

Three

1941–1956

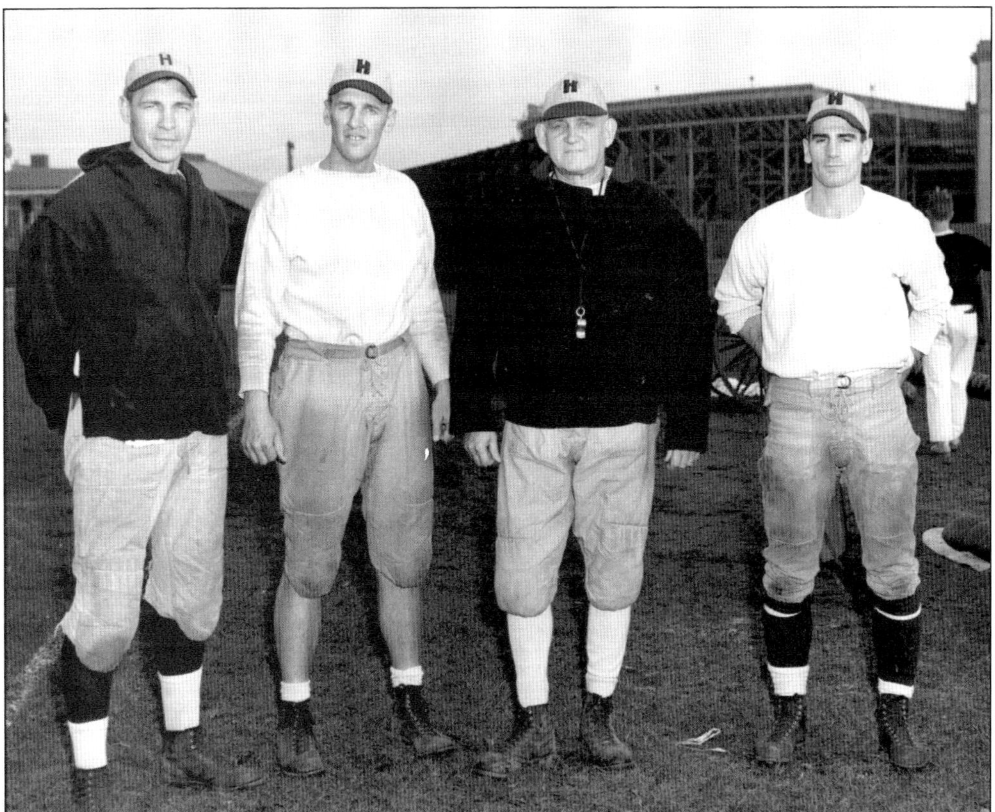

HARLOW WITH THE POSTWAR COACHING STAFF. Coach Dick Harlow (third from left) is pictured with assistant coaches, from left to right, Harry Jacunski, Hal Kopp, and Bob Margarita.

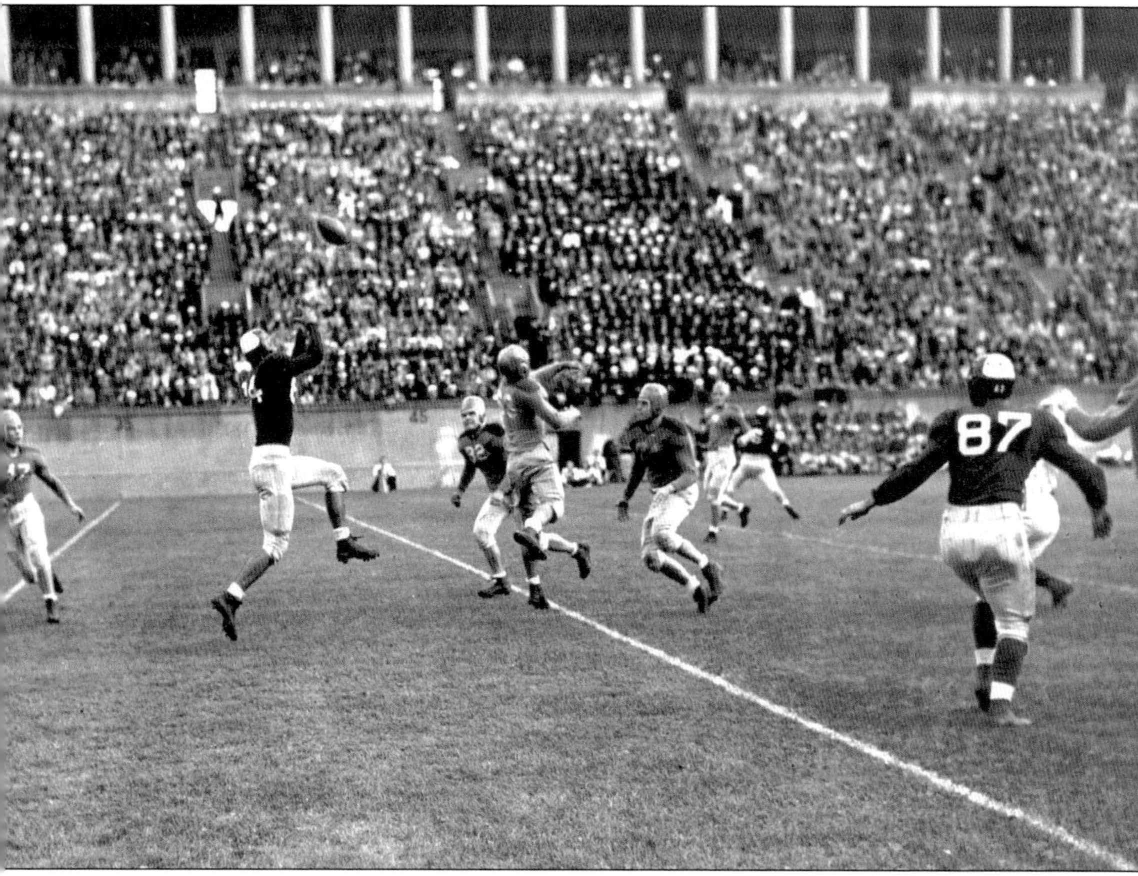

HARVARD VERSUS TUFTS, 1945. Harvard lost to local rival Tufts University (light jerseys) 7-6 in the 1945 season opener. The result was a disappointment to returning head coach Dick Harlow, who had served as a naval lieutenant commander in the Pacific theater. The Harvard 1943 and 1944 teams had been designated as informal due to World War II, but players on those squads were later awarded major "H" letters.

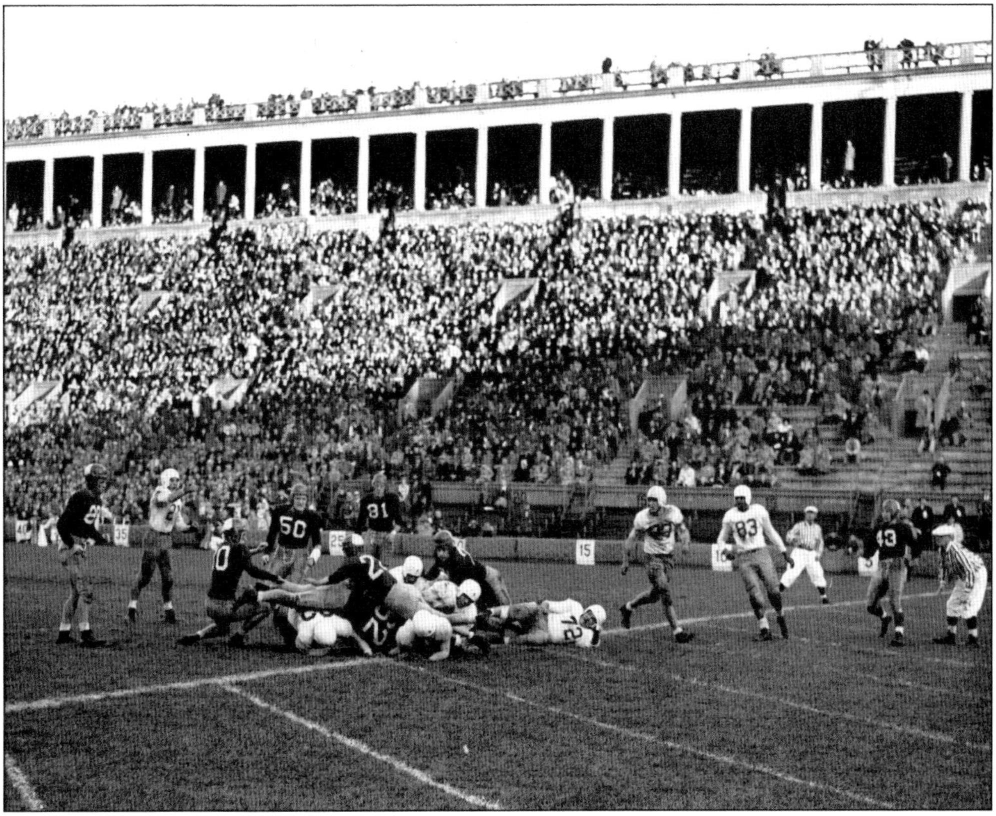

HARVARD VERSUS RUTGERS, 1947. The Crimson rolled to a 5-0 season start in 1947 before being upset by Rutgers 13-0. Rutgers halfback Grimsley plunges over the goal line from two yards out for the Scarlet Knights' first score in the third quarter.

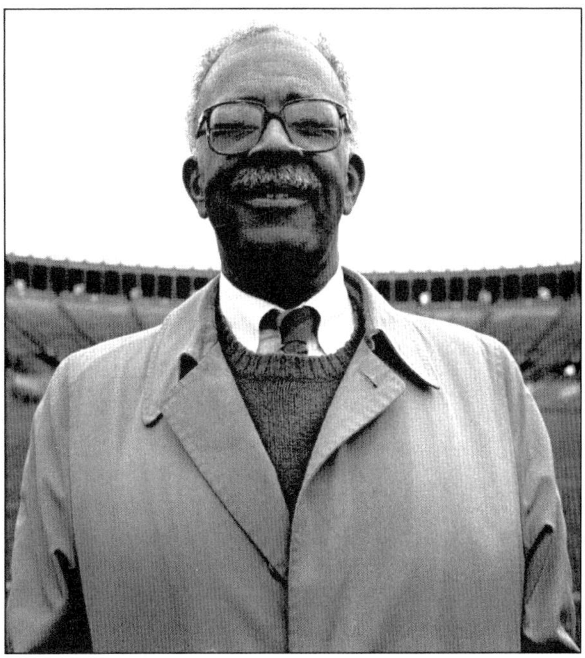

CHET PIERCE '48. Chet Pierce made history in 1947. The Harvard tackle became the first African American ever to play with or against an all-white team below the Mason-Dixon Line. His appearance in a game versus the University of Virginia at Charlottesville came after a unanimous pregame vote of approval by the Cavalier players. Virginia dominated the game, defeating Harvard 47-0. Dr. Chet Pierce went on to a career in Harvard's Department of Psychiatric Medicine.

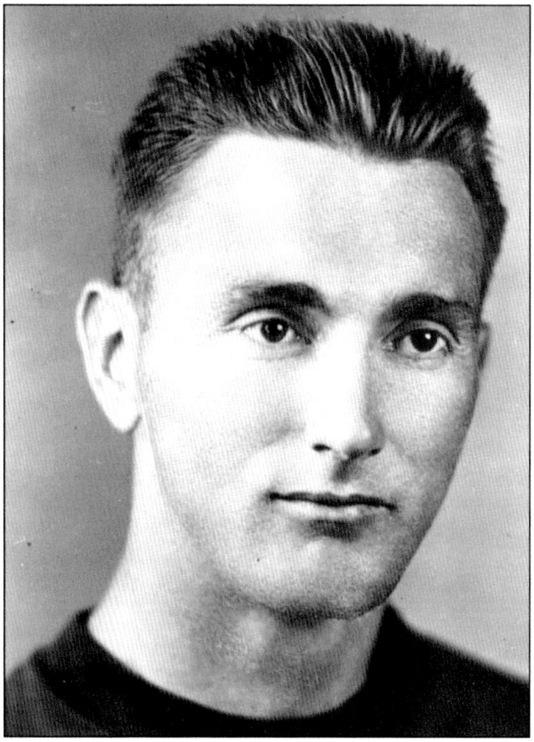

KENNY O'DONNELL '49. Kenny O'Donnell was an outstanding two-way back for the post-war Crimson (1946–1948). The starting quarterback of the 1947 team, O'Donnell is still Harvard's career leader in interceptions, with 15. A close friend of teammate Robert Kennedy, O'Donnell became one of the most powerful and influential men in John F. Kennedy's White House as special assistant to the president. O'Donnell is a member of the Harvard Varsity Club Hall of Fame.

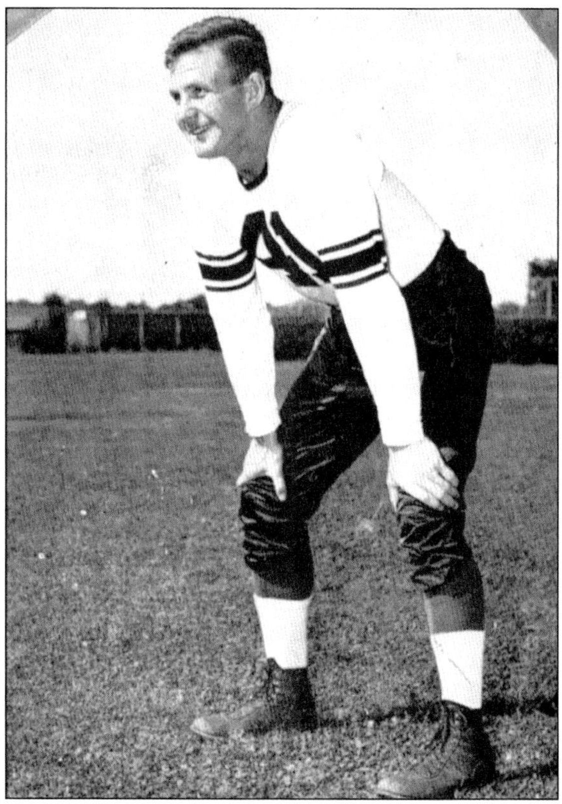

CHIP GANNON '50. A star halfback from 1946 to 1948, Thomas "Chip" Gannon was a three-sport standout, exhibiting his all-around athletic prowess on the basketball court and baseball diamond as well. Gannon is a member of the Harvard Varsity Club Hall of Fame.

VINCE MORAVEC '48 (CAPTAIN, 1947). Vince Moravec captained the ill-fated 1947 Crimson, Dick Harlow's last team. In addition to the loss to Virginia, Harvard was trounced by Rutgers and Princeton on successive weeks—31-7 versus the Scarlet Knights and 33-7 against the Tigers. Alas, captain Moravec, a rock-solid 200-pound fullback out of western Pennsylvania, did not play in either game. His season had ended by a broken kneecap in the Virginia game. The son of a steelworker, Moravec later rose to vice president of Bethlehem Steel.

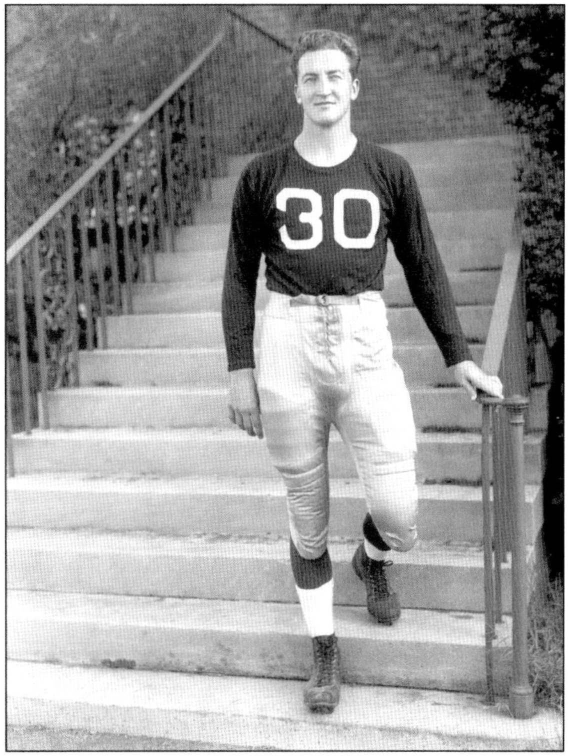

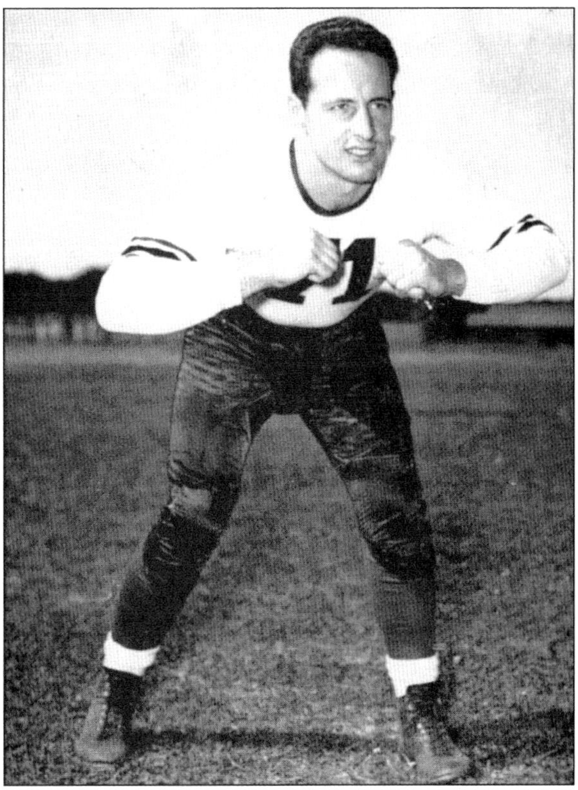

HOWARD HOUSTON '50 (CAPTAIN, 1949). Howie Houston was one of the Crimson's best lineman of the postwar period, playing both guard and tackle. The captain of the 1949 team, Houston also participated in crew and was recipient of the Francis H. Burr Scholarship for his combination of "character, leadership, scholarship and athletic ability" in 1950.

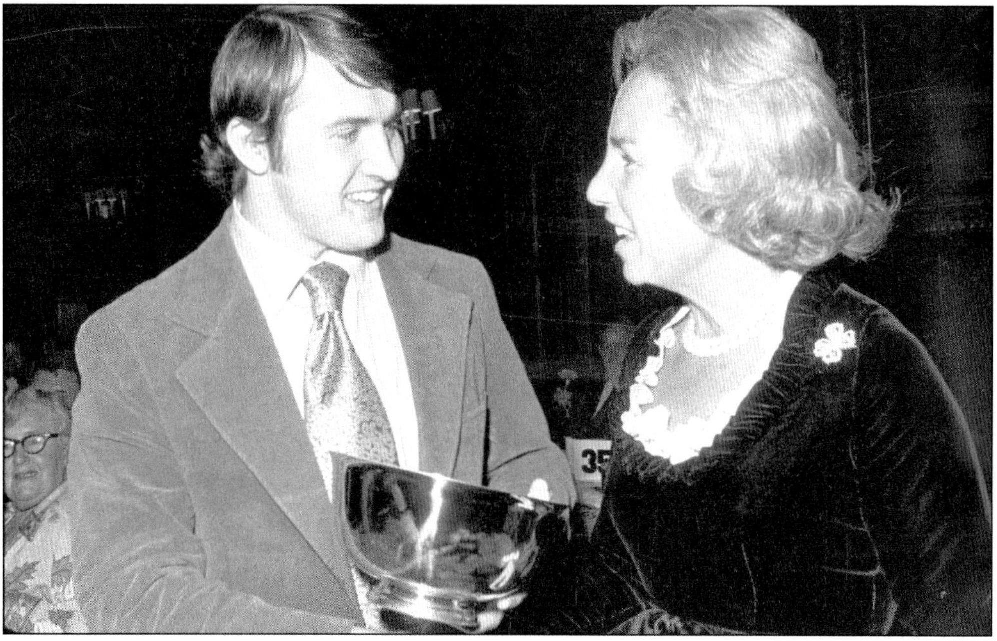

NEAL MILLER '76 WITH ETHEL KENNEDY. The teammates of Bobby Kennedy (who played football for Harvard from 1945 to 1947) established the Robert F. Kennedy Award in 1975. The award, a Paul Revere bowl, is given annually to that member of the varsity football team who, through his desire, determination, and willingness to work, has made himself a valuable member and thereby has gained the respect and admiration of his teammates and coaches. The late senator's widow, Ethel Kennedy, presents the award to fullback Neal Miller, the first player to be honored.

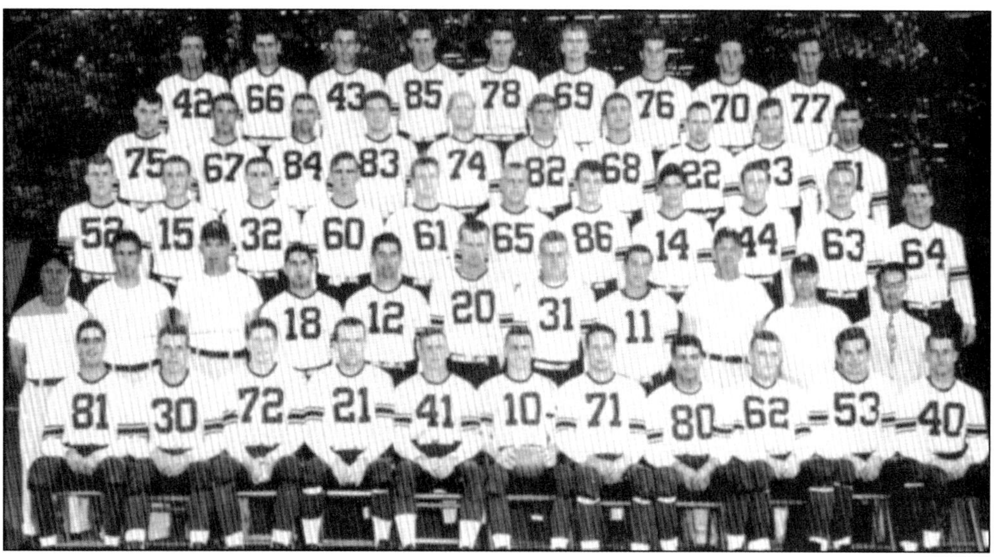

THE 1948 TEAM. The first Harvard team under the direction of head coach Arthur Valpey finished the season at .500 with a final record of 4-4, winning three of the last four games. The season highlight was unquestionably a 20-7 victory over Yale at Harvard Stadium. Captain Kenny O'Donnell, who had suffered a hairline leg fracture in the Princeton game two weeks earlier, scored the winning touchdown despite playing with a heavy cast.

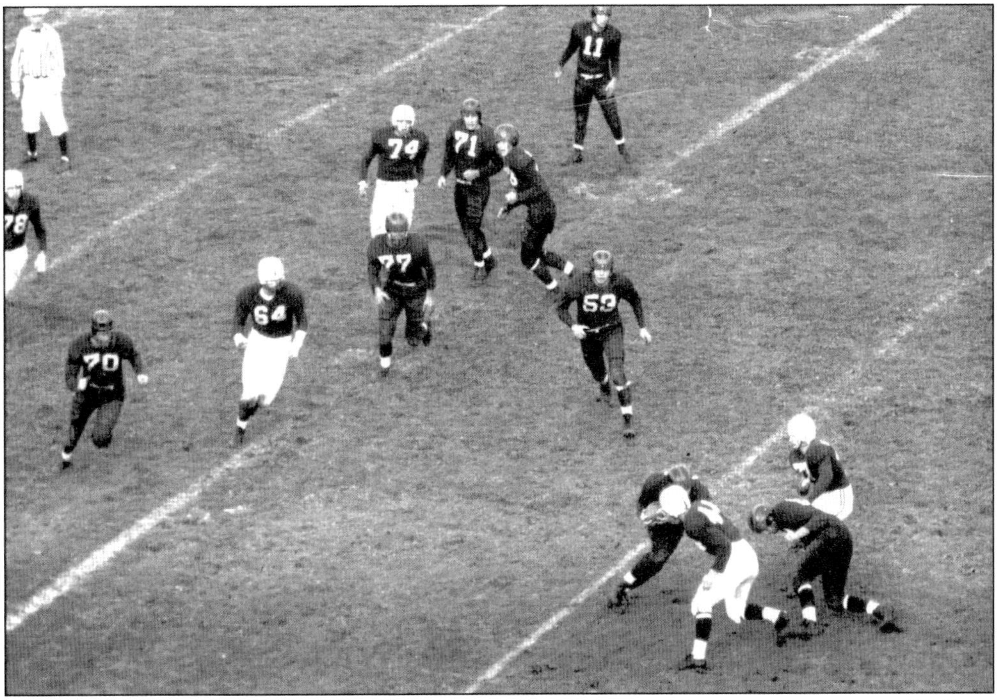

HARVARD-YALE ACTION, 1949. James Noonan completes a third-quarter pass to William Henry for a Harvard first down at the Yale Bowl in the 1949 renewal of the Game.

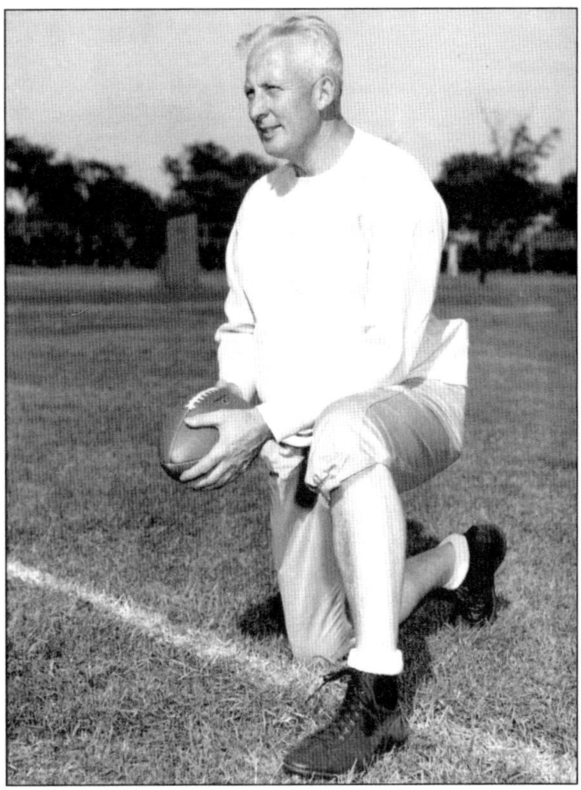

LLOYD JORDAN (COACH, 1950–1957). Lloyd Jordan became the 21st head coach of the Harvard Crimson in 1950. The selection came as somewhat of a surprise since for 18 years the 50-year-old Jordan had been the head coach at Amherst, where he had also served as athletic director. Jordan had three winning seasons during his seven-year tenure as head coach, compiling a career mark of 24-31-3 (.440).

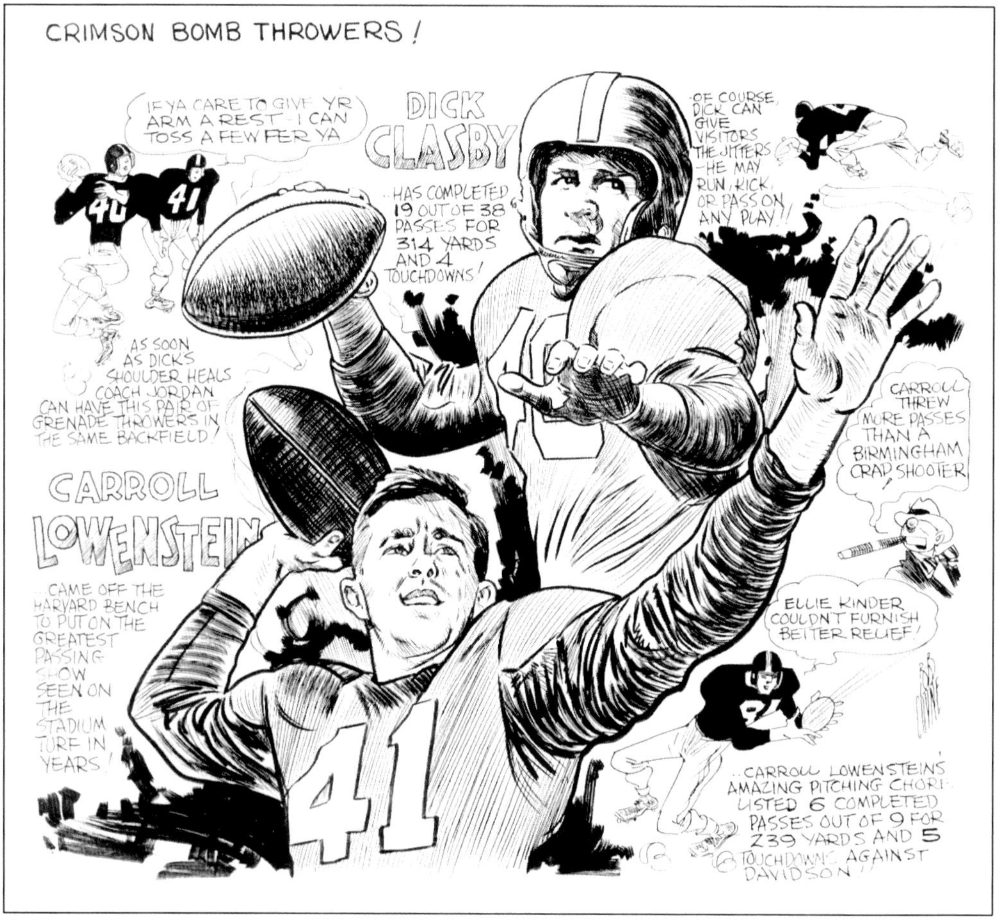

A Dick Clasby and Carroll Lowenstein Cartoon. This cartoon by Boston newspaper legend Bob Coyne depicts the Crimson's two-headed passing threat during the 1953 season: Dick Clasby and Carroll Lowenstein. Lowenstein's five touchdown passes versus Davidson College remains Harvard's single-game mark almost a half-century later. Lowenstein captained the 1951 team.

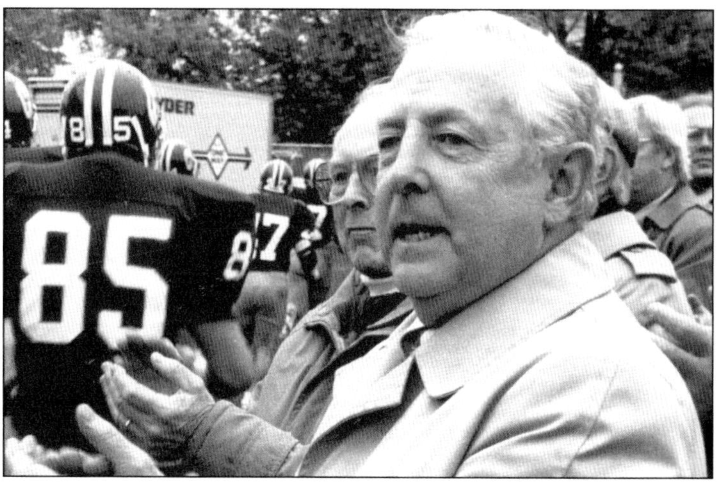

Carroll Lowenstein '52. Back on campus some four decades later, former quarterback Carroll Lowenstein applauds the men of Harvard as they run past onto the field of battle before a 1992 game. Lowenstein is a member of the Varsity Club Hall of Fame for his esteemed gridiron exploits.

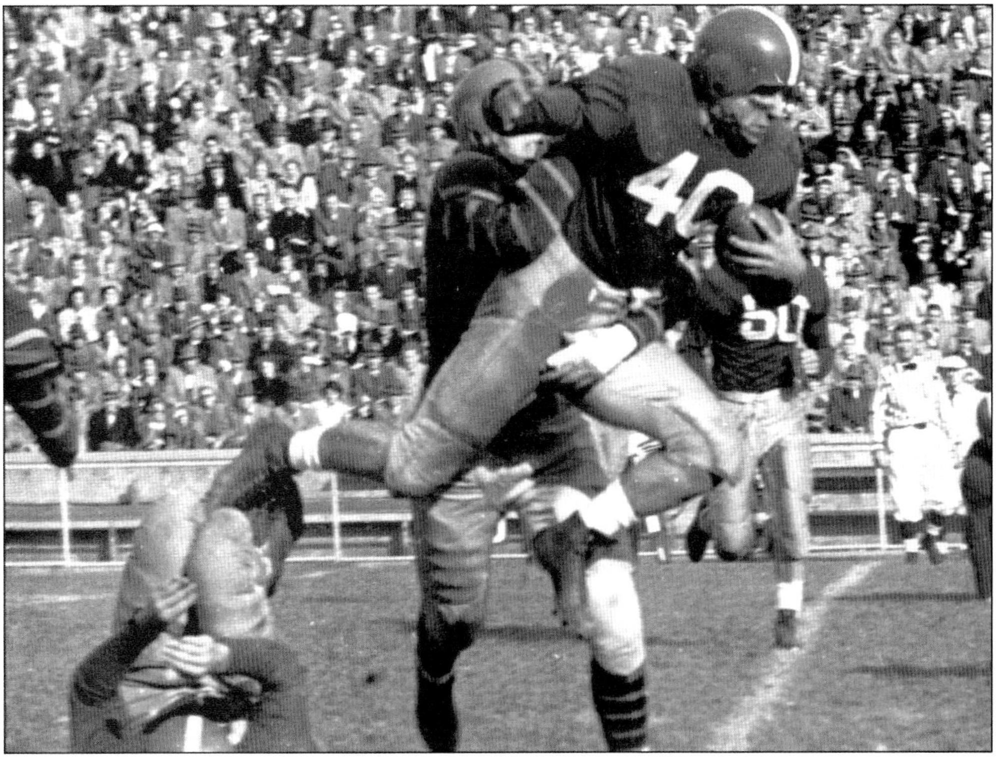

Dick Clasby '54 versus Princeton, 1952. Dick Clasby remains one of Harvard's greatest all-around athletes. A three-sport standout in the tradition of George Owen '23 and Barry Wood '31, Clasby starred in hockey and baseball, in addition to his considerable double-threat (running and passing) ability on the football field. He still ranks fifth on the Crimson all-time rushing list, with 1,825 yards and 13 touchdowns. Clasby carries the ball here at Princeton in a November 1952 game. He is a member of the Harvard Varsity Hall of Fame in the all-around performance category.

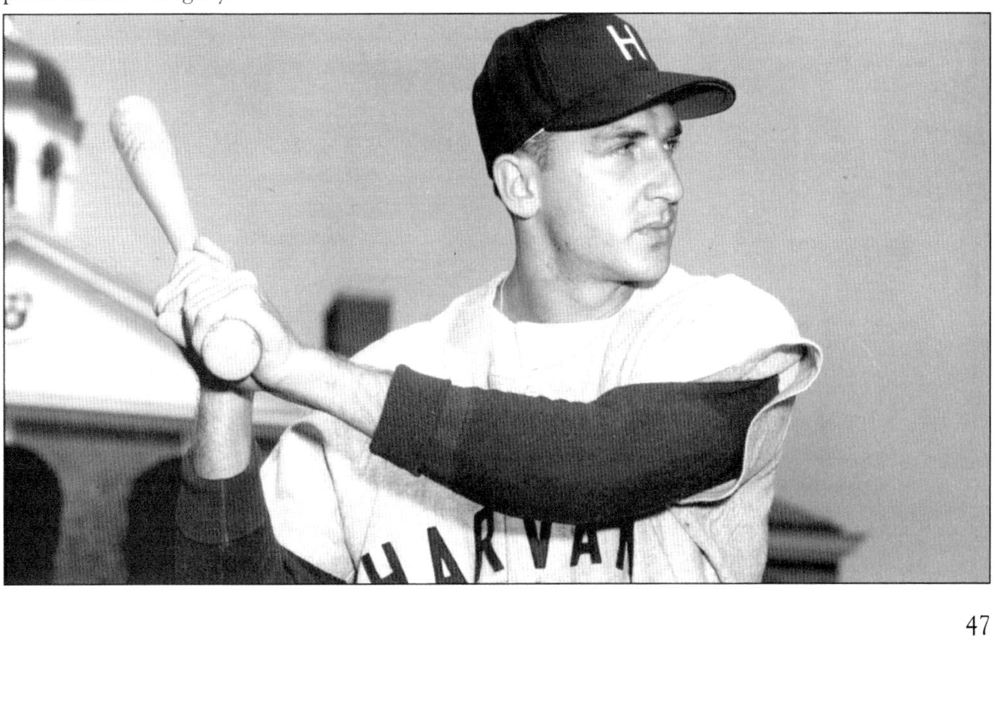

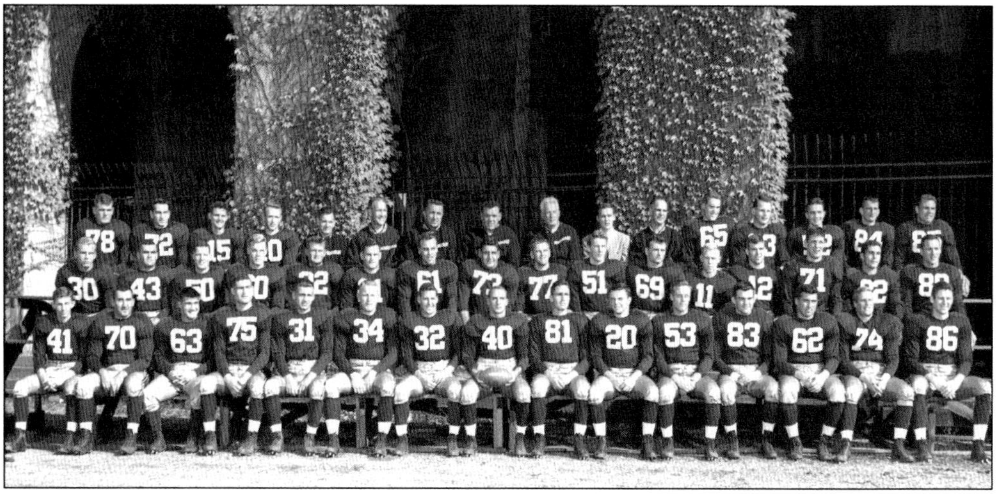

The 1953 Team. Lloyd Jordan's best—the 1953 squad—finished with a 6-2 record, the Crimson's finest since the 1946 team (7-2). Losses to Columbia and Princeton by identical 6-0 scores were the only two defeats for the Dick Clasby–captained 11. The season culminated in a 13-0 victory over Yale in New Haven.

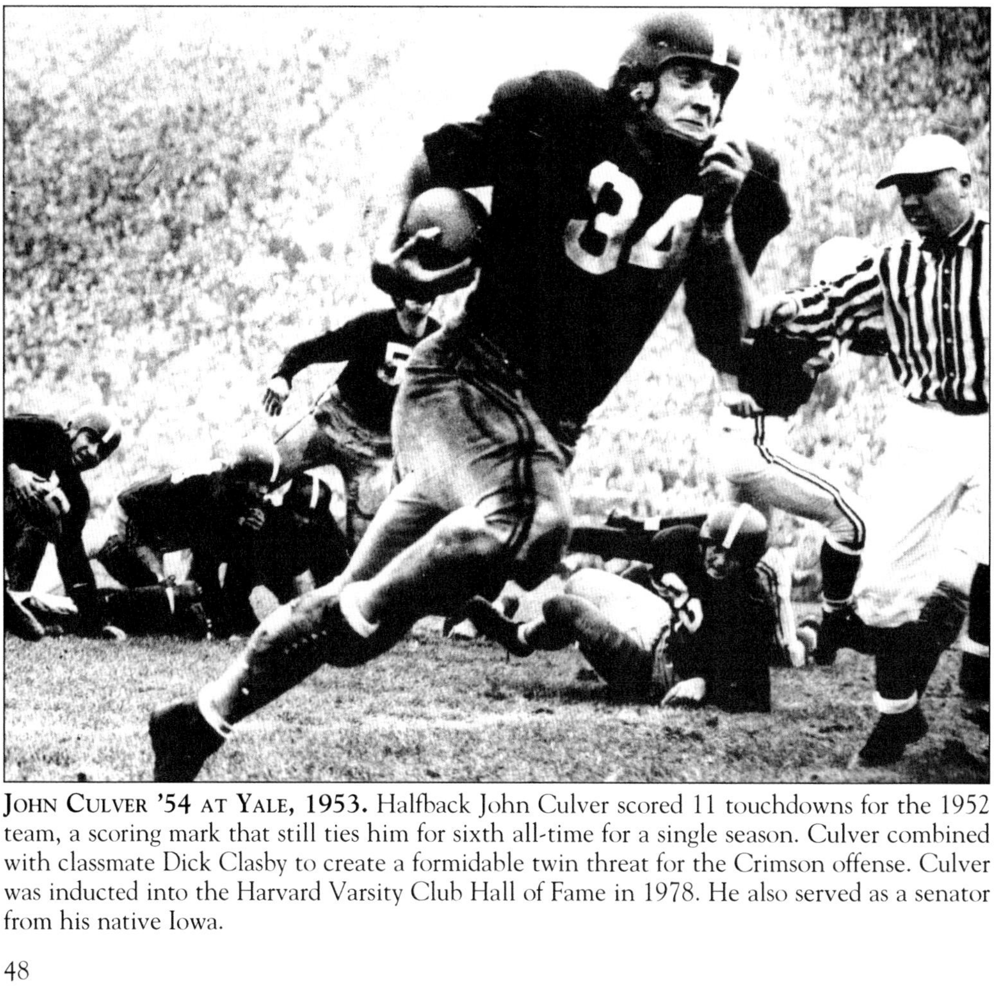

John Culver '54 at Yale, 1953. Halfback John Culver scored 11 touchdowns for the 1952 team, a scoring mark that still ties him for sixth all-time for a single season. Culver combined with classmate Dick Clasby to create a formidable twin threat for the Crimson offense. Culver was inducted into the Harvard Varsity Club Hall of Fame in 1978. He also served as a senator from his native Iowa.

TIM ANDERSON '55 (CAPTAIN, 1954). Guard Tim Anderson captained the 1954 team. The 4-3-1 Crimson overall record was highlighted by wins over Princeton (14-9), the program's 500th in 81 years of competition, and Yale (13-9), for the team's first Big Three title since 1941. The Crimson losses were all razor close—two 13-7 setbacks versus the University of Massachusetts and Dartmouth, along with a 7-6 loss to Columbia.

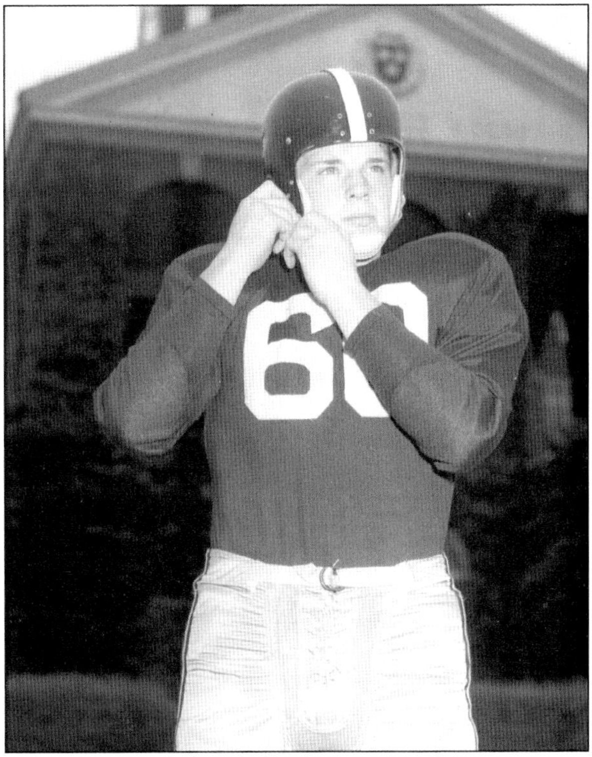

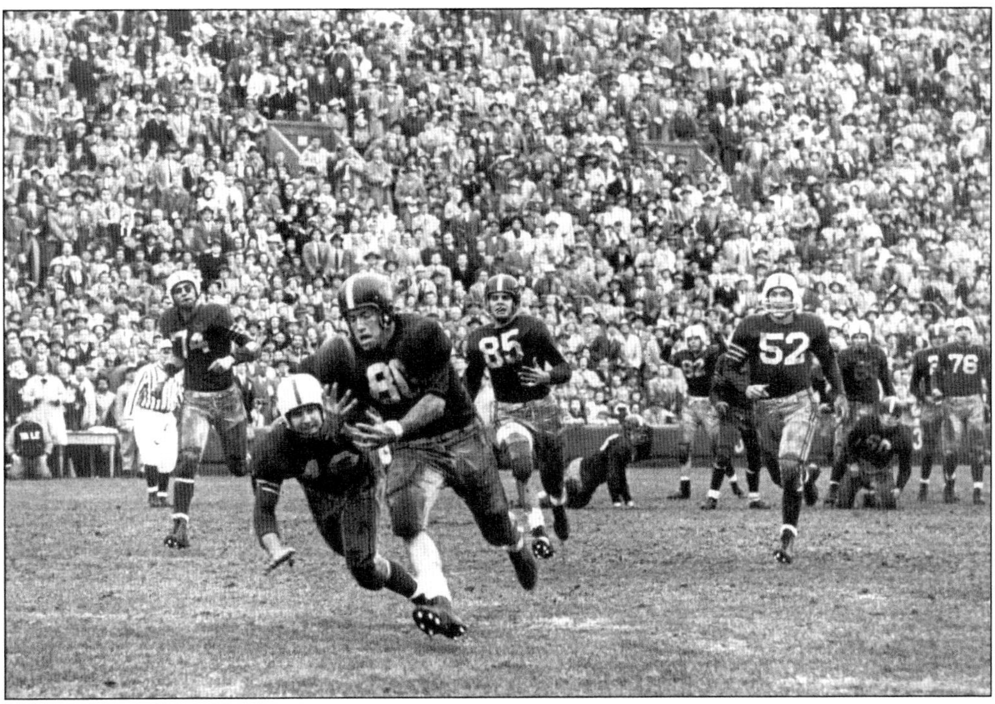

THE 1954 YALE GAME. Bob Cochran hauls in a 23-yard reverse pass from Frank White for the winning score in a 13-9 Harvard victory over Yale. Cochran juggled the ball before racing down the sideline for the touchdown. Harvard rallied from a 9-0 third-quarter deficit.

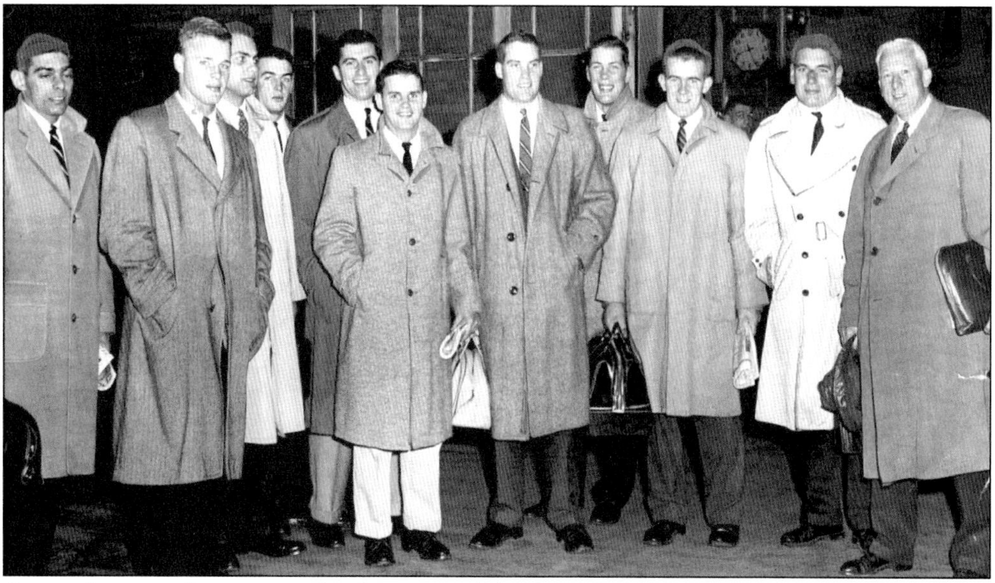

SOUTH STATION, BOSTON, 1954. Train travel for the Harvard football team remained popular in the mid-1950s. Here the Crimson, with captain Tim Anderson (second from left) and coach Lloyd Jordan (right), gets ready to leave South Station for a game at Princeton in 1954.

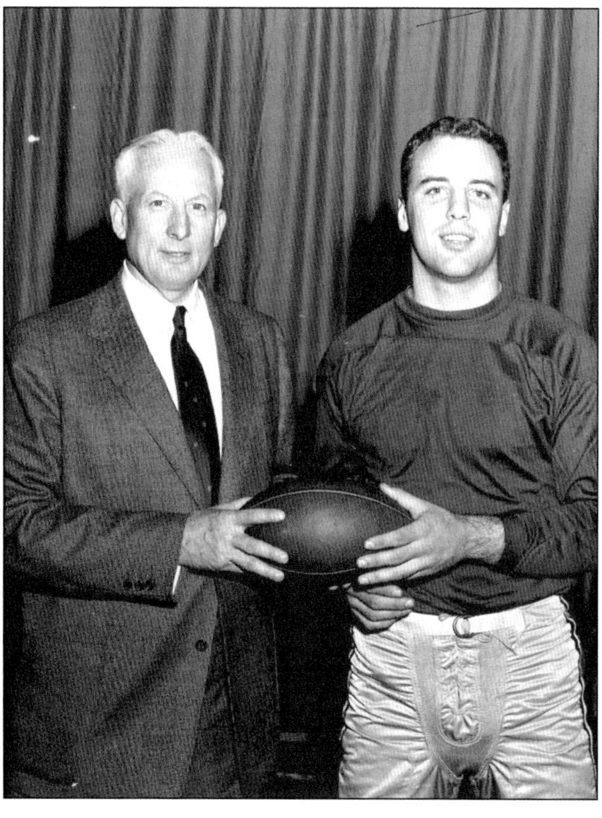

WILLIAM MEIGS '56 (CAPTAIN, 1955). Bill Meigs (right), who had played at the guard position with Tim Anderson the previous year, was elected captain of the 1955 team. He shares the football with coach Lloyd Jordan.

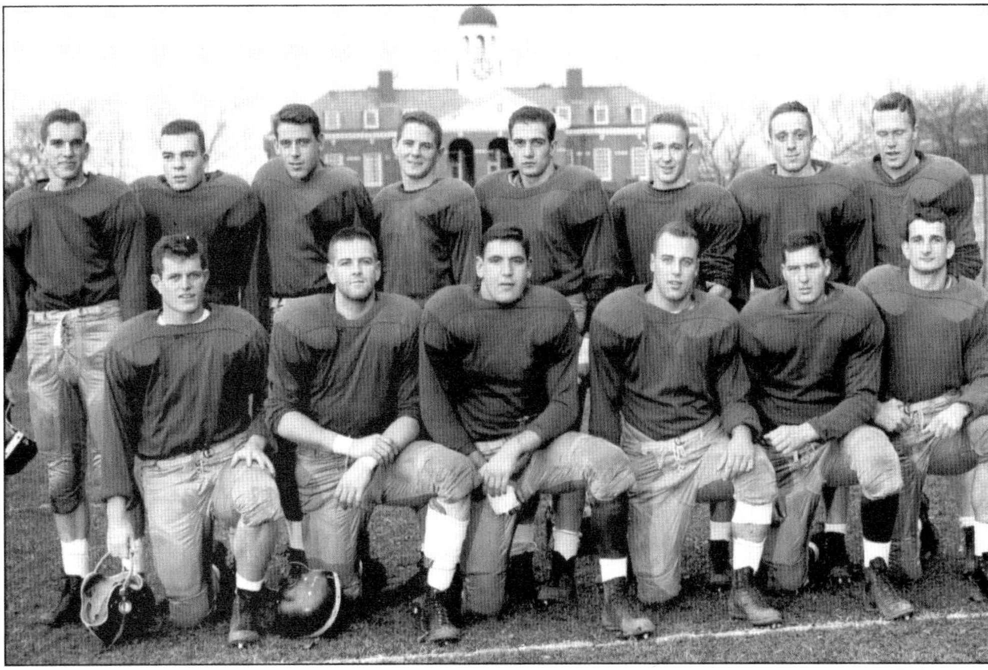

THE SENIOR CLASS OF 1955. An undermanned team throughout the season, Harvard slumped to a 3-4-1 overall mark. A 7-6 victory over Princeton was the season's only real highlight. Future senator Edward M. Kennedy '54 (front left) was a solid performer at the end position and scored Harvard's only touchdown in a 21-7 loss to Yale in New Haven, the last varsity game for this group of 14 seniors.

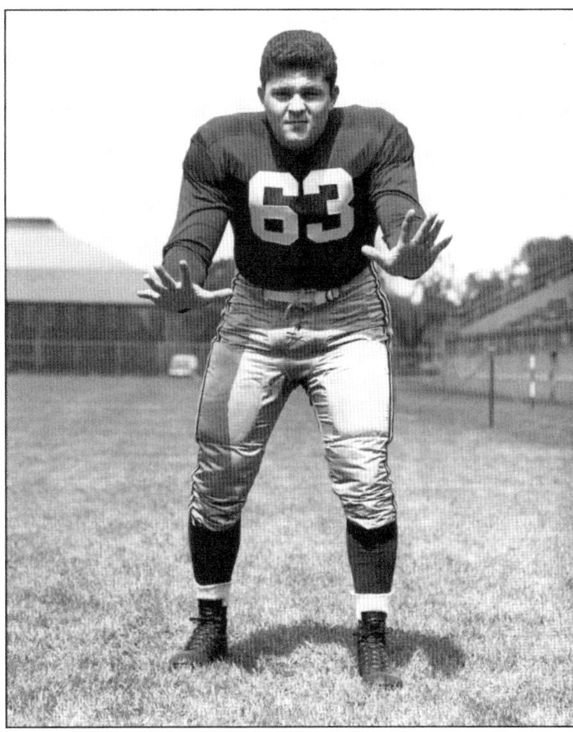

THEODORE METROPOULOS '57 (CAPTAIN, 1956). Ted Metropoulos captained the first Harvard team to compete in the newly formalized Ivy League in 1956. A native of Aliquippa, Pennsylvania, he was the lone returning veteran on the line. His outstanding effort under difficult circumstances all season earned him the distinction of being the first Crimson All-Ivy selection, receiving the honor for his play at the guard position.

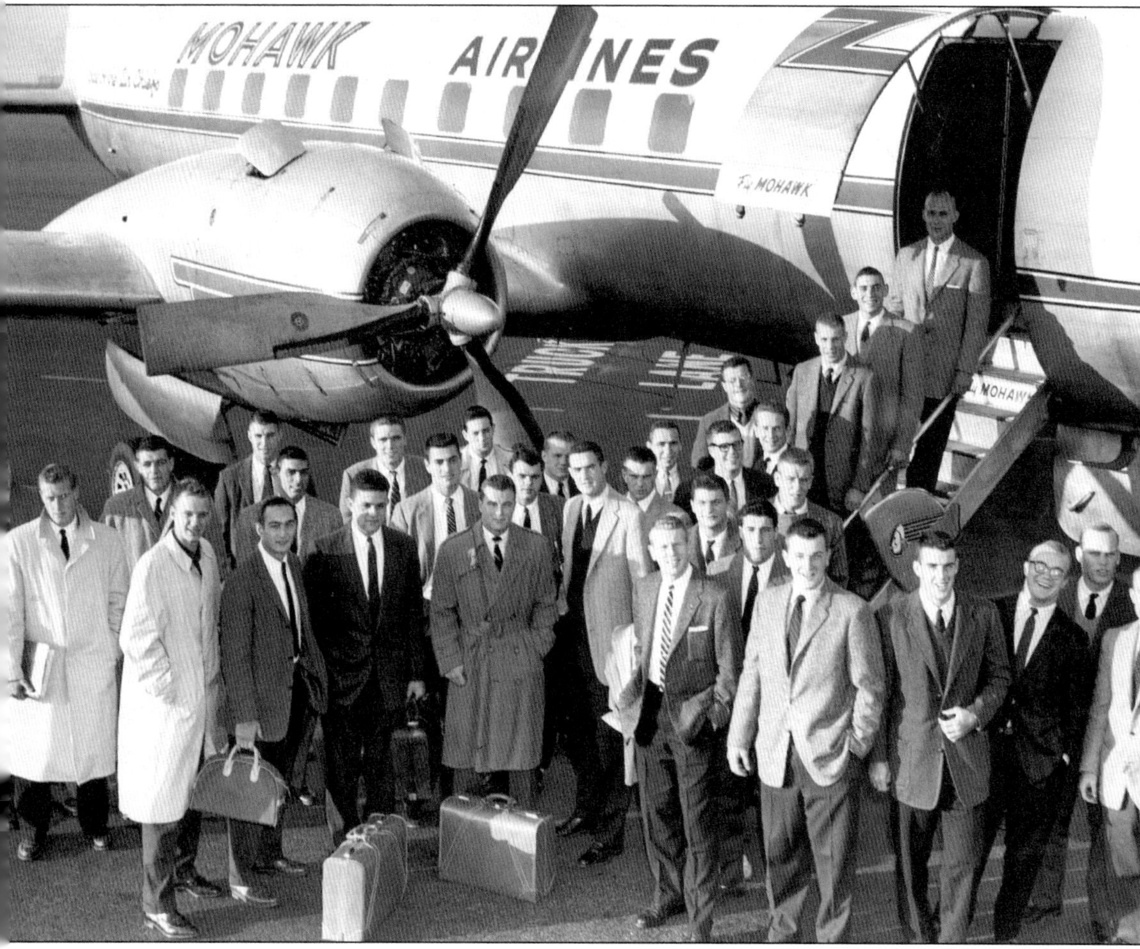

AN AIR TRIP TO CORNELL, 1956. Air travel was a relatively new experience for college sports teams. Here a dapper group of gridders prepares to board a Mohawk Airlines prop plane for a trip to Cornell in 1956. The mode of travel must have agreed with the Crimson, as evidenced by the 32-7 victory that followed.

Four

1957–1967

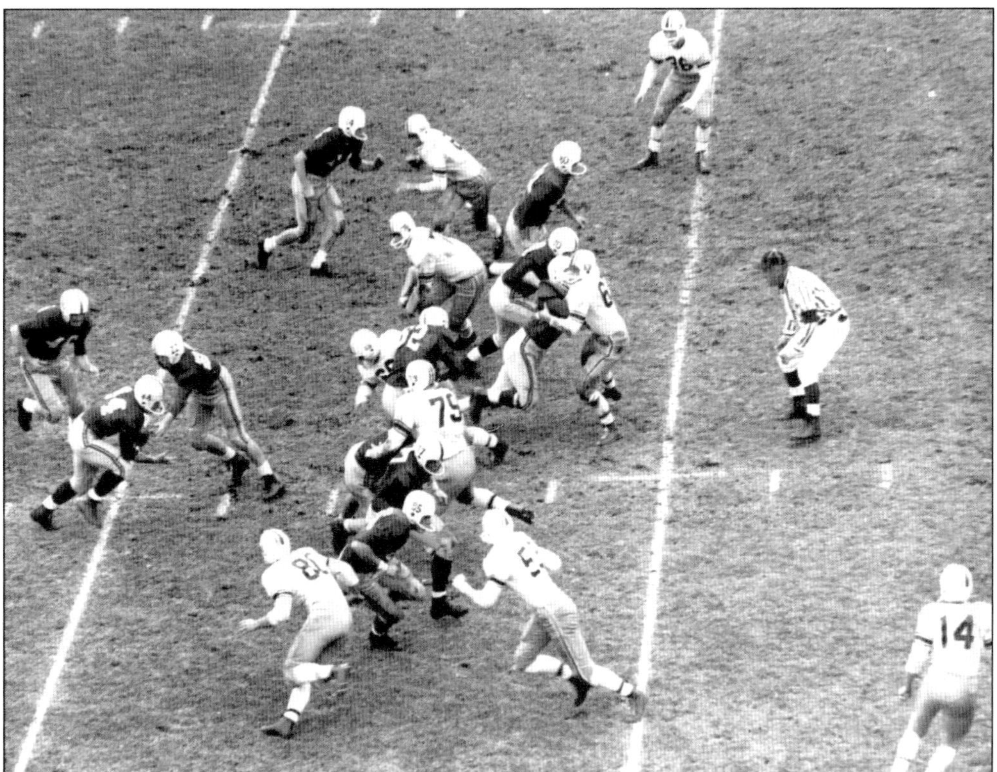

CHRIS HAUGHIE '60 VERSUS BROWN UNIVERSITY, 1958. Halfback Chris Haughie picks up five yards in action versus Brown at Harvard Stadium in November 1958. A 23-22 Crimson lead disappeared on the final play of the game as the Bears' Frank Finney scored the winning touchdown for a wild 29-22 Brown victory.

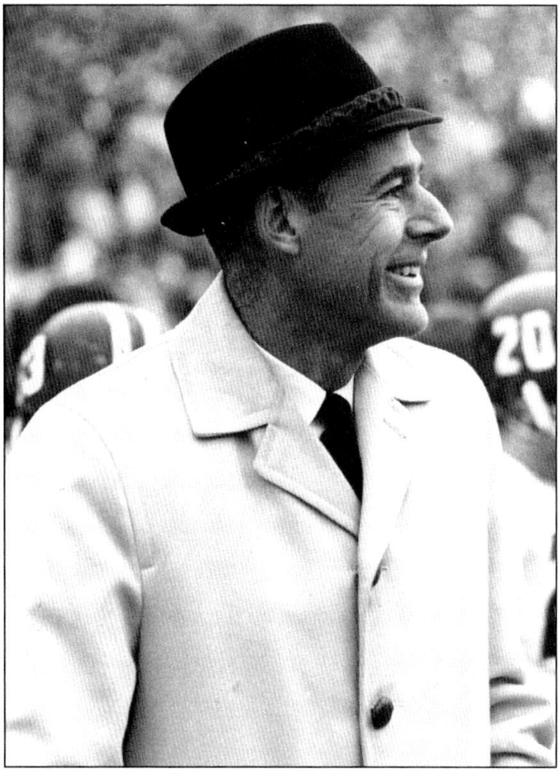

JOHN YOVICSIN (COACH, 1957–1970). John Yovicsin, a Pennsylvanian, succeeded Lloyd Jordan as head coach in 1957. The 22nd head coach in Harvard's 84-year history, Yovicsin came to Cambridge after five very successful years (32-11) as head coach at Gettysburg College. Former Harvard coach Dick Harlow gave the new Crimson mentor a strong recommendation. A gracious, articulate, and earnest man, Yovicsin faced a formidable task in turning around the overall fortunes of the football program.

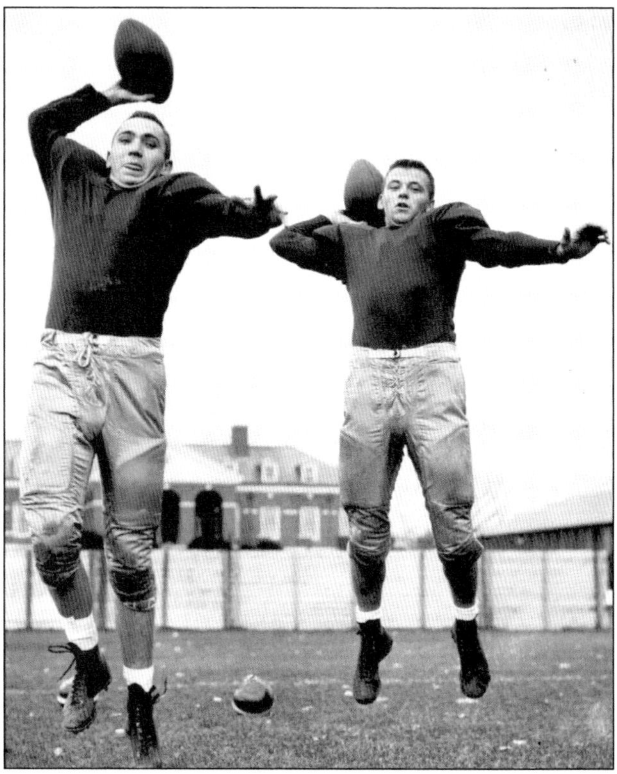

QUARTERBACKS DICK MCLAUGHLIN AND RON JOHANSON, 1957. A pair of juniors, Dick McLaughlin '59 and Ron Johanson '59, saw action at the quarterback position for Yovicsin's first team. McLaughlin was the early season starter until an injury forced him out of the Penn game. Johanson, called up from the junior varsity, responded with a touchdown, leading the Crimson to a 13-6 win over the Quakers.

BOB SHAUNESSY '59 (CAPTAIN, 1958). Bob "Shag" Shaunessy, a returning All-Ivy tackle, was chosen to captain the 1958 Harvard squad. A strapping 6 feet 2 inches and 223 pounds, he led a young Crimson team to victories over Ivy League champion Dartmouth (16-8) and Yale (28-0), holding the Eli to just 35 yards in total offense. Shaunessy was later honored by induction into the Harvard Varsity Club Hall of Fame.

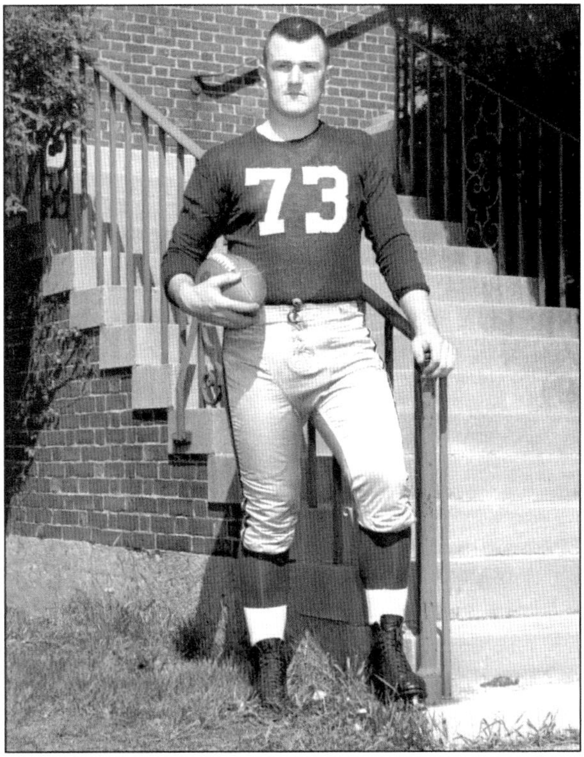

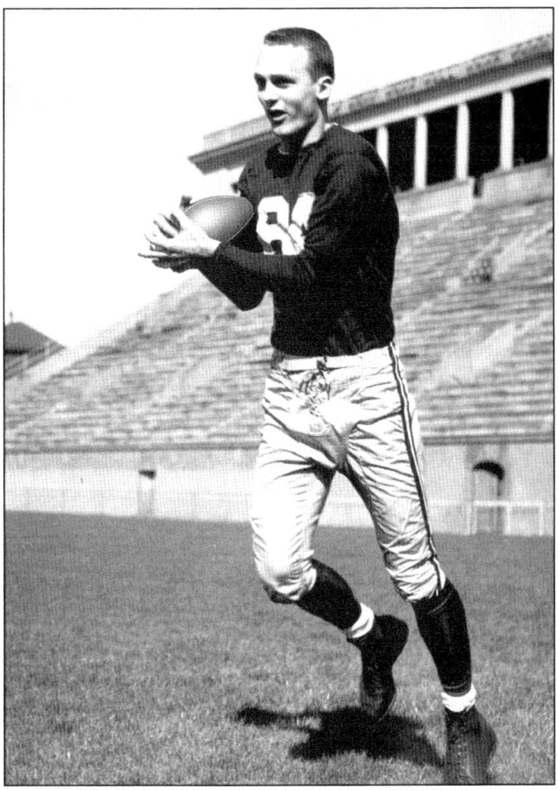

HAROLD KEOHANE '60 (CAPTAIN, 1959). The 1959 team began an impressive run of 10 straight winning seasons under Yovicsin. The 6-3 record could have been even better with a few breaks. Harold Keohane, a native of Arlington, Massachusetts, captained the team and still holds the Crimson record for longest touchdown reception—an 85-yard toss from Chet Boulris versus Yale.

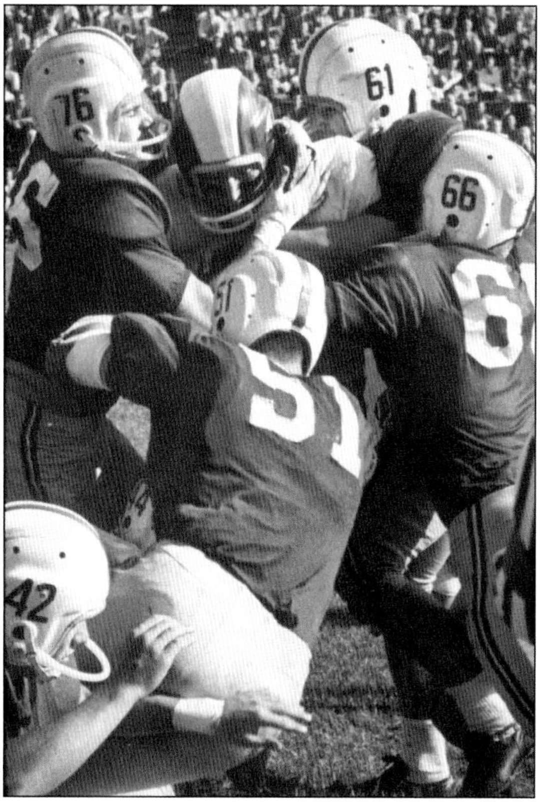

THE CRIMSON DEFENSE, 1959. The Crimson defense demonstrates the gang tackle, as Cornell's George Telesh is surrounded by Bruce MacIntyre (42), Glenn Haughie (44, on the ground), Pete Eliades (51), Darwin Wile (76), Bill Swinford (61), and Roger Wilson (66). Despite this swarming defensive effort, the Crimson lost a heartbreaker to the Big Red 20-16 on a 76-yard touchdown pass with 24 seconds remaining. Both Swinford and Wile were All-Ivy selections in 1961.

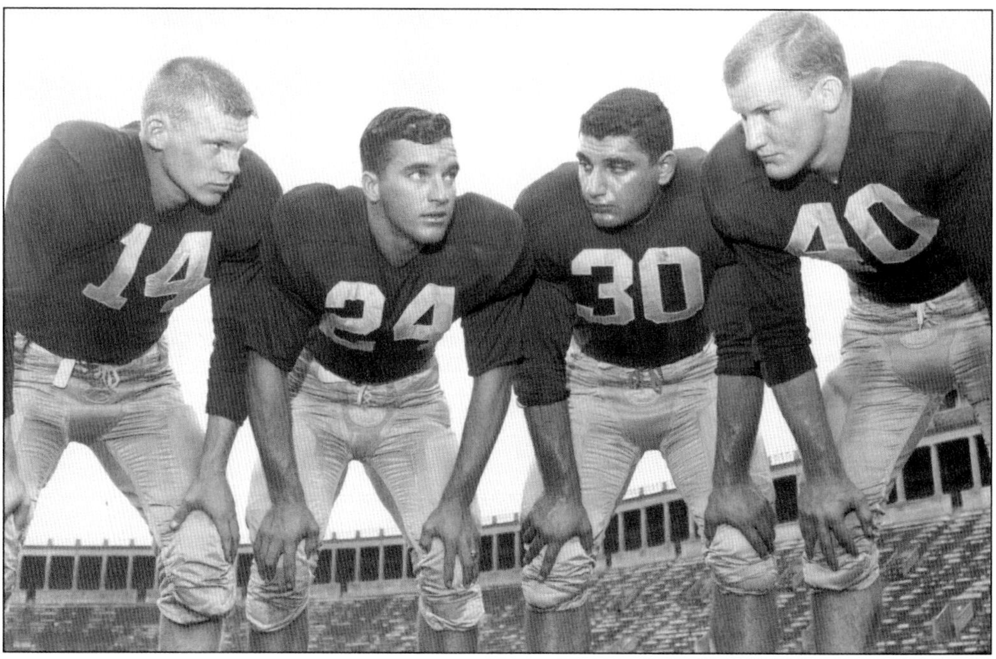

THE HARVARD BACKFIELD, 1959. The 1959 backfield confers. Shown, from left to right, are halfback Larry Repsher, quarterback Charley Ravenel, fullback Sam Halaby, and halfback Chet Boulris. Each man was a three-year letter winner.

Chet Boulris '60. A hard-running product of Springfield, Massachusetts, Chet Boulris was twice a first-team All-Ivy selection as halfback (1958 and 1959). He is a member of the Varsity Club Hall of Fame and was named to the All-Ivy Team of the Decade.

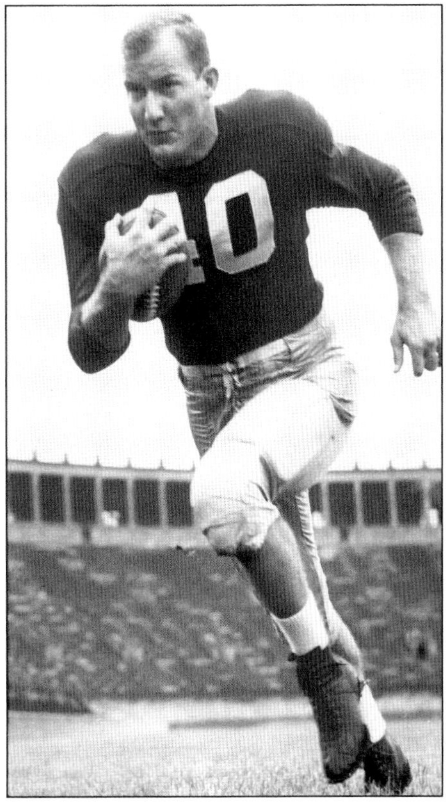

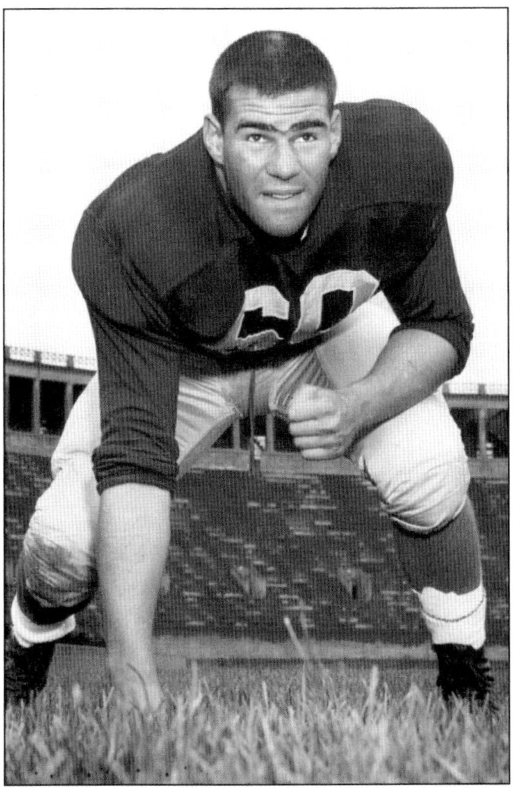

Terry Lenzner '61 (Captain, 1960). Terry Lenzner's 1960 season exemplified his team's frustration and disappointment. Captained by Lenzner, a solid, spirited player, Harvard was the preseason favorite to win the Ivy League championship. However, knee injuries to quarterback Charley Ravenel and Lenzner dashed the high expectations of the squad.

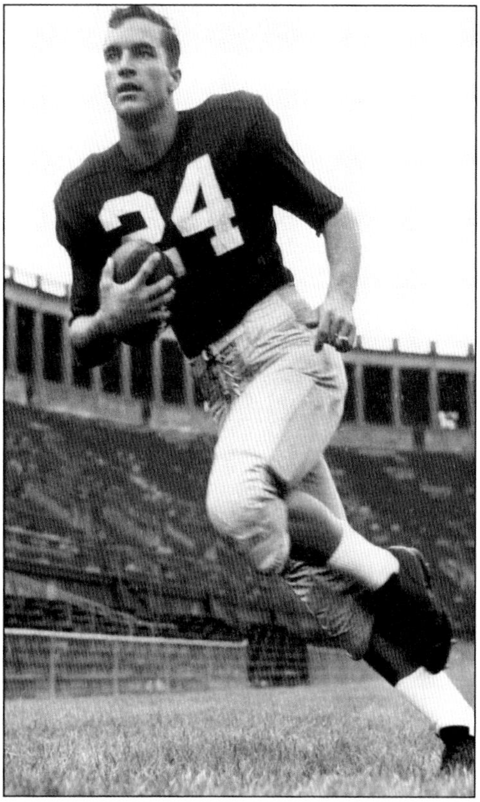

CHARLEY RAVENEL '61 (FOOTBALL, BASEBALL). A fiery, emotional player, Charley Ravenel was dubbed the "Riverboat Gambler" for his risk-taking style and inspirational play at quarterback. The Charleston, South Carolina, native (via Exeter) led the team in scoring in 1958 and 1959. In the spring Ravenel was one of the Ivy League's best hitters for the Crimson baseball team.

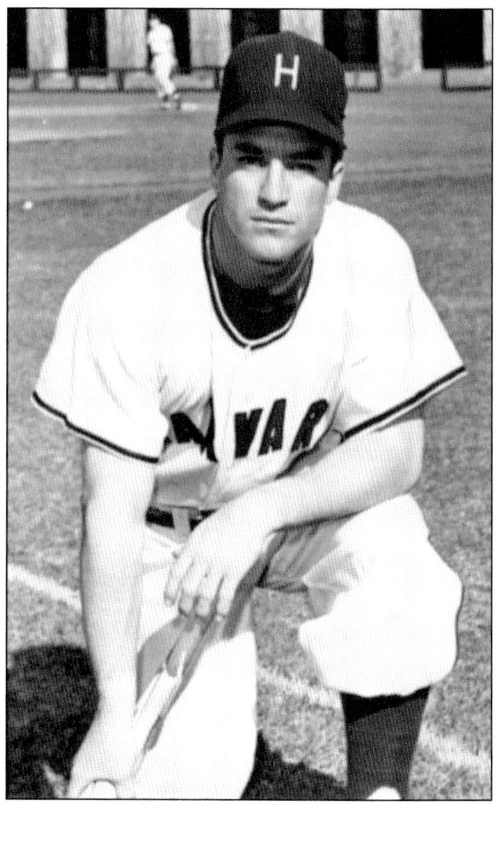

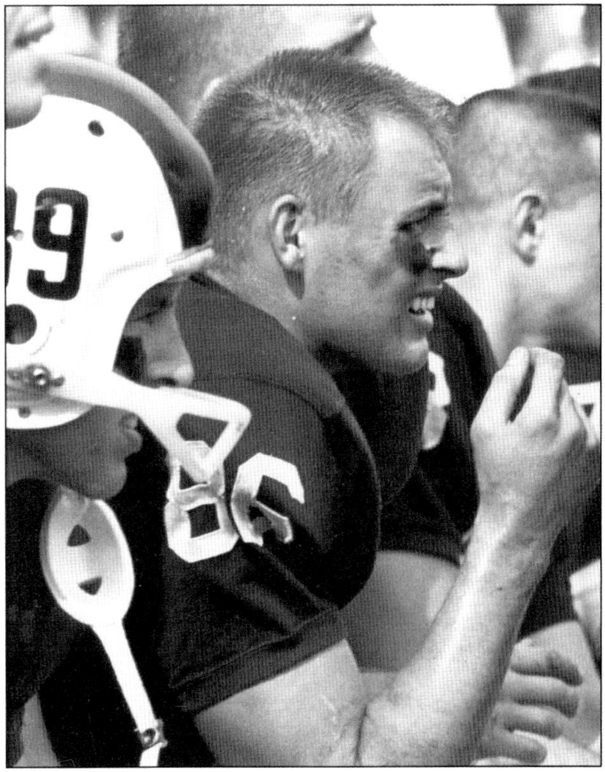

Pete Hart '62 (Captain, 1961) in Action versus Yale. Pete Hart holds the distinction of captaining the Crimson's first Ivy League championship team in 1961. A seventh-place preseason pick in the eight-team league, Harvard closed out the season with five straight victories. A two-way starter at tight end and defensive end, Hart played briefly with the AFL's Boston Patriots before going into business, rising to become president and chief executive officer of MasterCard International. Hart (86), in a game versus Yale at New Haven, closes in on quarterback Leckonby in Harvard's resounding 27-0 shutout victory.

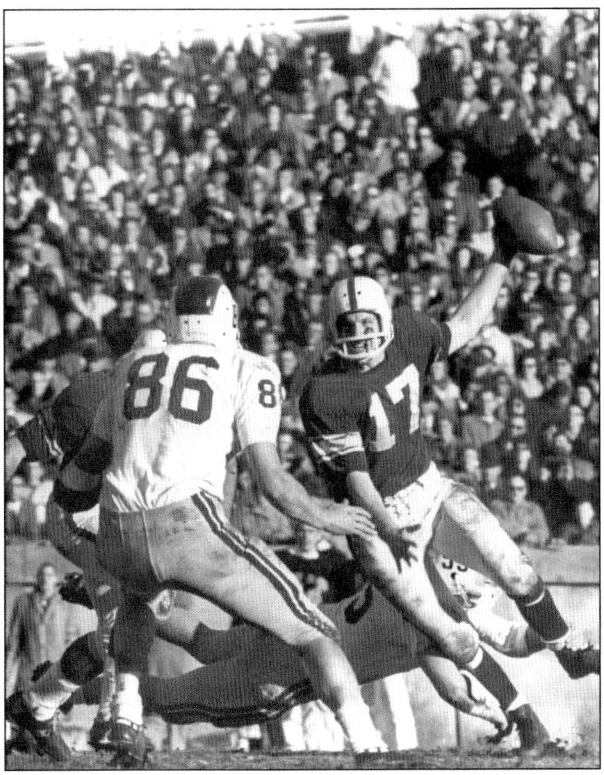

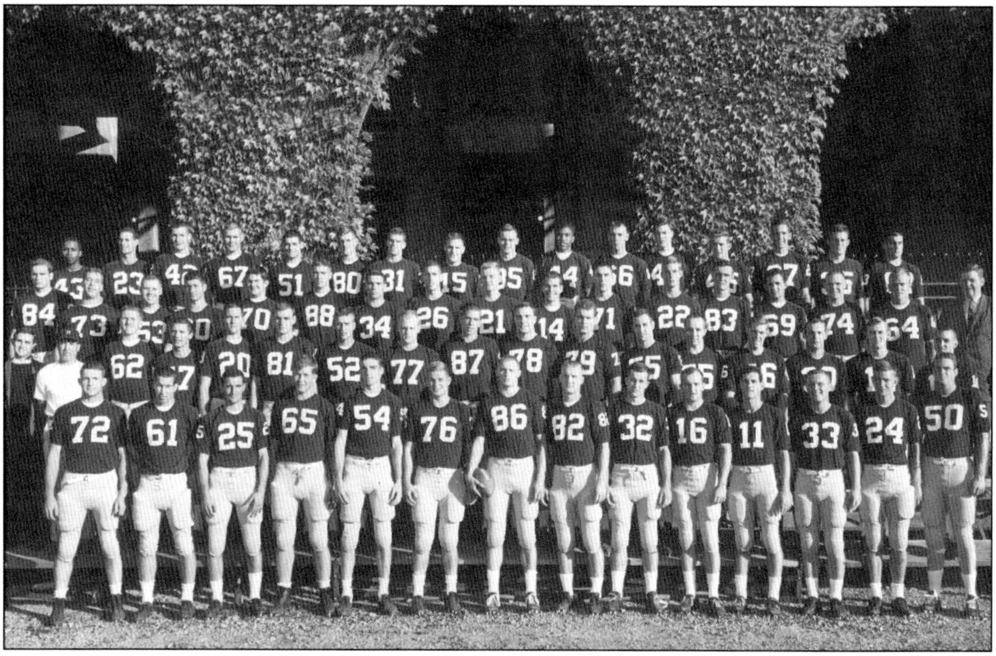

THE 1961 TEAM AND THE IVY LEAGUE TROPHY. The 1961 team featured an unyielding defense that only allowed 34 points during its five-game season-ending winning streak. Despite the loss of 16 key seniors from the previous year, the Crimson showed great resilience and saved the very best for last. Winner of the Big Three title, Harvard more importantly seized a share of the Ivy League title (with Columbia) by posting a 6-1 league record. Shown below are the spoils of war: the Ivy League trophy encircled by the game balls from each Ivy contest.

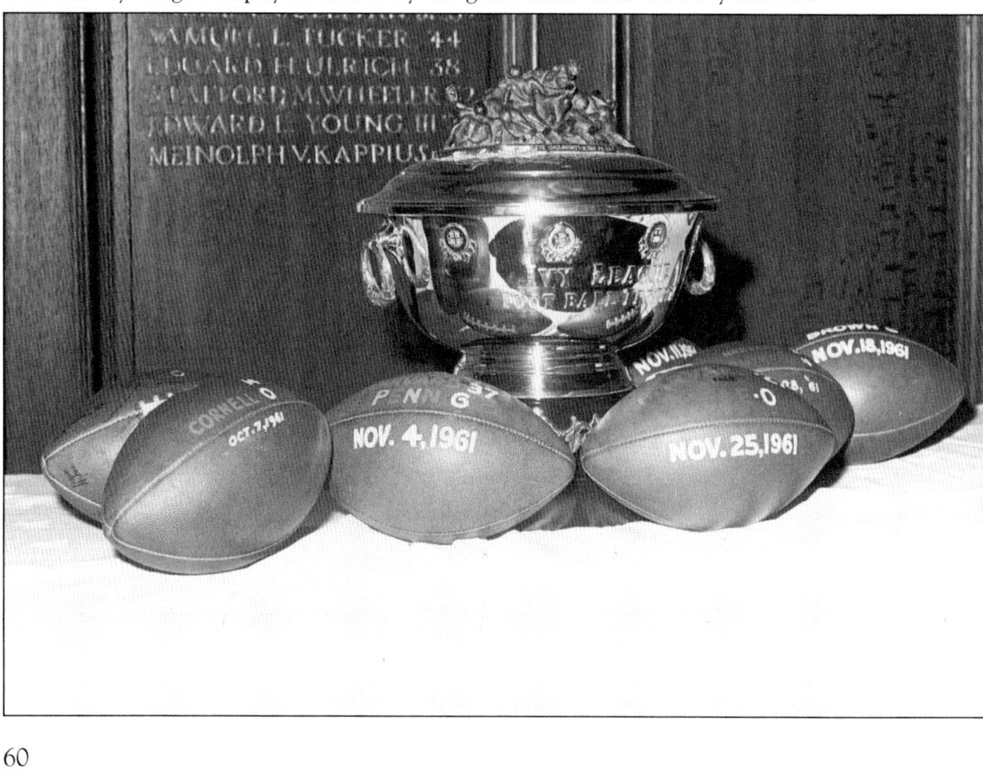

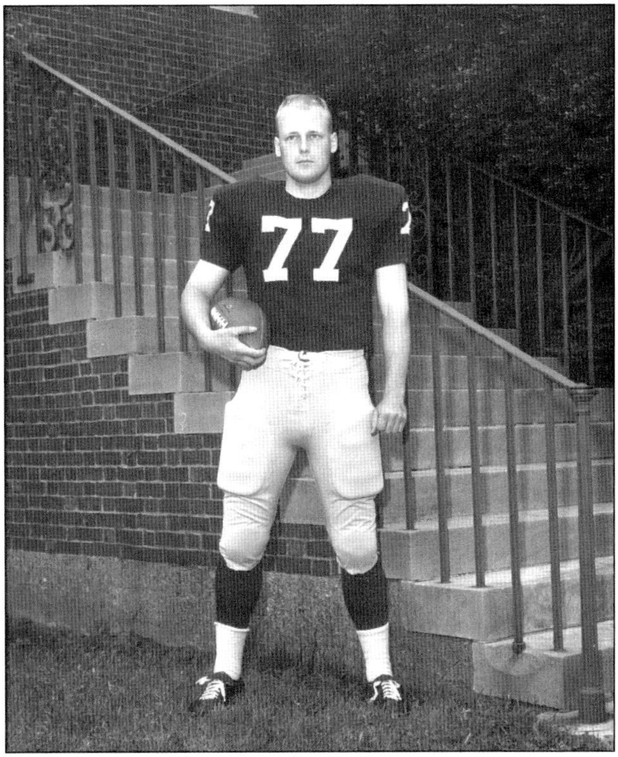

Richard Diehl '63 (Captain, 1962). Dick Diehl, the only returnee on the line from the 1961 starting group, was a solid leader by example on the field. The tackle from Choate via Pittsburgh, Pennsylvania, showed good quickness on the defensive side, which factored prominently in the Yale game, as the Crimson consistently stifled the Yale offense.

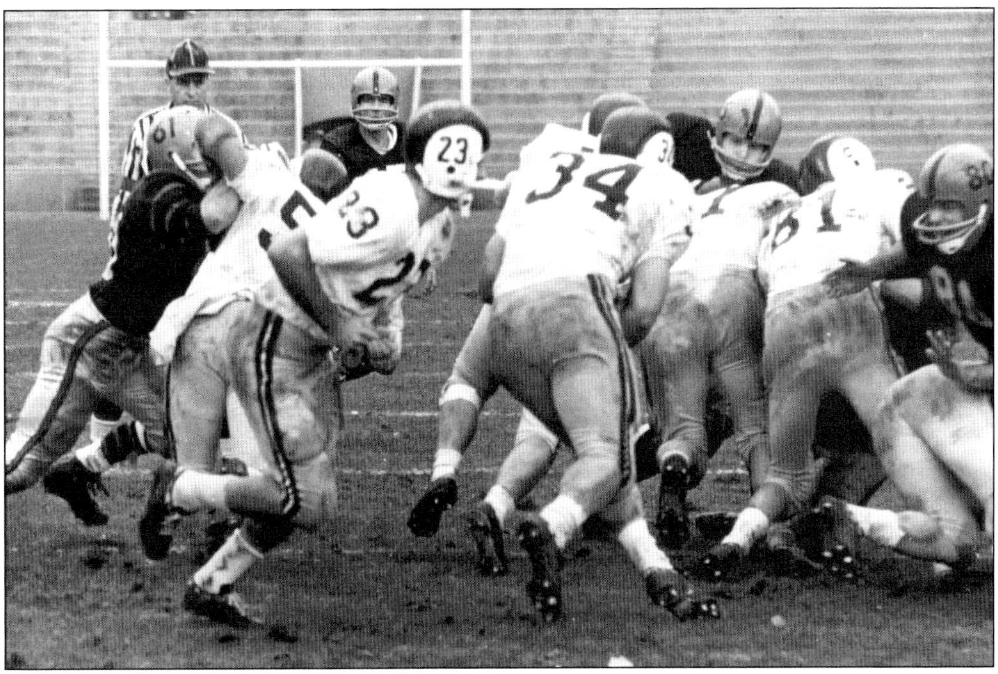

Harvard versus Princeton, 1962. Fullback Bill Grana '64 takes the handoff from quarterback Mike Bassett and smashes into the middle of the Princeton defensive front in 1962 road action at Palmer Stadium. Grana scored twice, and Bassett made a multitude of big plays in Harvard's 20-0 shutout victory.

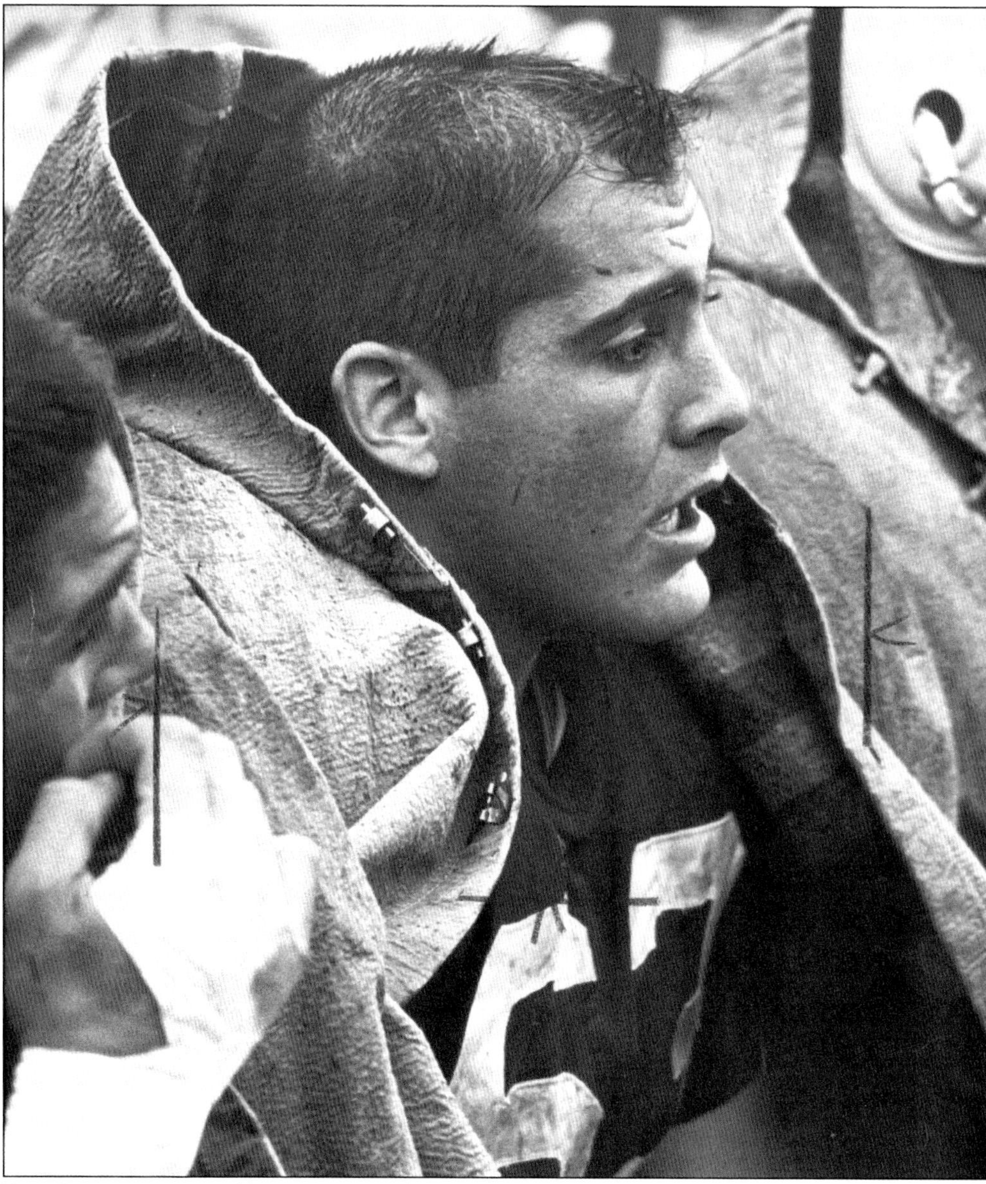

BILL SOUTHMAYD '64 (CAPTAIN, 1963). Bill Southmayd continued a 10-year run of linemen as Crimson captains in 1963. Harvard stayed in the Ivy League race despite an upset loss at Penn (7-2) and a tie versus Columbia (3-3) at Harvard Stadium. The Crimson did end Dartmouth's 15-game winning streak (17-13) and surprised Princeton (21-7) to keep hopes of an Ivy title alive. Southmayd, an All-Ivy selection, went on to a career in sports medicine as a noted orthopedic surgeon.

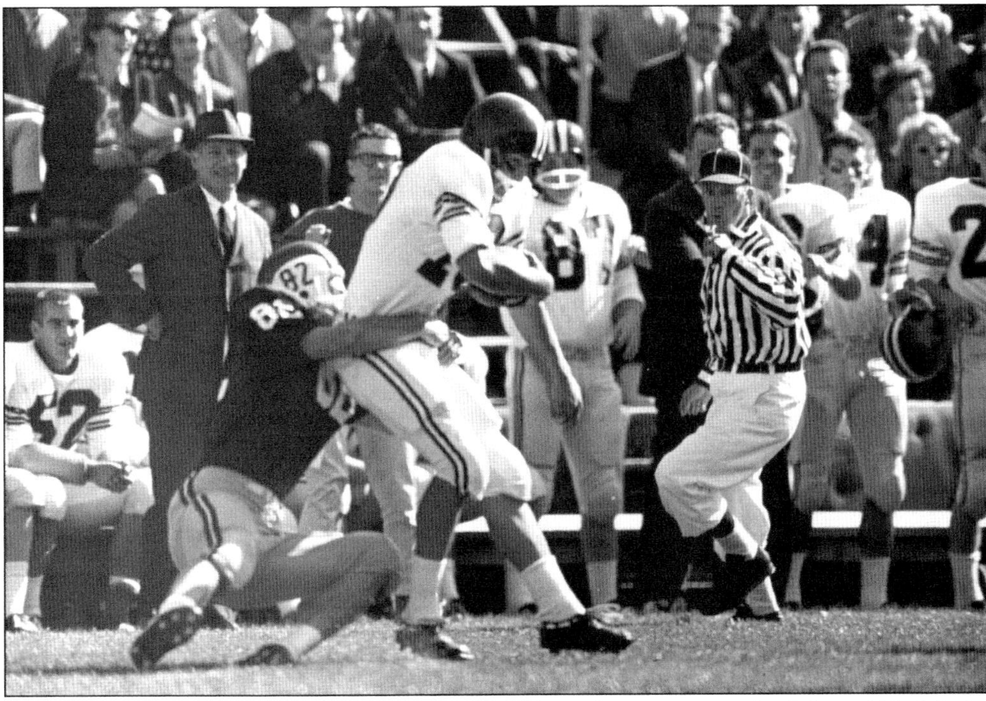

HARVARD VERSUS UMASS, 1963. University of Massachusetts quarterback Jerry Whelchel is sacked by Harvard's Paul Barringer for a five-yard loss. The Minutemen and Crimson played to a scoreless tie in the 1963 season opener at Harvard Stadium.

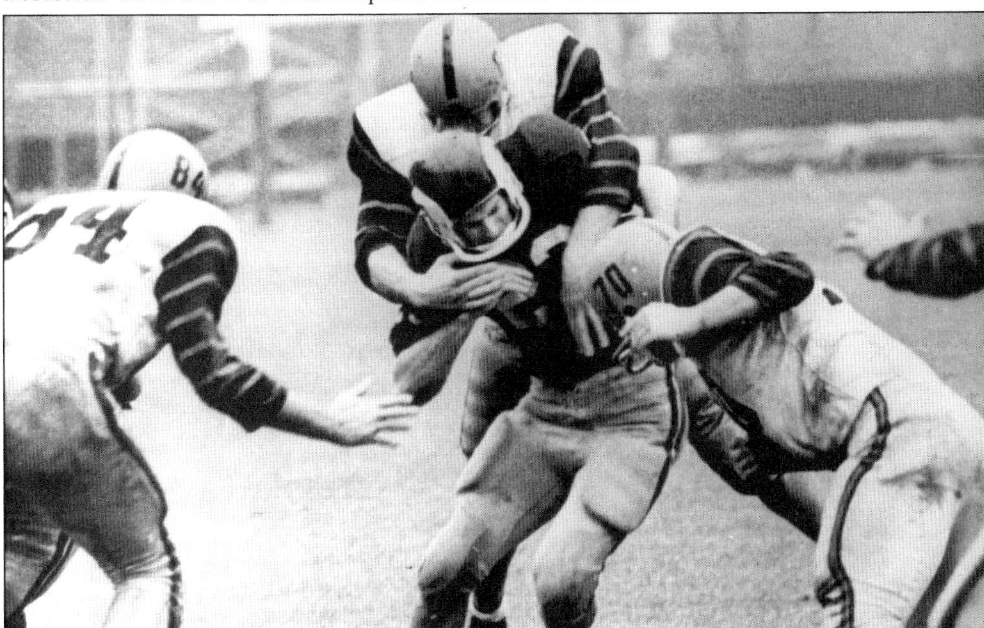

QUARTERBACK MIKE BASSETT VERSUS PRINCETON, 1963. Harvard's Mike Bassett, surrounded by three Princeton players, appears to be stopped. The Crimson quarterback escaped the Tigers' claws to pick up five more yards and a touchdown. On this day the Crimson knocked Princeton from the ranks of the unbeaten with a 21-7 victory.

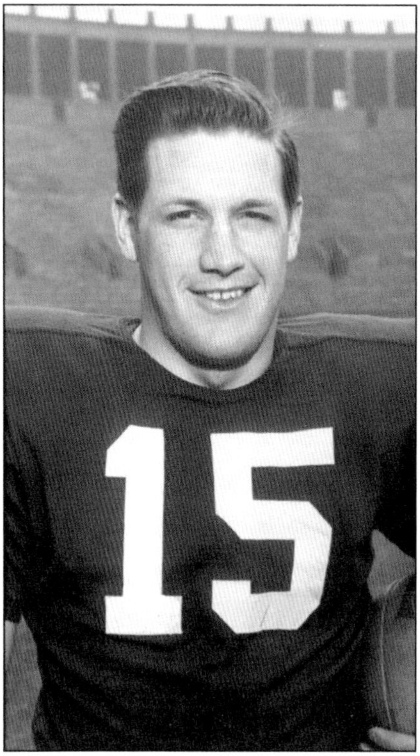

Scott Harshbarger '64. Sophomore halfback Scott Harshbarger scrambles into the end zone for the first Harvard touchdown in the 27-0 rout of Yale. A native of State College, Pennsylvania, Harshbarger was another in the long line of Crimson football players to go on to public service. Harshbarger was the longtime Middlesex County district attorney.

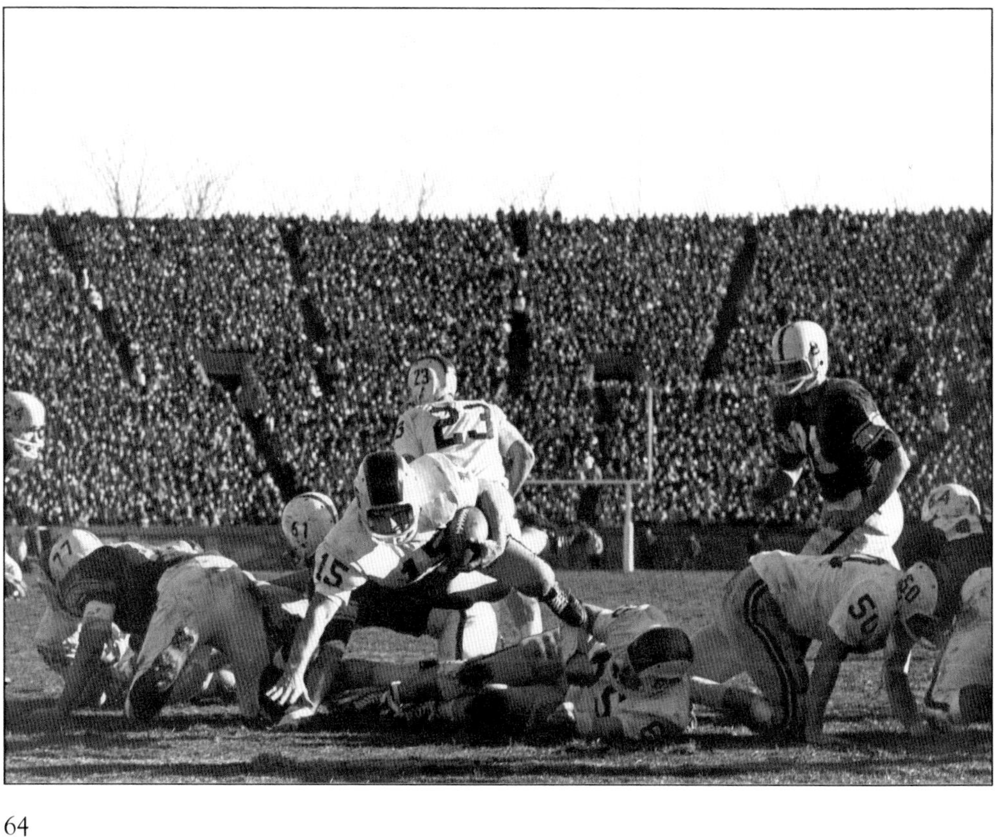

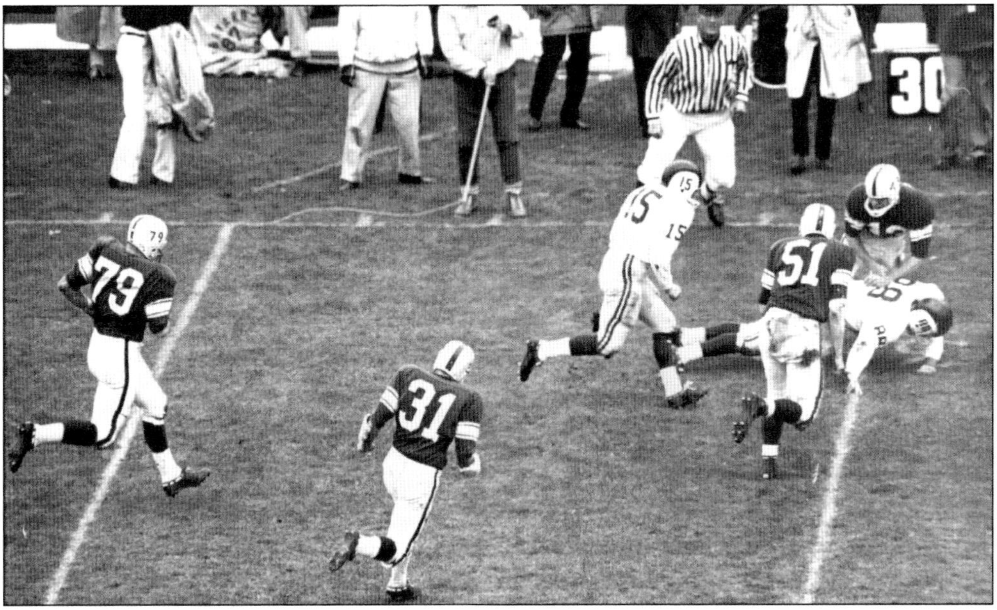

SCOTT HARSHBARGER AND TOM STEPHENSON VERSUS YALE, 1963. The Game of 1963 was pushed back a full week because of the assassination of President Kennedy '40 on November 22. Kennedy had been a spectator at that year's Columbia game. Played on November 30, Yale defeated Harvard 20-6 at the Yale Bowl, ending the Crimson's hopes for a piece of the Ivy crown. Halfback Scott Harshbarger '64 (15) gets a big block from end Tom Stephenson (88) and heads upfield.

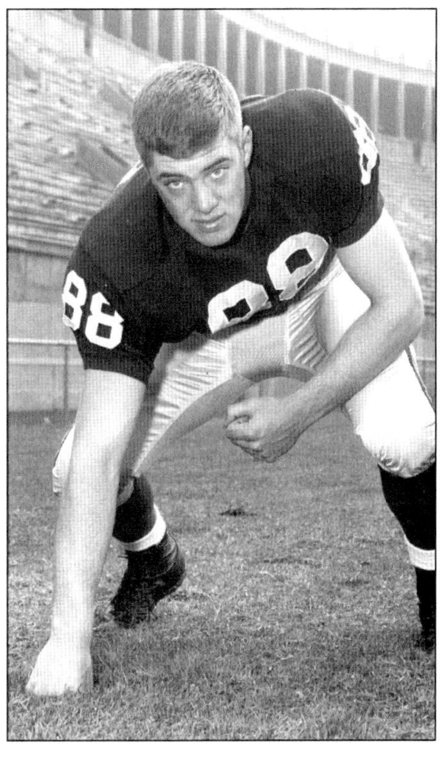

TOM STEPHENSON '64. A native of Wilmington, Delaware, Tom Stephenson lettered in 1962 and 1963 at the end position. In October 1994, Stephenson established a $2 million endowment fund that supports the head football coach in much the same way that an endowed chair supports a professor. Stephenson chose to name the fund for his family, which has been an active participant in the Harvard community for four generations.

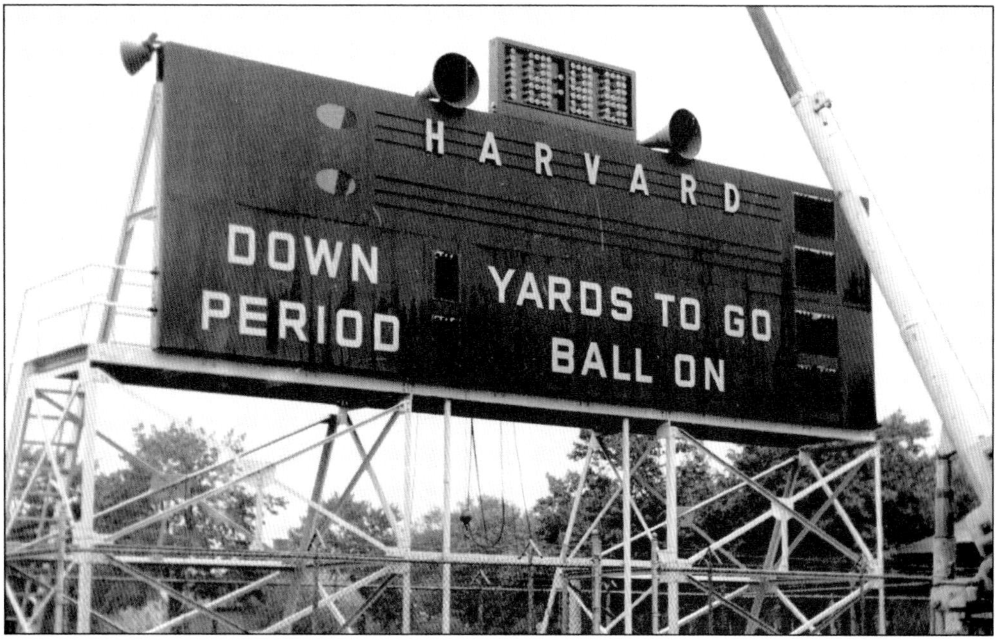

THE NEW STADIUM SCOREBOARD, 1964. A new state-of-the-art scoreboard was unveiled at Harvard Stadium to begin the 1964 season. The Crimson lit up its side for 20 points in a victory over UMass (20-14) in the home opener.

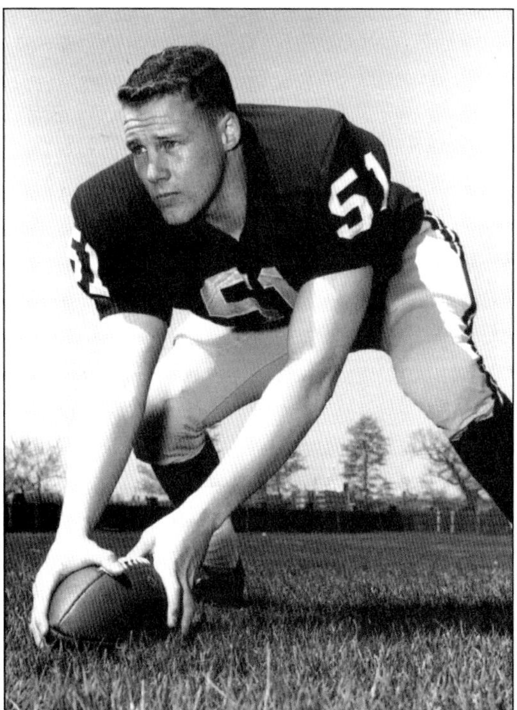

JOHN O'BRIEN '65 (CAPTAIN, 1964). A local boy from Brockton, Massachusetts, center John O'Brien captained the 1964 team to a record of 6-3. Harvard amazingly played in five shutout games—three for and two against in its five Ivy League contests. The Crimson finished the year on a high, rallying from a 14-12 deficit on a 46-yard touchdown dash by sophomore Bobby Leo for a 19-14 victory over Yale at Harvard Stadium.

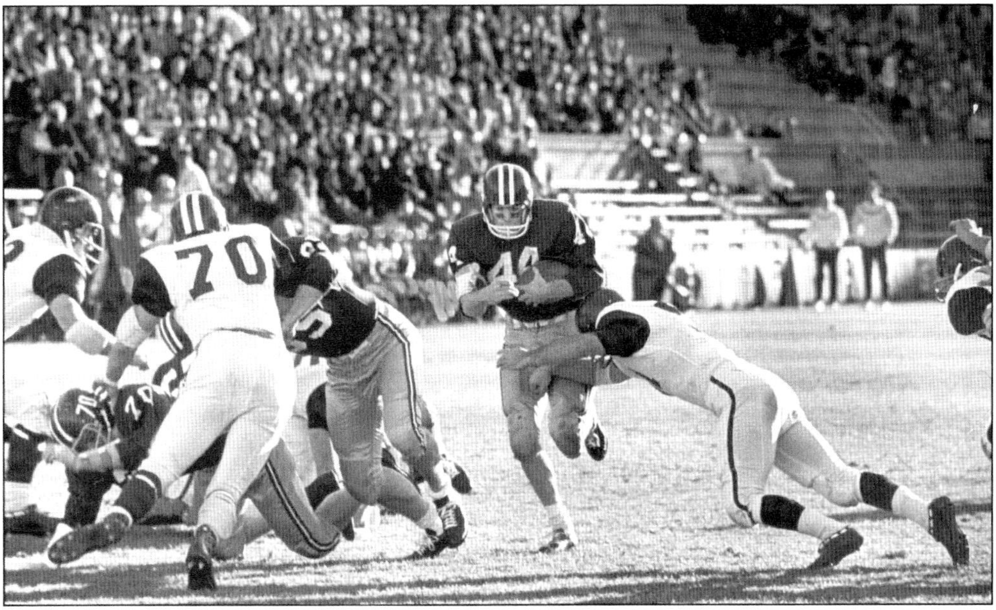

JOHN DOCKERY '66. John Dockery enjoyed a stellar athletic career at Harvard, playing both football and baseball. Dockery was an impact player both offensively and defensively as a halfback and defensive back. His 100-yard interception return for a touchdown versus Cornell in 1964 remains an Ivy League record. Dockery was also a baseball Most Valuable Player (MVP) in the spring of 1965. He went on to a professional football career as a defensive back for the New York Jets (1968–1971) and Pittsburgh Steelers (1972–1973), earning a Super Bowl ring with Joe Namath and the 1968 Jets as a National Football League (NFL) rookie. Dockery has been a successful nationally-known sports broadcaster for many years.

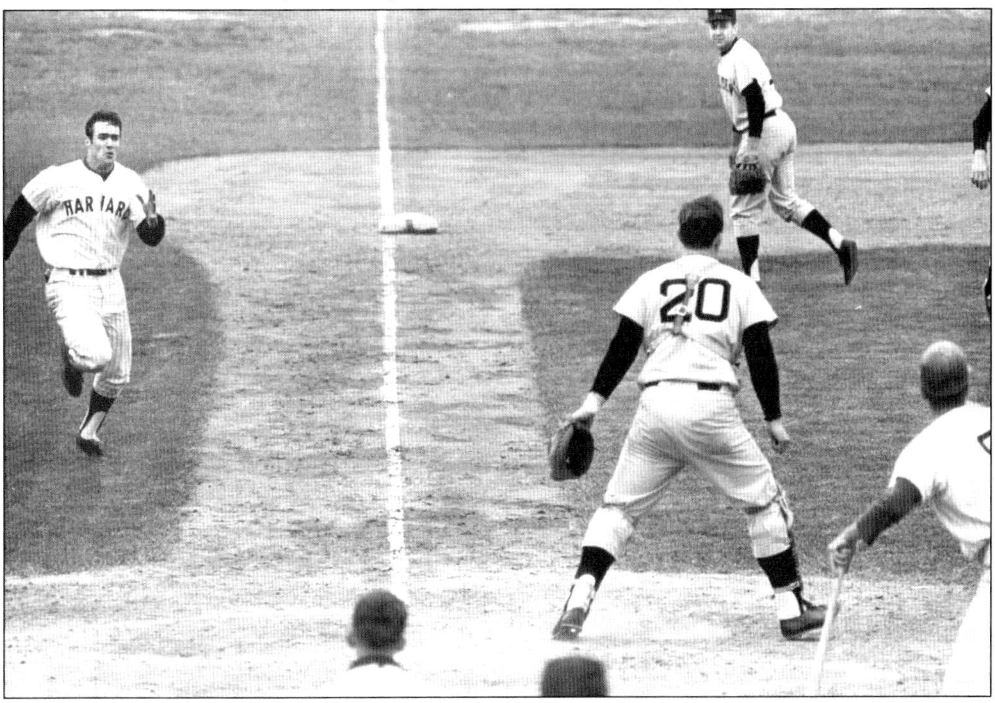

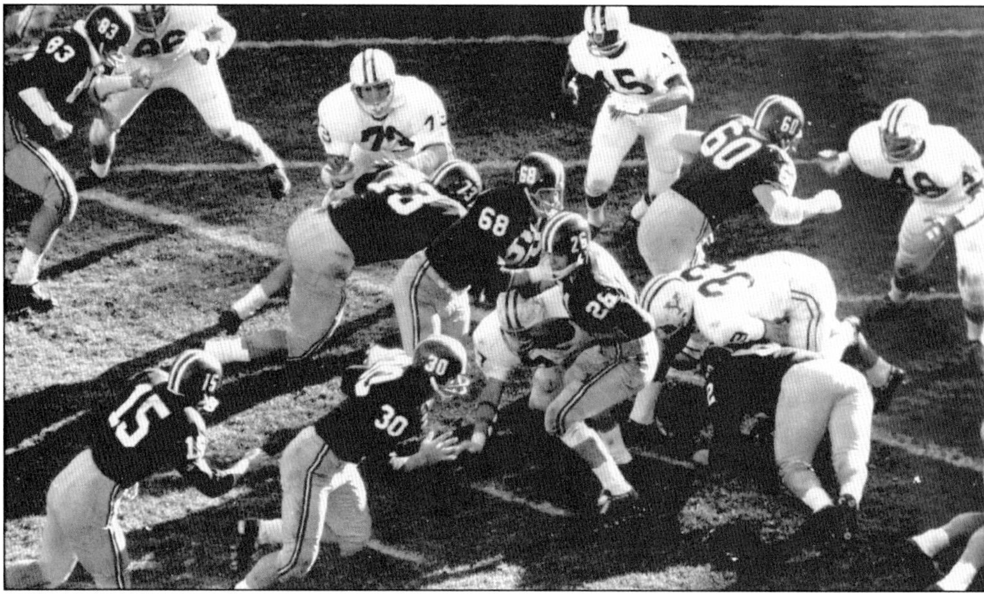

Action versus Yale, 1966. The blocking of Joe O'Donnell (60), Bob Brooks (73), and Bob Flanagan (68) leads to a Harvard touchdown in a 17-0 win over Yale on November 19, 1966. Bobby Leo (below) dashes for the end zone and the winning touchdown in the Game at Harvard Stadium. "The greatest back I ever coached" is how John Yovicsin described Leo when the halfback finished his playing career at Harvard in 1966. A first-team All-Ivy member, Varsity Club Hall of Famer, and winner of the George Bulger Lowe Award as New England's best player in 1966, the former Everett, Massachusetts, high school star set a Harvard career mark of 5.5 yards per carry over three seasons. In each of those years, he scored the winning touchdown against Yale. He went on to play two years (1967 and 1968) for the Boston Patriots.

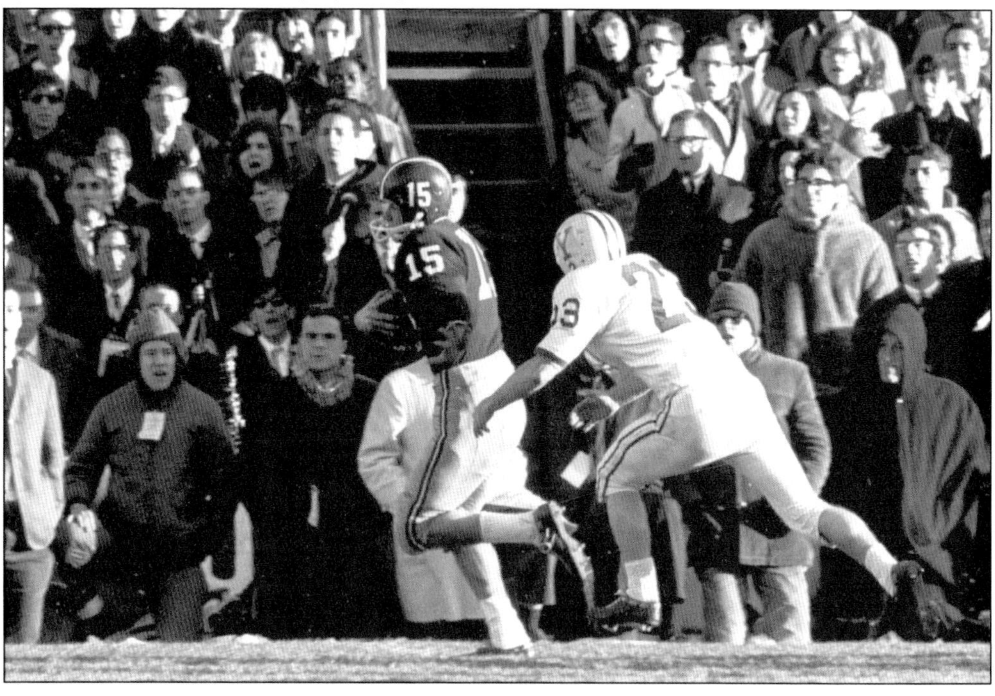

KEN BOYDA '66 (CAPTAIN, 1965). Ken Boyda was captain of the 1965 team that compiled a 5-2-2 overall record. The defense was outstanding, allowing the fewest points in Ivy League play: 62. An 0-2-2 mid-season stretch was followed by victories against Brown and Yale to finish off the season. Boyda, an end from Carnegie, Pennsylvania, was named first-team All-Ivy along with tackle Steve Diamond and safety Dave Poe.

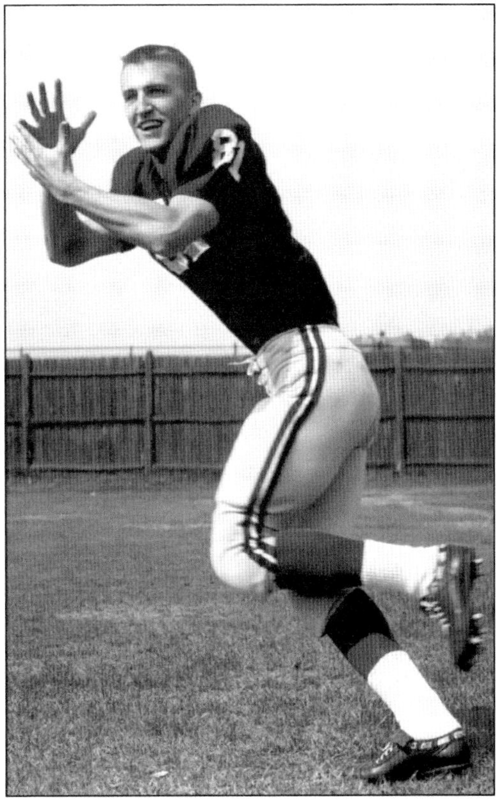

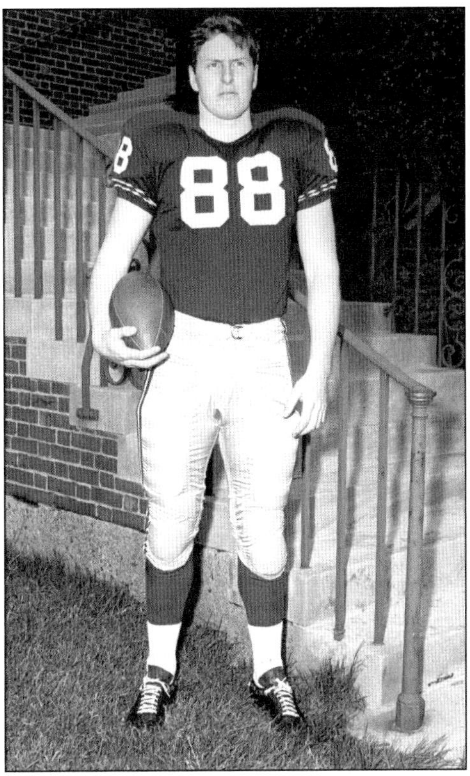

JUSTIN HUGHES '67 (CAPTAIN, 1966). The 1966 team grabbed a share of the Ivy title. Harvard's 6-1 league record was matched by Dartmouth and Princeton. An 8-1 overall mark was tainted only by an 18-14 loss at Princeton, as the Tigers marched 93 yards in the final quarter. The emergence of left-handed quarterback Ric Zimmerman and sophomore halfback Vic Gatto bolstered the offensive contributions of veterans Bobby Leo and Tom Choquette, as the Crimson scored 111 more points than the previous year. Justin Hughes, another local product from nearby Natick, Massachusetts, captained the 1966 team from his end position.

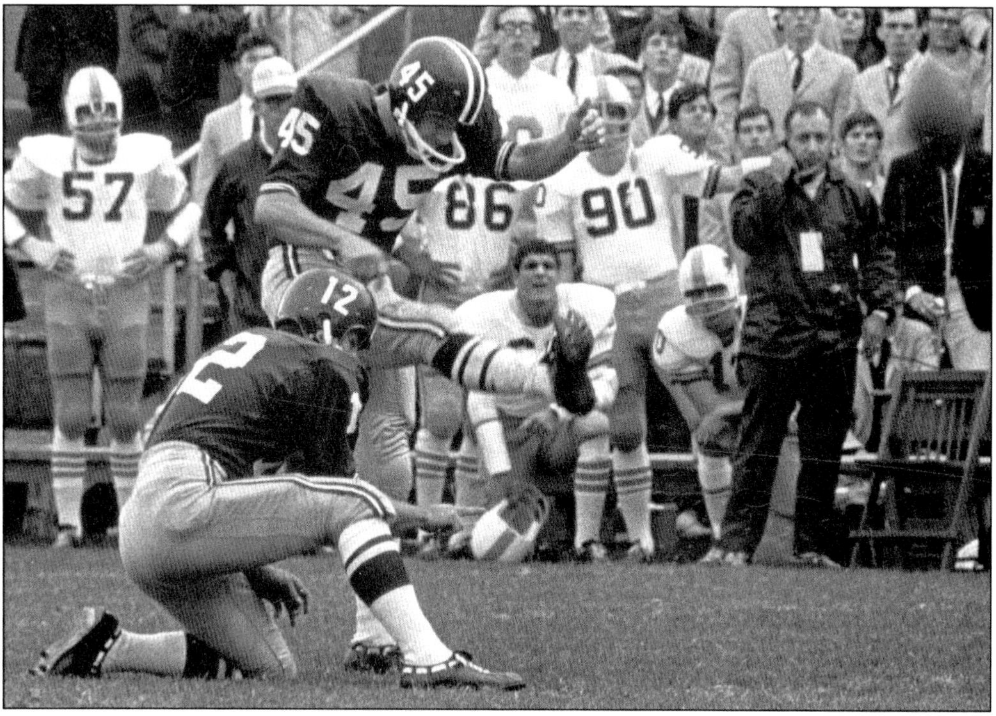

TOM WYNNE'S RECORD-SETTING FIELD GOAL, 1967. The Crimson, captained by two-time All-Ivy selection linebacker Don Chiofaro, broke from the gate with four straight victories in 1967. The highlight of the team's Ivy League victory of the season over Columbia was a record-setting 51-yard field goal by Tom Wynne '69.

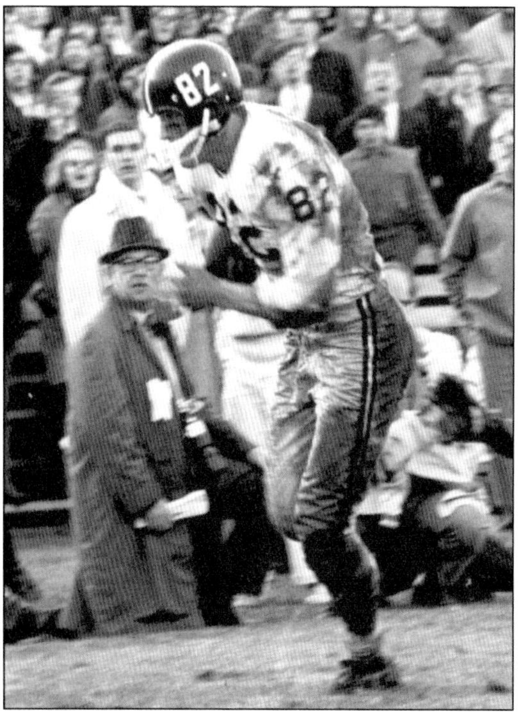

CARTER LORD '67. Carter Lord was a first-team All-Ivy selection in 1967. Called "the finest end I've ever coached" by coach John Yovicsin, Lord was instrumental as Harvard rallied from a 17-0 deficit to a 20-17 lead at New Haven versus Yale (7-0 record). Eli quarterback Brian Dowling marched his team back to a winning score with just 2 minutes and 16 seconds left, despite being held to just 5 completions in 20 attempts.

Five

1968–1970

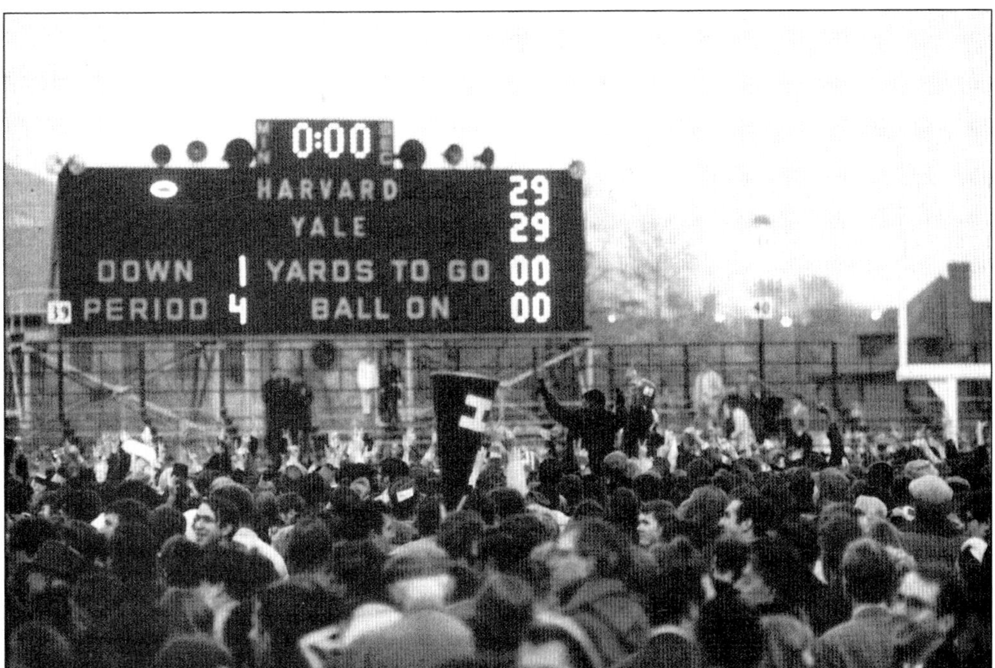

THE 29-29 "VICTORY." The momentous final minute is over. The scoreboard tells the story. The fans mob the field to celebrate Harvard's stunning 29-29 "victory" over Yale.

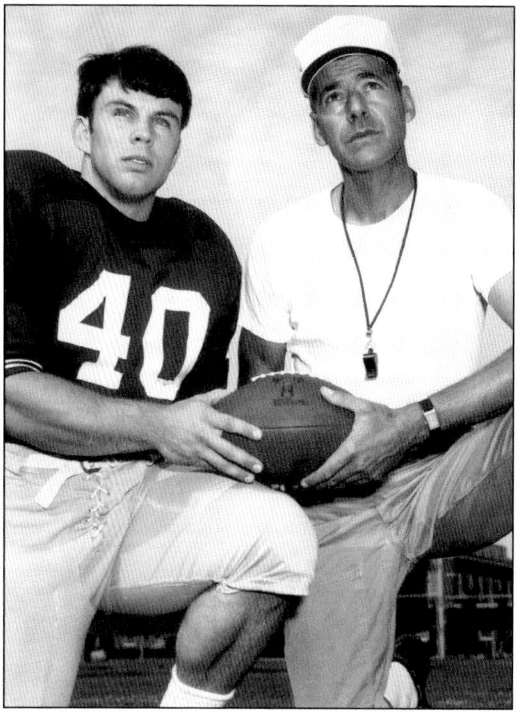

Coach John Yovicsin and Captain Vic Gatto. The 1968 Harvard team began the season with low expectations but watched its stock rise quickly. A suffocating defense allowed only 61 points through their first eight games—all victories. Captain Vic Gatto (left), along with Ray Hornblower, paced the running attack for an efficient if unspectacular Crimson offense directed by quarterback George Lalich.

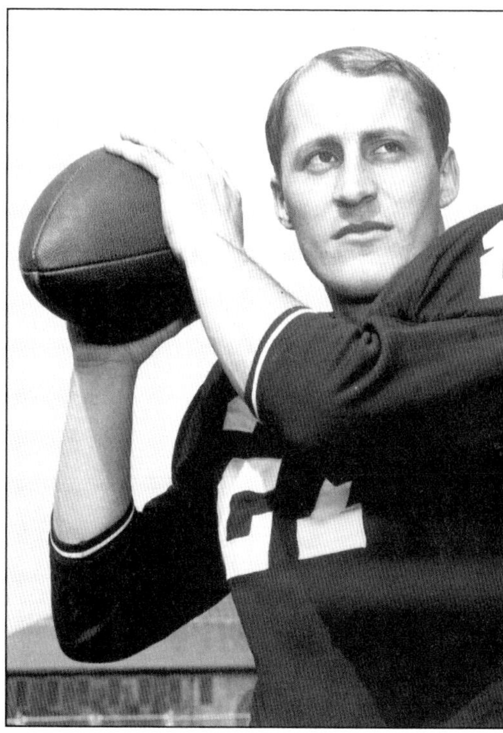

Frank Champi '70. For eight-and-a-half games in 1968, Everett, Massachusetts, native Frank Champi was a backup quarterback. Coming off the bench to rally Harvard in the second half against Yale, Champi turned 42 seconds of action into a career. He gave up football in the early weeks of the 1969 season.

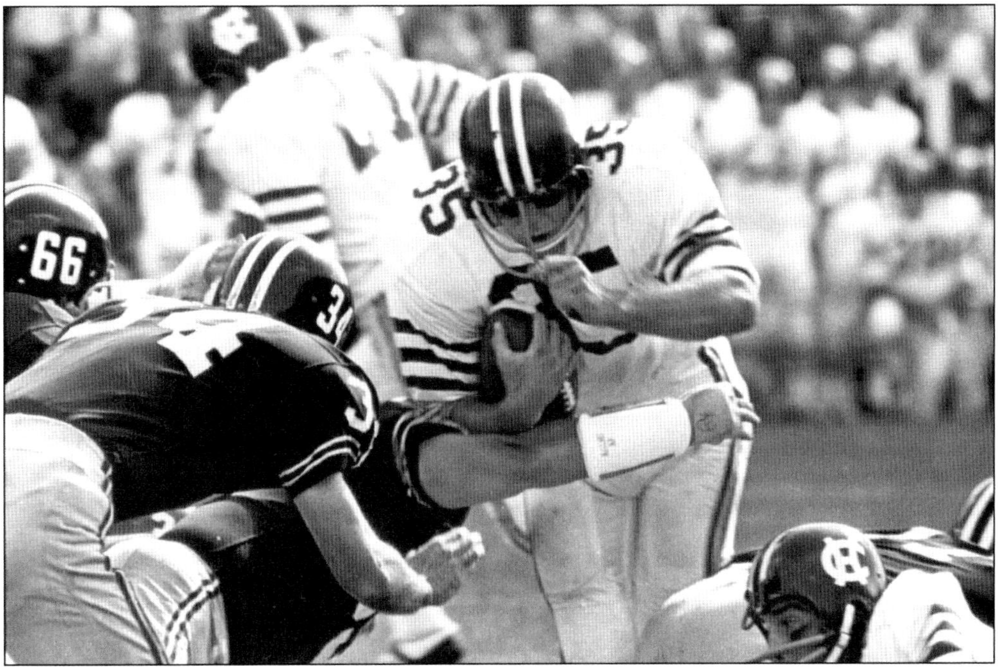

The Harvard Defense versus Bucknell and Holy Cross, 1968. The defense was the hallmark of the 1968 Ivy League co-champion Crimson. Defensive end Pete Hall, linebacker John Emery, and safety Pat Conway received All-Ivy recognition. The gang-tackling, swarming style is evidenced by these two plays versus Bucknell and Holy Cross.

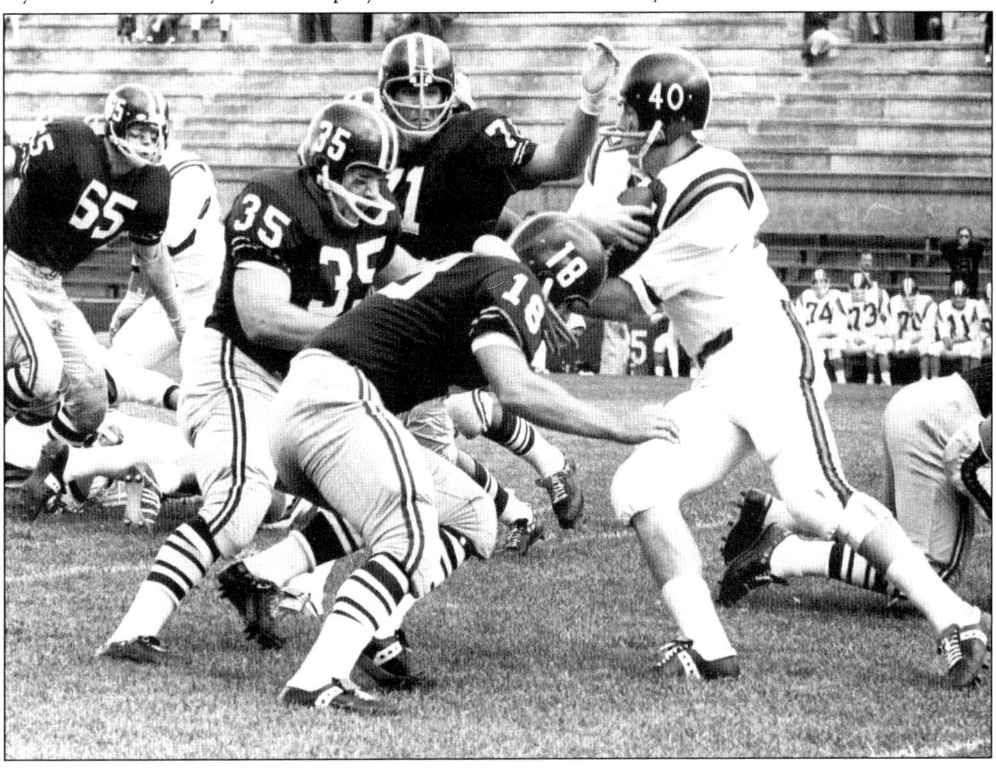

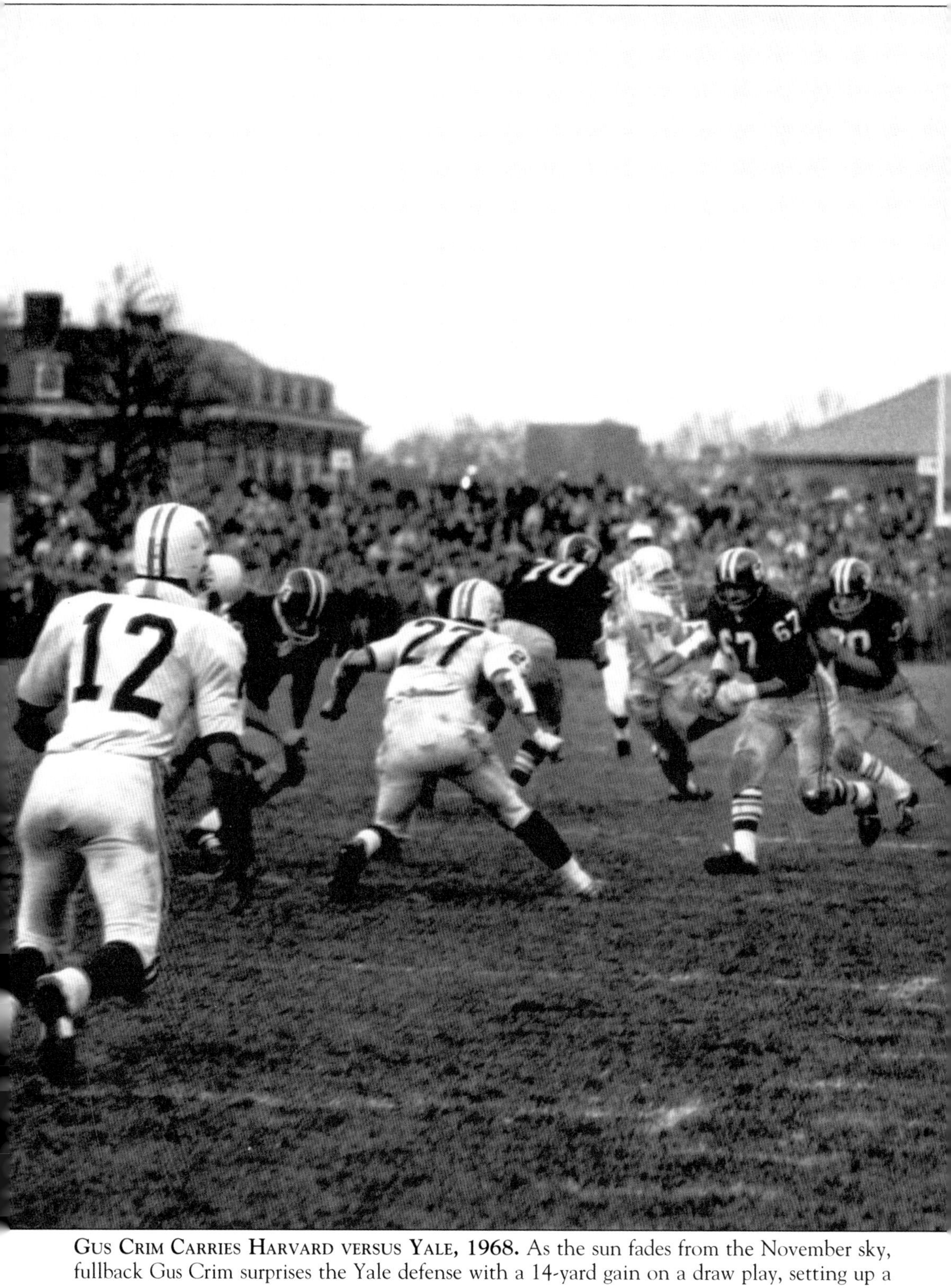

Gus Crim Carries Harvard versus Yale, 1968. As the sun fades from the November sky, fullback Gus Crim surprises the Yale defense with a 14-yard gain on a draw play, setting up a

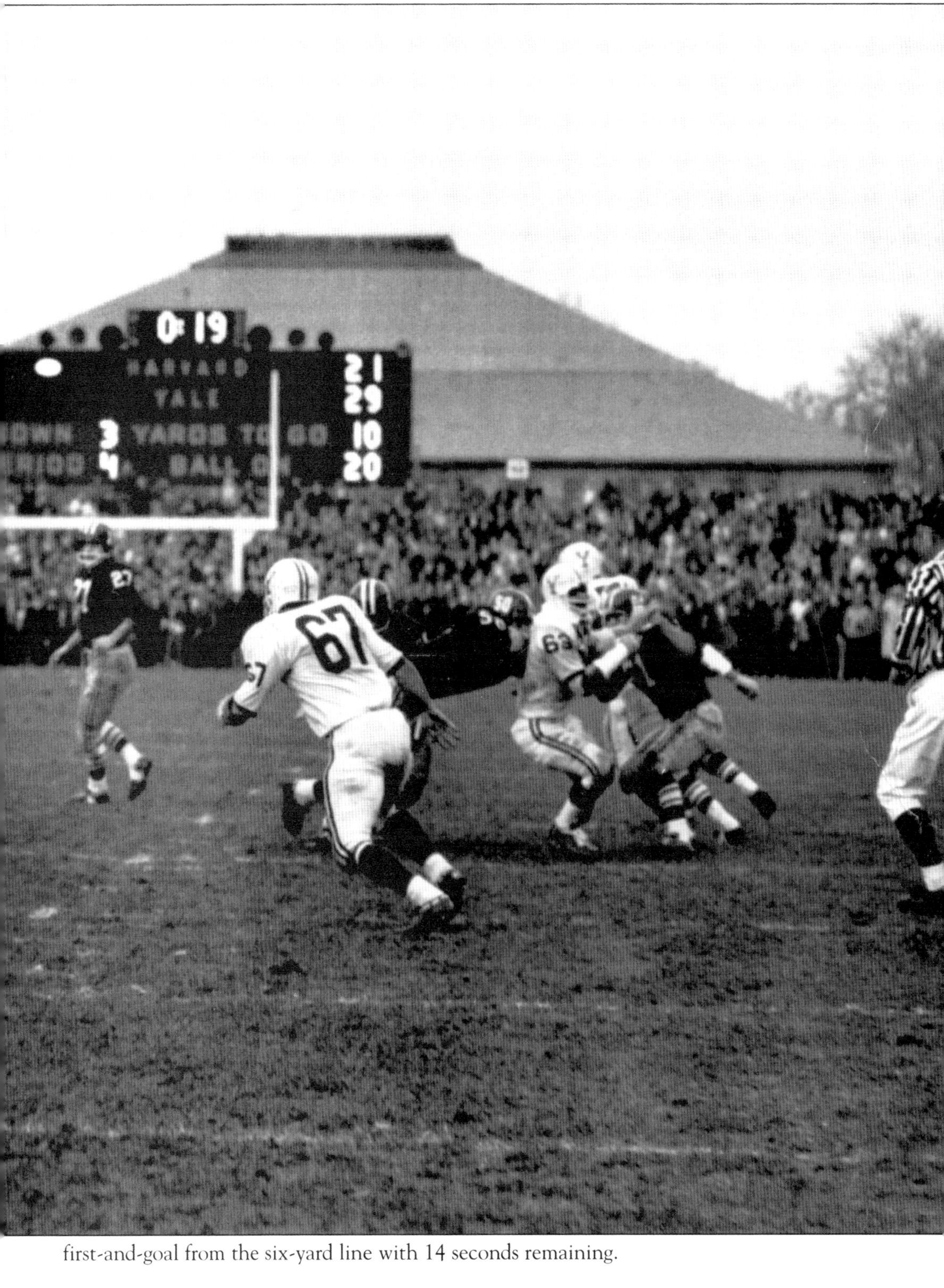

first-and-goal from the six-yard line with 14 seconds remaining.

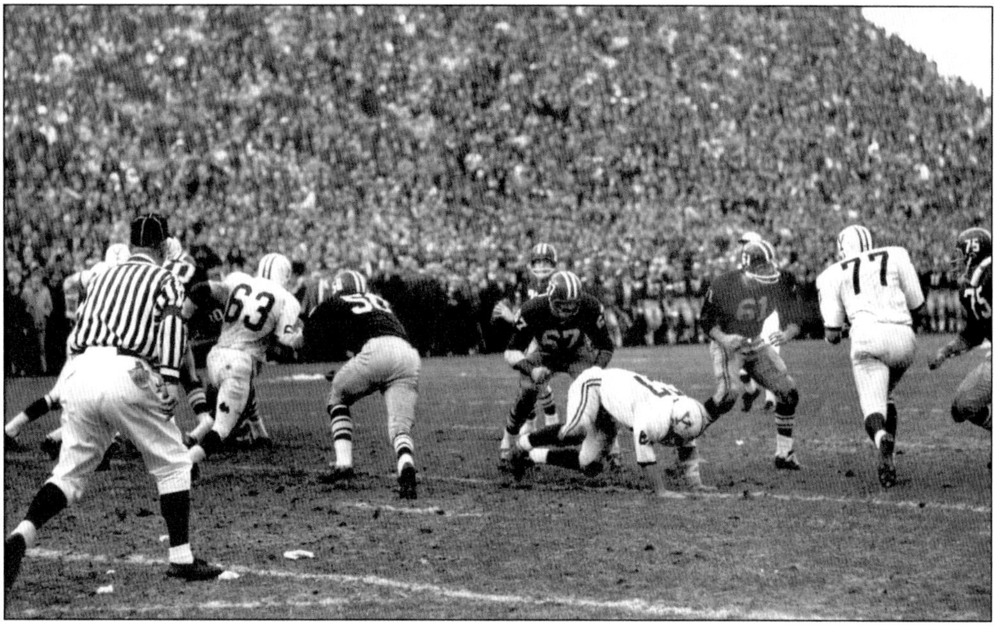

FRANK CHAMPI THROWS TO VARNEY. Time had already expired on the field when Harvard, trailing 29-27 after Vic Gatto's touchdown, lined up to attempt the two-point conversion for the tie. Quarterback Frank Champi tossed in the direction of tight end Pete Varney, who had run a curl-in pattern on Yale defensive back Ed Franklin.

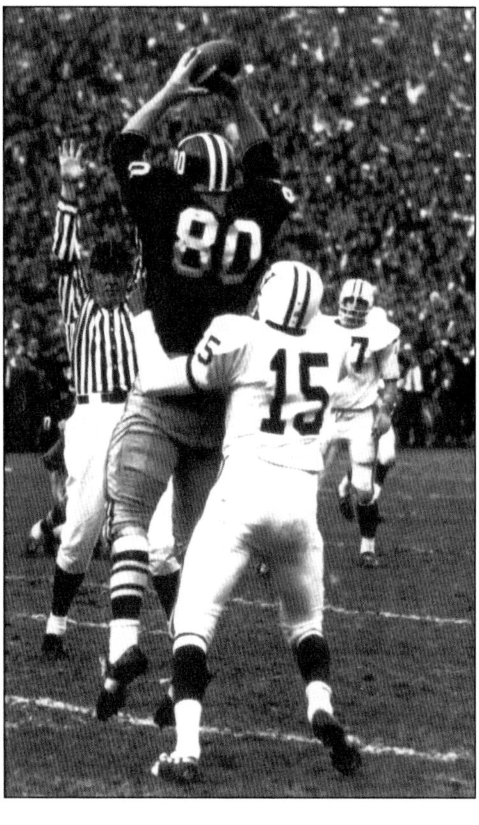

PETE VARNEY IN THE END ZONE VERSUS YALE, 1968. With no time left on the clock, quarterback Champi completes the Crimson's miracle rally (16 points in 42 seconds) for the 29-29 "victory" over Yale. Tight end Pete Varney, a 6-foot 4-inch 240-pound target, holds the ball aloft after receiving the two-point conversion pass just over the Yale goal line.

BILL KELLY '71. A sophomore backup defensive back from Reading, Massachusetts, Bill Kelly joined Frank Champi on the list of unlikely Crimson heroes. Kelly's onside kickoff recovery at the Yale 49-yard line made the Harvard miracle comeback possible. "The kickoff came to my side but it didn't bounce right, and I thought, 'Uh-oh, this isn't what we practiced.' Then the Yale player fumbled and I saw the ball lying on the ground with no one around it. I thought, 'This is amazing, all I have to do is fall on it.' "

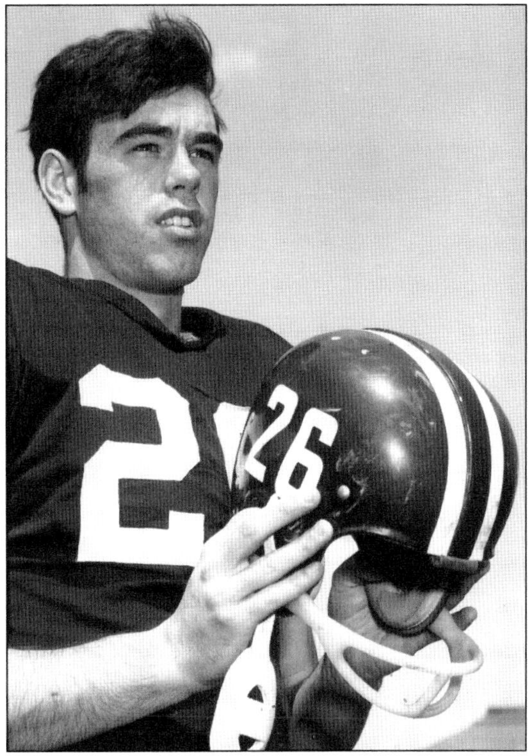

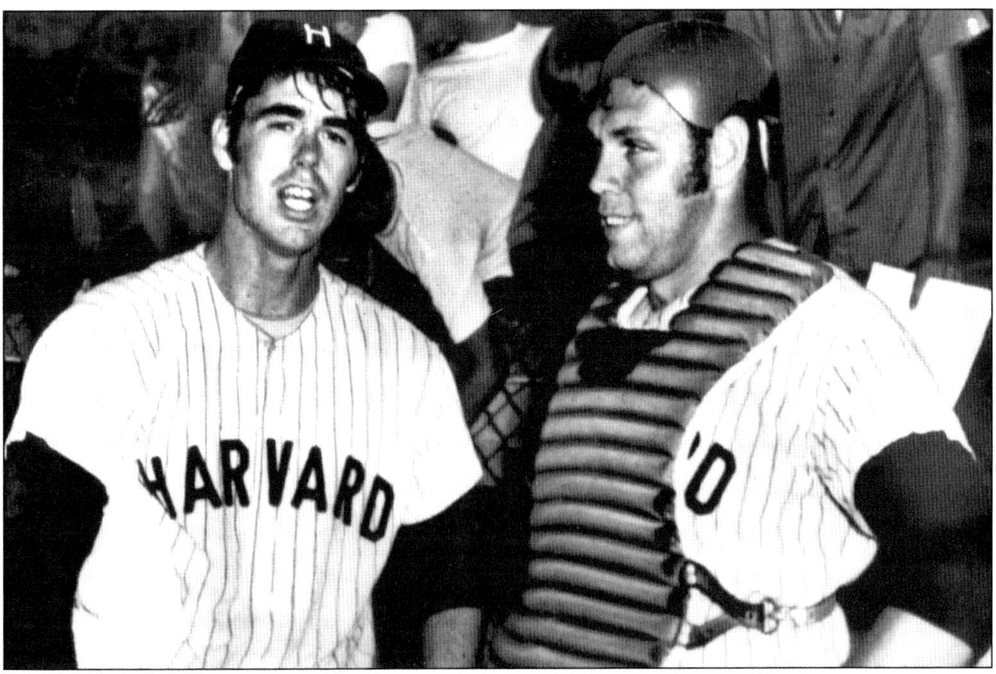

KELLY AND VARNEY (BASEBALL). The two key players in Harvard's famed 1968 29-29 tie with Yale also starred for the Harvard baseball team. Kelly was the winning pitcher, and catcher Varney hit a two-run homer in a 4-1 victory over Brigham Young at the 1971 College World Series. The victorious battery celebrates moments after the game in Omaha, Nebraska.

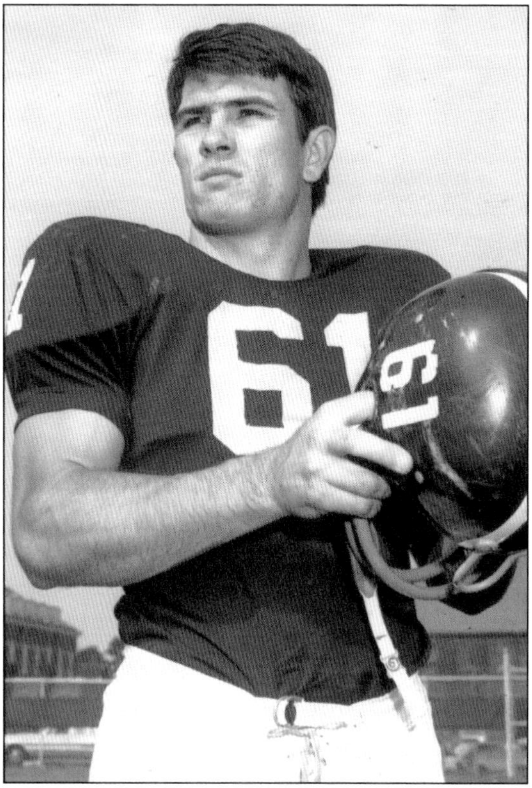

TOMMY LEE JONES '69. Born and raised in Texas, guard Tommy Lee Jones was one of Harvard's six All-Ivy selections in 1968—along with halfback Vic Gatto, who finished as Harvard's all-time career rushing leader, safety Pat Conway, linebacker John Emery, defensive end Pete Hall, and punter Gary Singleterry. Jones moved on to Hollywood and a successful acting career, starring in a multitude of blockbuster movies. He is pictured (below) in 1983's *Savage Island.*

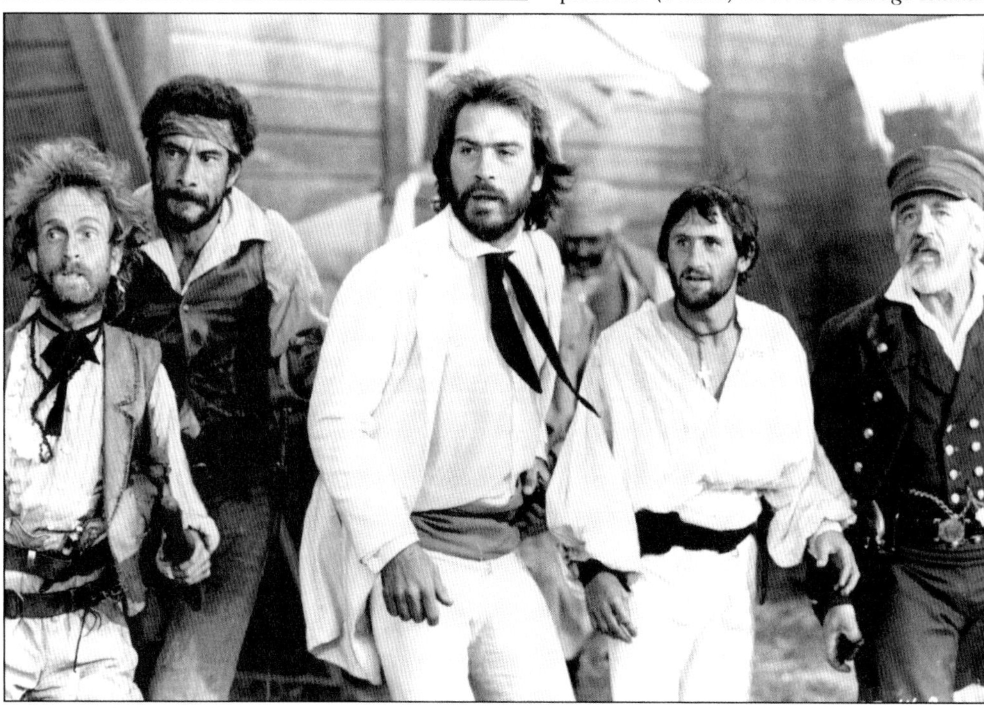

JOHN CRAMER '70 (CAPTAIN, 1969). The 1968 undefeated season proved to be a tough act to follow. The 1969 team slumped to a 3-6 record, with just a 2-5 mark in Ivy play. A strong defensive effort in New Haven was not enough, as the Crimson lost to archrivals 7-0. Tom Cramer, a defensive end from Portland, Oregon, captained the Crimson.

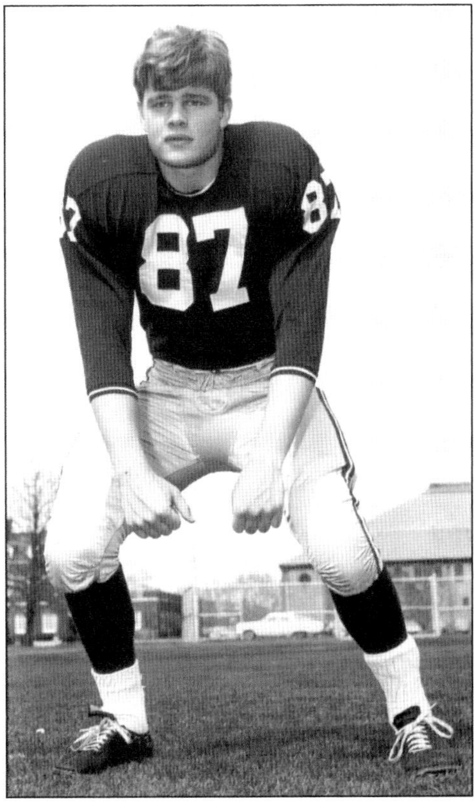

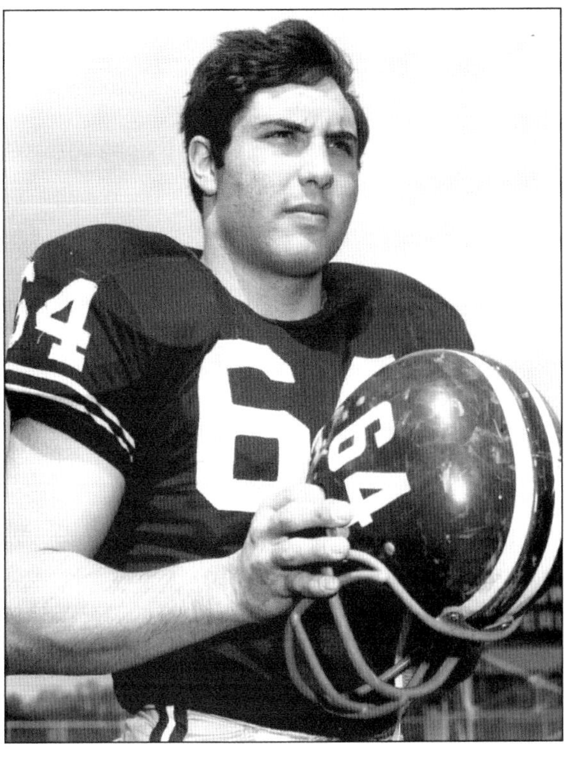

GARY FARNETTI '71 (CAPTAIN, 1970). The Crimson rebounded nicely to send off coach John Yovicsin on a winning note in 1970, his final season. Harvard rolled to a 7-2 finish (5-2 in the Ivy), losing only to eventual league champions Dartmouth and Columbia. Hard-hitting linebacker Gary Farnetti captained the team and anchored the Crimson defense. The defense was never better than in the season finale, successfully protecting a 14-0 lead for a 14-12 victory over Yale at Harvard Stadium in John Yovicsin's last game.

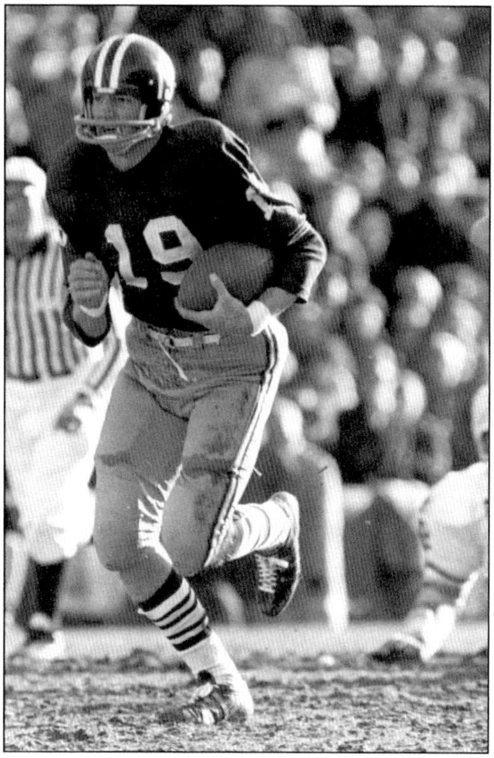

Rod Foster '73 and Eric Crone '73. Rod Foster and Eric Crone acted as a two-headed quarterback monster for the Crimson, beginning as sophomores in 1970. Foster was noted more for his shifty moves and breakaway speed, while Crone was more the traditional quarterback with the stronger arm. Both had their moments and made their share of big plays during their careers.

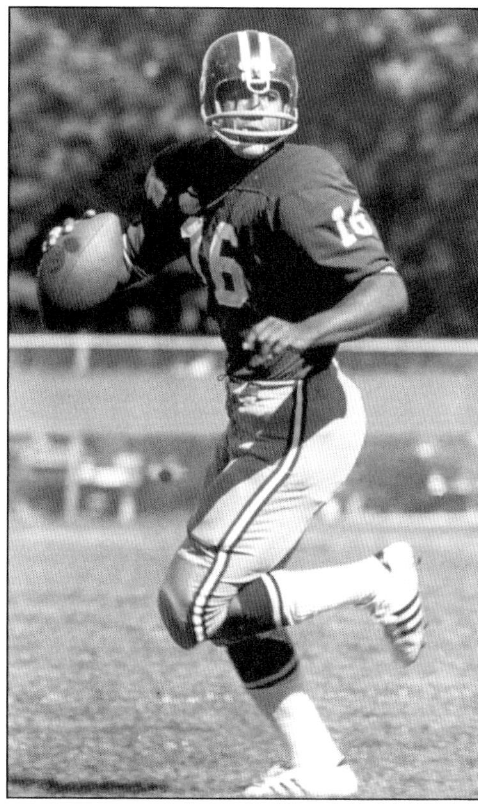

Six

1971–1979

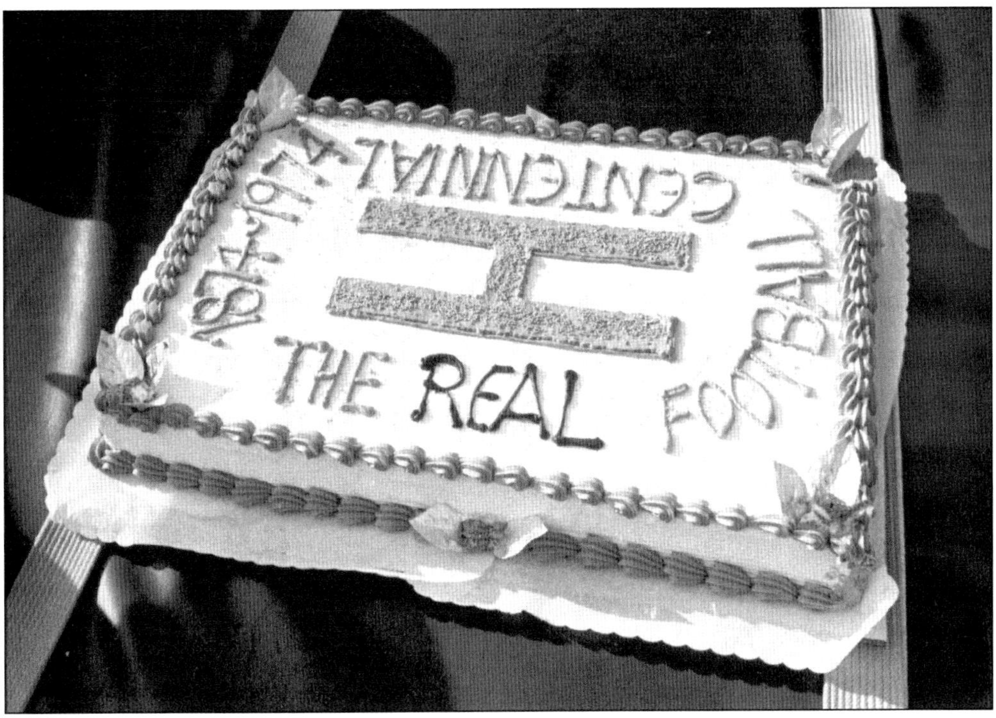

The "Real" Football Centennial, 1974. Harvard referred to the 1974 season as the "real" football centennial. Although Princeton and Rutgers celebrated college football's centennial in 1969, commemorating their 1869 first meeting, the Crimson contended that Harvard's game versus McGill in May 1874 was played under rules more closely associated with modern football and was the "real" centennial of the college game.

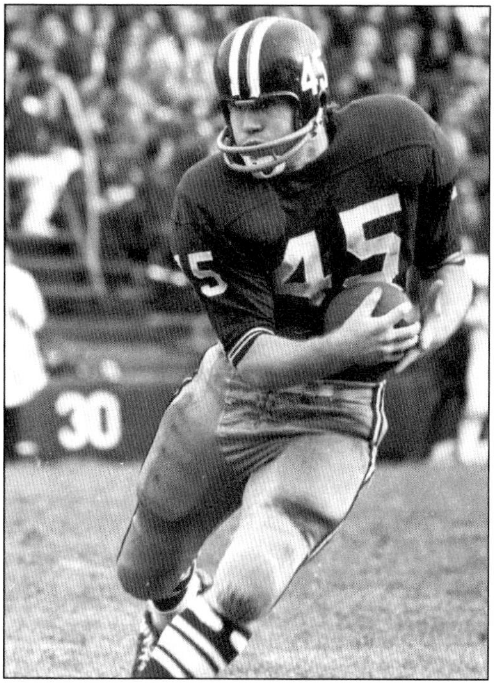

TED DEMARS '73. A solid, all-around halfback from Providence, Rhode Island, Ted DeMars played a major role in the Crimson offensive attack for three varsity seasons. With his 1,899 career rushing yards, he is currently fourth on the all-time rushing list. His 5.1-yards-per-carry average ties him for first. The captain of the 1972 team, he is a member of the Varsity Club Hall of Fame.

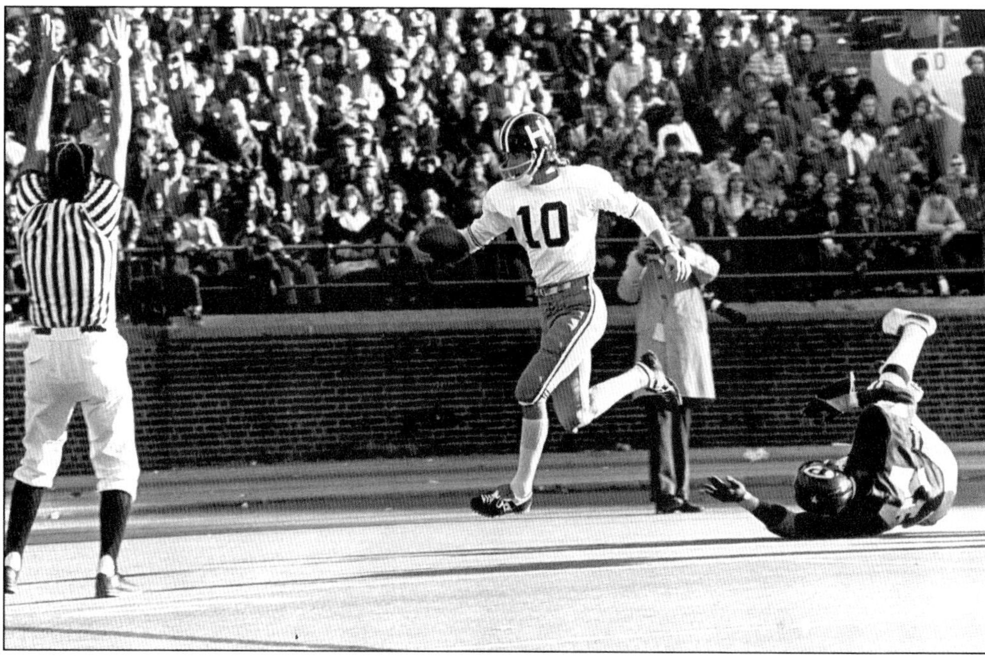

JIM STOECKEL '74 RUNNING VERSUS PENN. Joe Restic's complex "multiflex" offense always depended on an adept on-field tactician for maximum success. Restic's first discovery at the position was Jim Stoeckel, who stepped in and saw immediate action as a sophomore in 1971. Stoeckel debuted against Dartmouth, completing 20 of 37 passes for 230 yards. Stoeckel, the 1973 Ivy League Player of the Year (Harvard's first so honored), runs in for a touchdown in a 34-30 victory over Penn at Franklin Field the same year. Stoeckel rewrote the Crimson single-game passing record on this day, completing 27 of 48 passes for 291 yards.

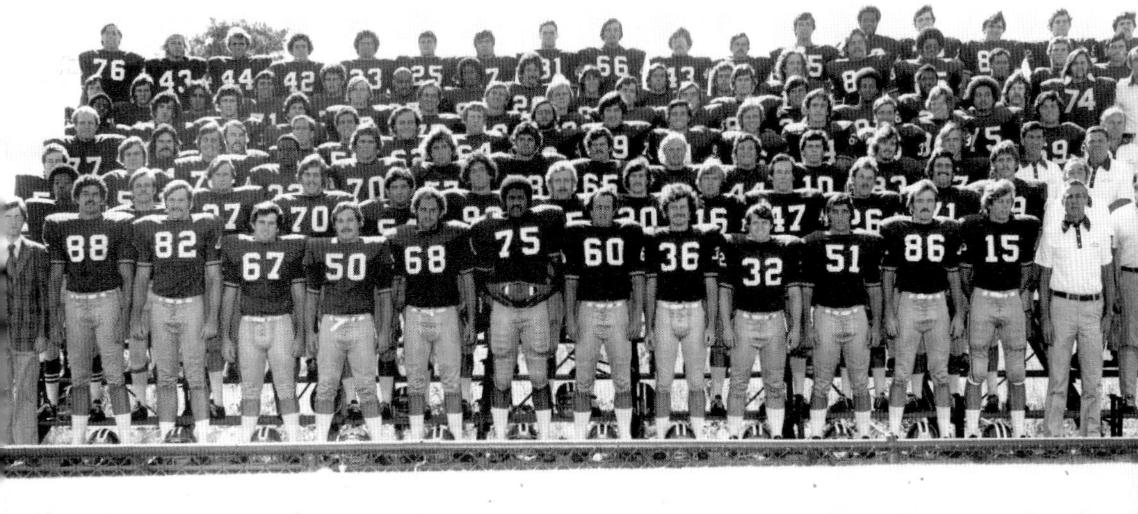

The 1975 Team. The 1975 Harvard team was the program's first to achieve the distinction of being crowned undisputed Ivy League champions. A third straight 7-2 season record was spoiled only by an early-season upset loss (13-9) to Boston University and a late-season defeat versus Princeton (24-20) when starting quarterback Jim Kubacki was sidelined with a shoulder injury. Joe Restic's resilient team rallied to sweep Brown and Yale to win the league crown outright.

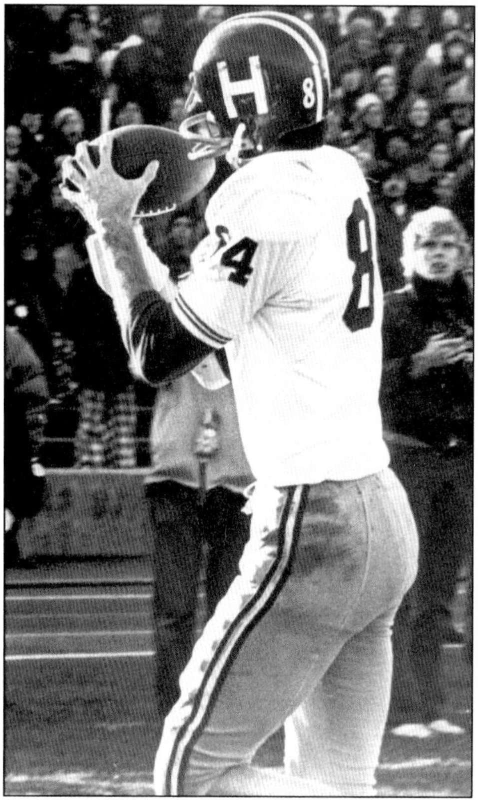

Pat McInally '75. Californian Pat McInally, at six feet six inches, was the favorite target of Jim Stoeckel and later, Milt Holt. McInally finished his Crimson career with 108 receptions and 15 touchdowns, both records at the time. His 13 catches for 178 yards in the 1973 Brown game established single-game receiving standards. He doubled as the Crimson punter and was a member of the All-Ivy team at both split end and punter in 1974. He became Harvard's first All-American since "Chub" Peabody in 1941. McInally went on to a decade-long NFL career (1976–1985) with the Cincinnati Bengals, playing in the Super Bowl and being named All-Pro in 1982.

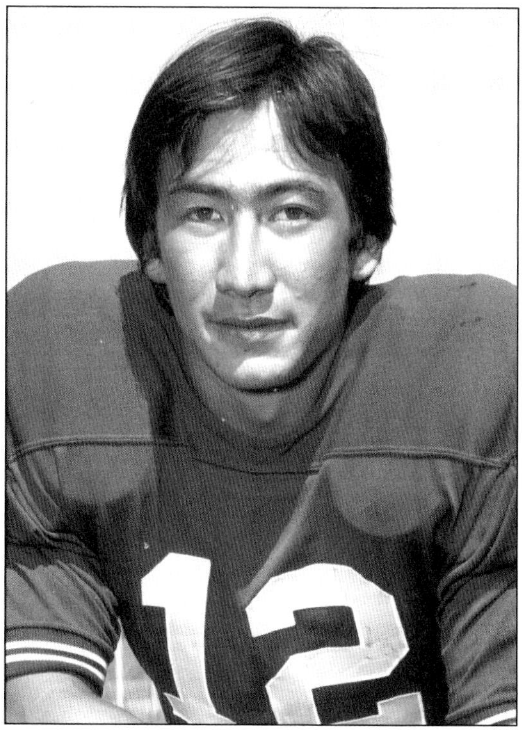

Milt Holt '75. Milt "Pineapple" Holt took the reins of the "multiflex" offense from Jim Stoeckel in 1974 and promptly guided the Crimson to a 7-2 season, matching the previous year's record. A native of Honolulu, Hawaii (via Andover Academy), Holt was a crowd favorite for his fashionable white shoes and risk-taking. His athleticism and adaptability made him a coach's favorite week after week. "I could adapt with him right on the sidelines, which made it difficult for a defense to know what we would do, even if they studied us," said head coach Joe Restic.

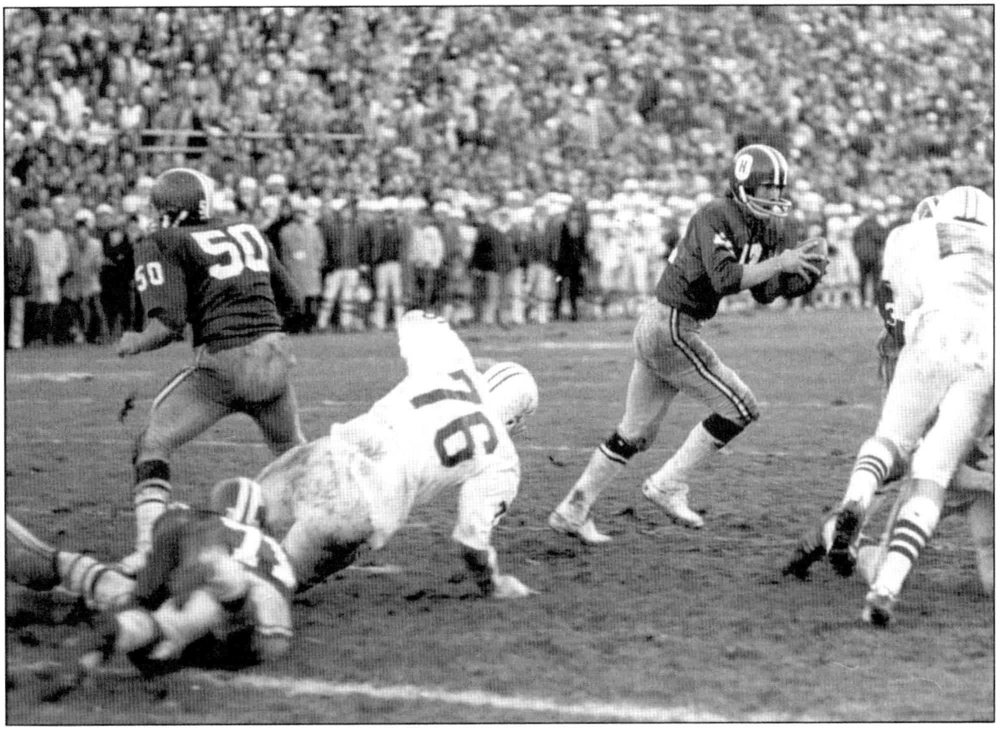

HOLT'S TOUCHDOWN VERSUS YALE, 1974. Holt is best remembered for his final drive as the Harvard quarterback who marched the Crimson 90 yards in the waning minutes of the Game for the winning touchdown over Yale, diving into the end zone from two yards away. The 21-16 victory gave Harvard a 6-1 Ivy League record, tying Yale for a share of the Ivy League title.

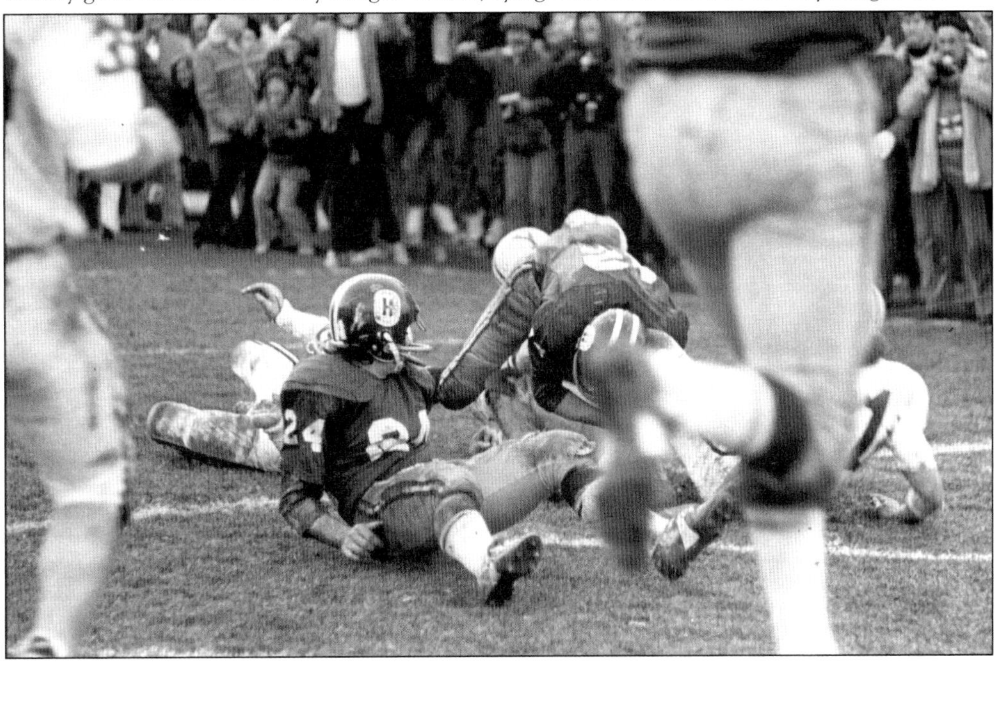

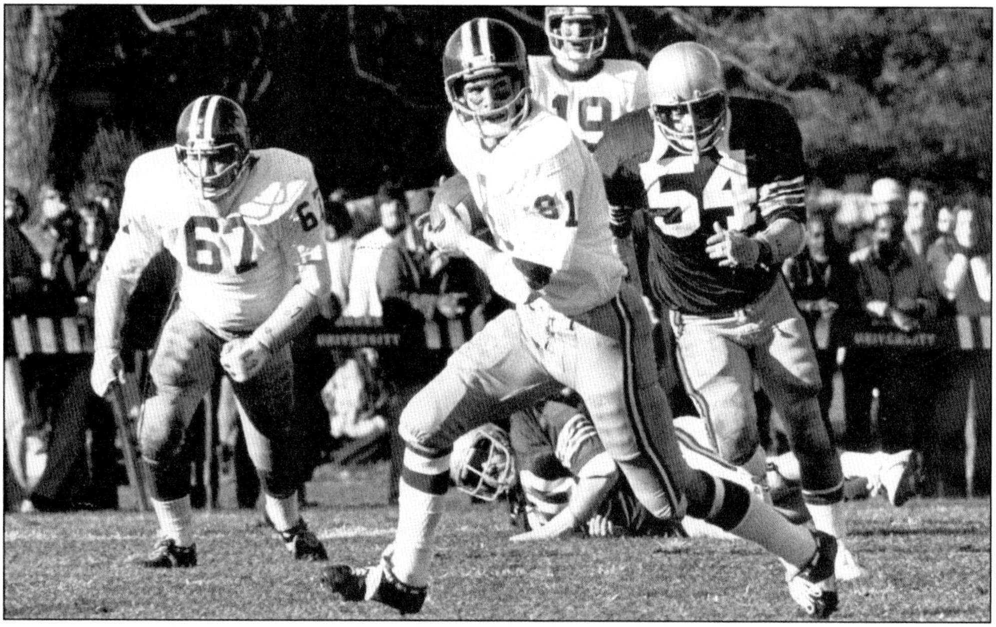

Bob McDermott '77. A sure-handed tight end, Bob McDermott made the clutch catch part of his job description. An All-Ivy selection in 1976, McDermott heads up field after the catch versus Brown in an ABC regionally televised game from Providence in 1975. The Crimson offense racked up 476 yards, as Harvard knocked the Bears from the ranks of the unbeaten by a score of 45-26. McDermott's life ended tragically when a fire engulfed his apartment in 1978.

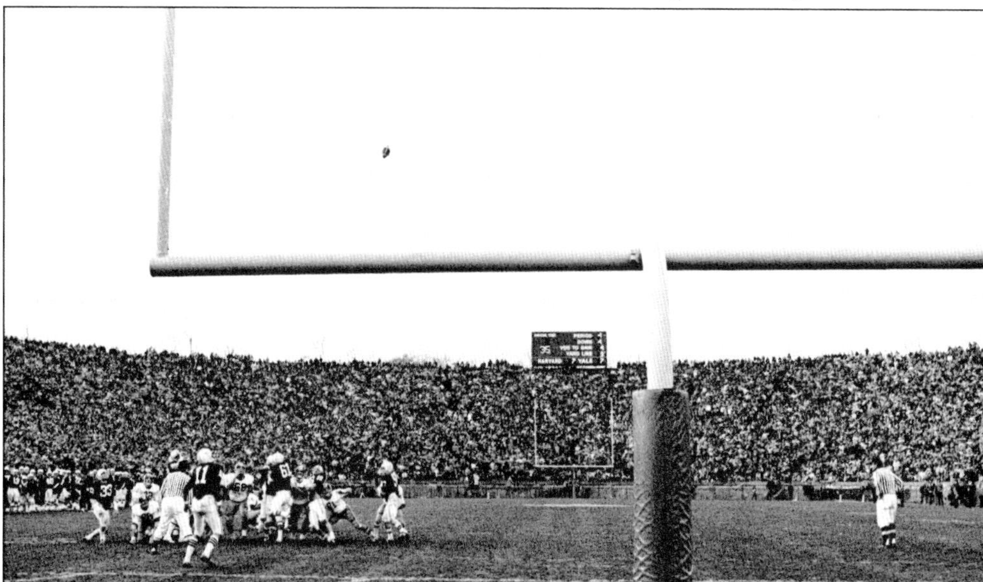

The Kick by Mike Lynch '77. The 100th anniversary of the first game between Harvard and Yale came down to the final minute. With 38 seconds remaining, kicker Mike Lynch atoned for a missed 42-yard field goal in the second quarter by booting the winning field goal from 26 yards out. "Late in the fourth quarter, Jimmy Kubacki led us on a 72-yard drive, the key play of which was a fourth-and-twelve pass to Bobby McDermott that kept us going," Lynch recounted. "When we got down to fourth and four from the nine it was up to me."

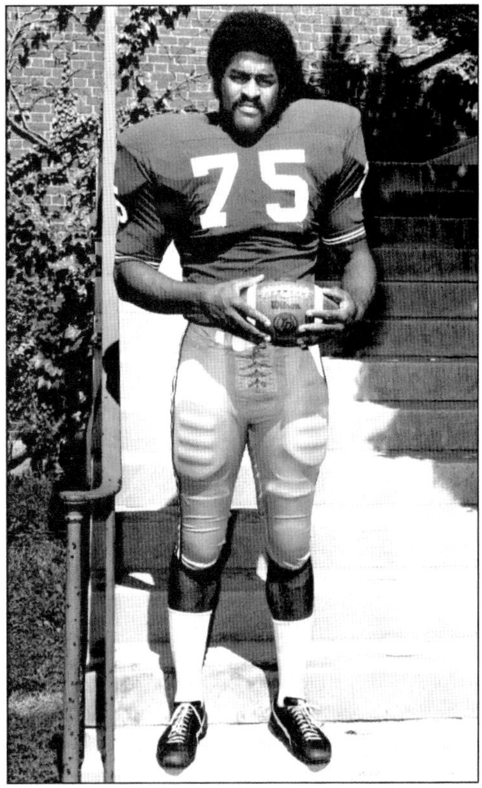

DAN JIGGETTS '76 (CAPTAIN, 1975). A two-time All-Ivy selection at offensive tackle, Dan Jiggetts anchored a solid Harvard offensive line. After leaving Cambridge, Jiggetts found a new home in Chicago, playing eight years for the National Football League Bears before retiring to the broadcast booth.

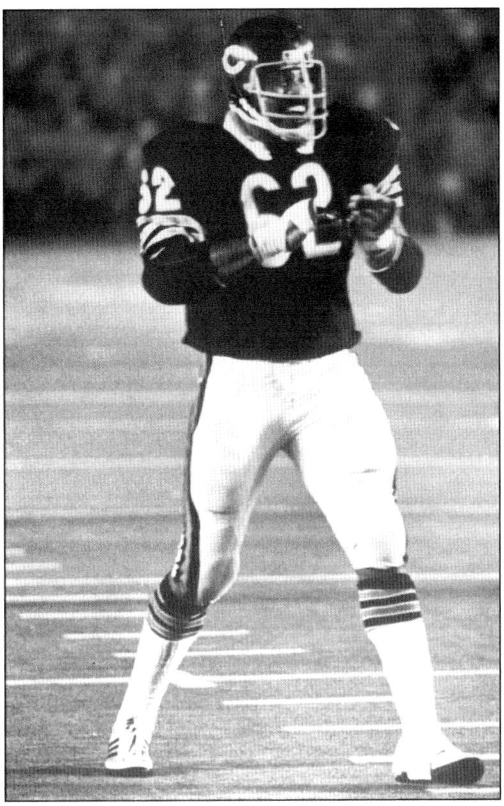

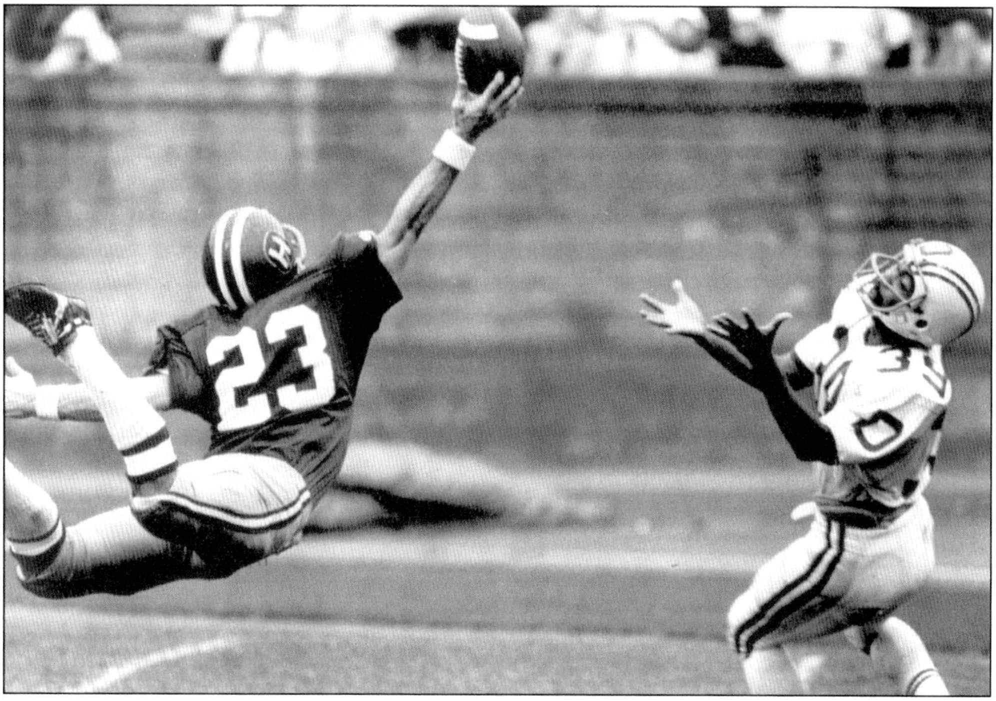

BILL EMPER '77. Cornerback Bill Emper makes a leaping breakup of a Dartmouth touchdown pass. A standout in the Crimson secondary, Emper was a two-time All-Ivy selection in 1975 and 1976, and captain of the 1976 team.

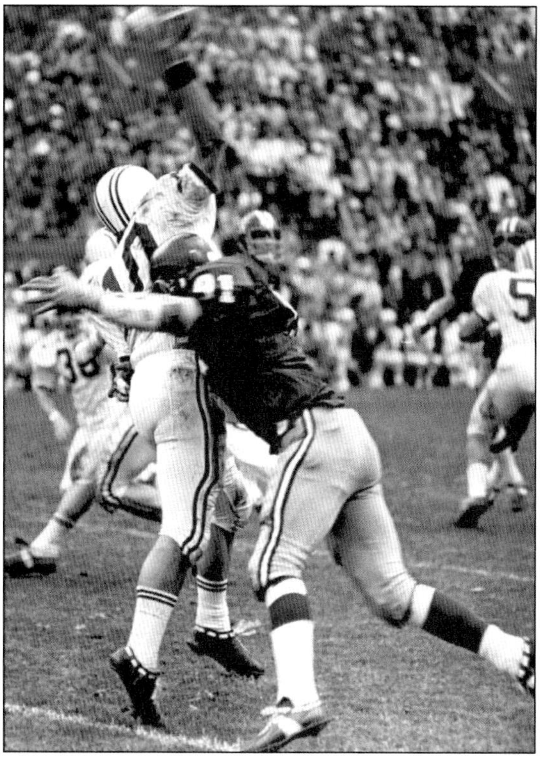

BOB BAGGOTT '78. Bob Baggott was a four-year varsity letter-winner at defensive end. His junior year (1976) was his best, as he made the All-Ivy defensive team.

JIM KUBACKI '77. Again coach Joe Restic turned to a southpaw signal-caller to direct his "multiflex" attack. Jim Kubacki stepped in to run the offensive show with efficiency, despite being plagued by injuries during the 1975 campaign. In the Columbia game, Kubacki set the Harvard single-game total-offense record with 310 total yards (236 passing, 74 running), as the Crimson prevailed over the Lions 35-30 at Harvard Stadium. Kubacki attained first-team All-Ivy recognition and is a member of the Varsity Club Hall of Fame.

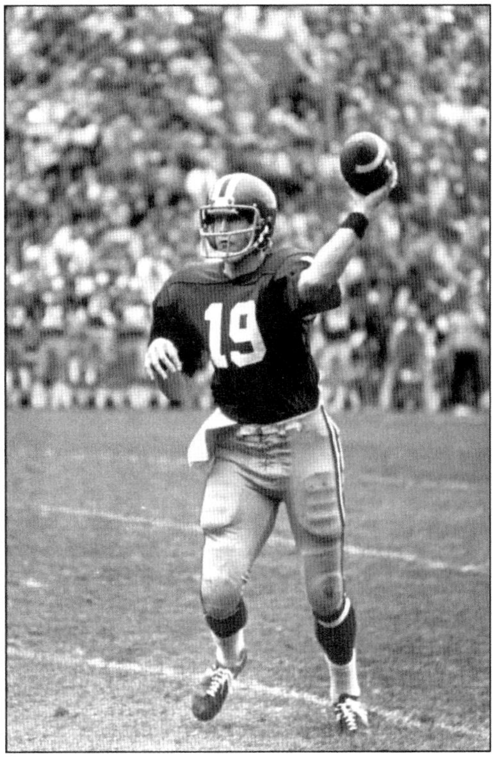

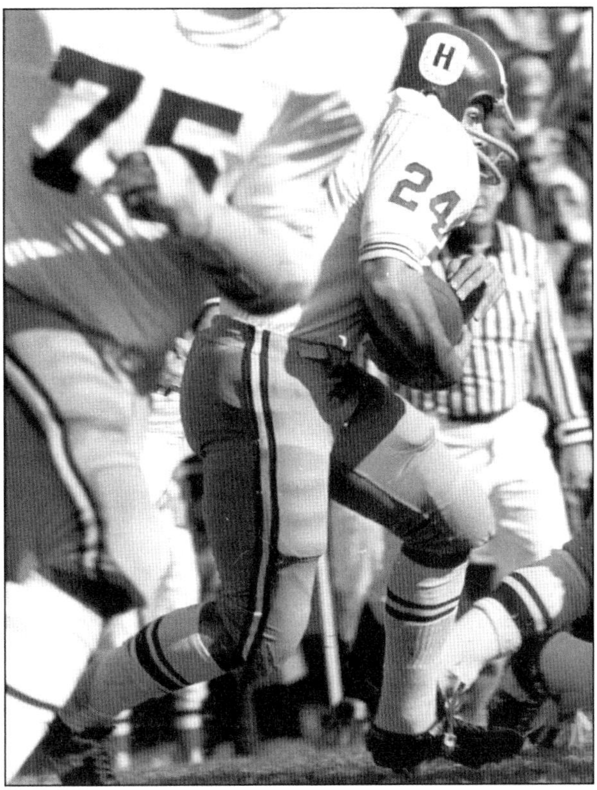

TOM WINN '77. Tom Winn, at 5 feet 8 inches and 170 pounds, was a model of consistency during the 1976 season. The diminutive halfback gained between 68 and 95 yards in eight of the Crimson's nine games. He finished as Harvard's fourth all-time leading rusher and fifth all-time leading receiver, a testament to his superior all-purpose skills. Winn ended his career with 1,719 yards and 11 touchdowns overall, still ranking him seventh all-time. The former Framingham, Massachusetts, North High School star was the recipient of the Crocker Award in 1976 as the player possessing "initiative, perseverance, courage and selflessness."

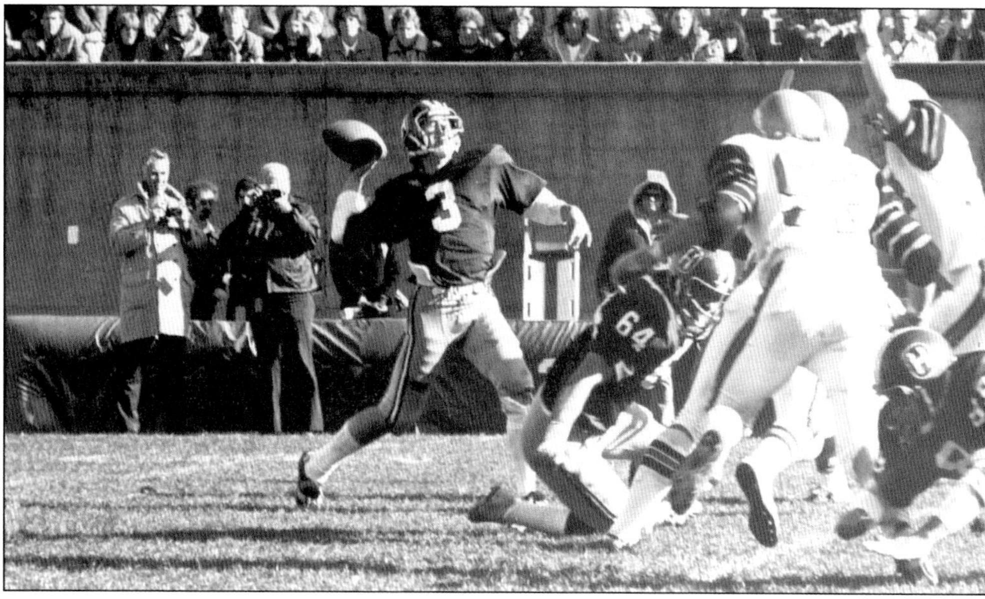

Larry Brown '79. Larry Brown, launching a pass downfield versus Princeton in 1977, ranks fifth among Harvard's all-time passing leaders. Brown emerged as the starter from a three-quarterback sweepstakes early in the 1977 campaign. A star baseball pitcher for the Crimson, Brown adapted nicely to coach Joe Restic's multiflex attack. He finished his career as Harvard's all-time passing leader and set a single-game mark against Penn in 1977 with 349 yards through the air. "People told me that Larry Brown would never be quarterback," said Restic. "And then he went out and set records."

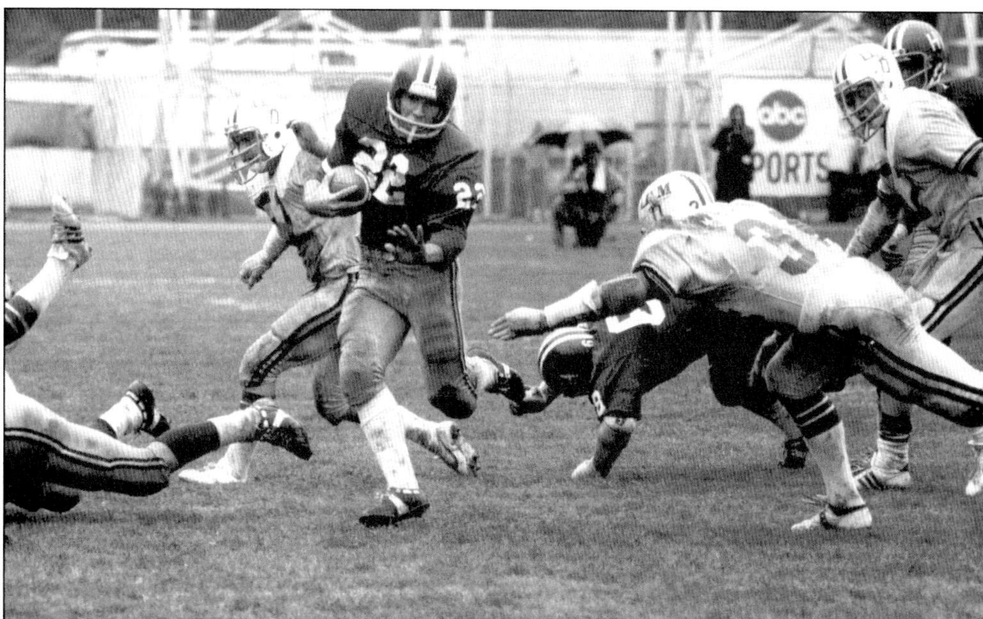

Ralph Polillio '79. Ralph Polillio, a fleet-footed halfback, completed the rare double play of leading the 1978 team in both rushing and receiving. Polillio burst through the line in a 10-0 shutout of UMass at Harvard Stadium, in a game televised regionally by ABC Sports.

Seven

1980–1989

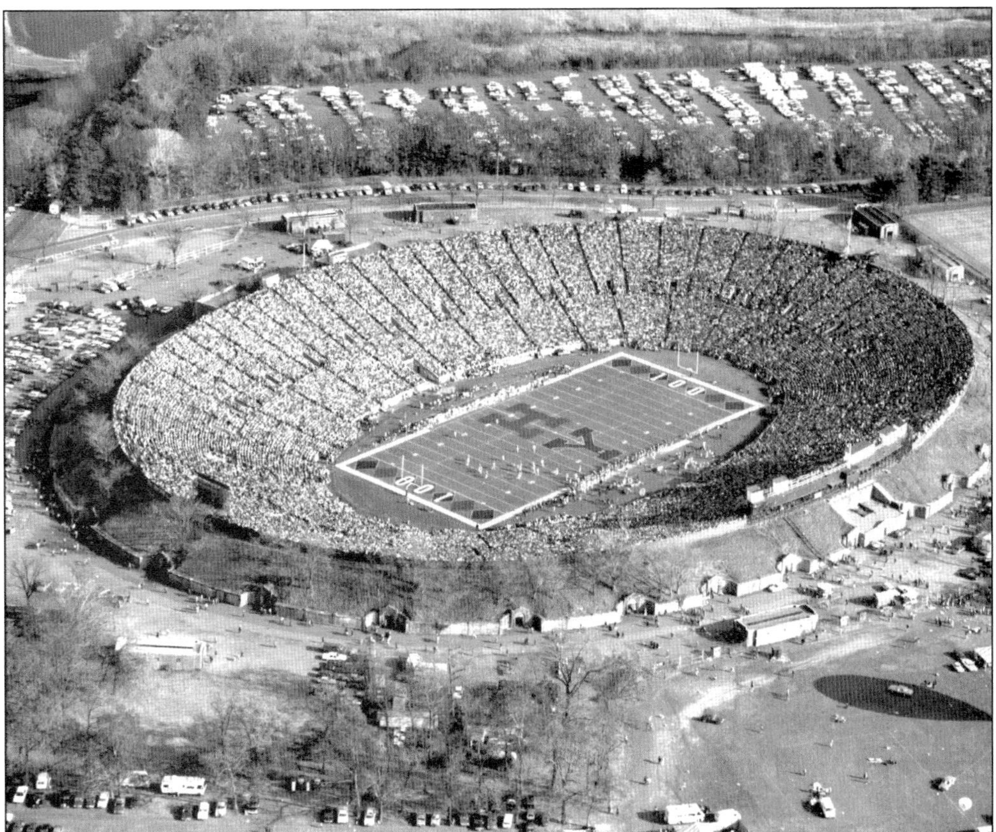

THE GAME TURNS 100, 1983. In this aerial view, the sun splashes into the Yale Bowl on November 19, 1983. The 100th playing of the Game produced a 16-7 Harvard win in New Haven, earning the Crimson a share of the Ivy crown.

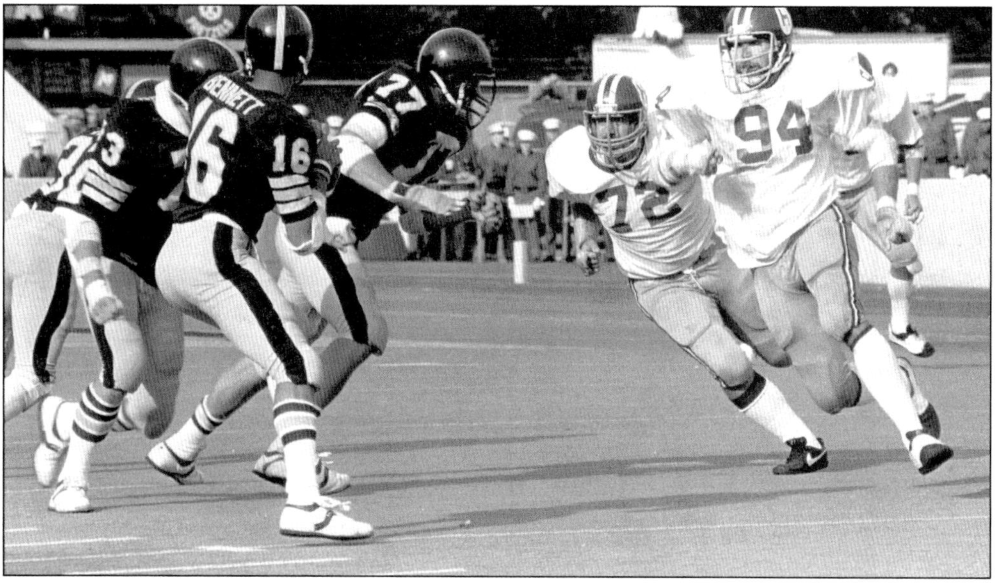

THE HARVARD DEFENSE VERSUS ARMY, 1980. The Harvard-Army series was renewed in 1980 after a 29-year hiatus. The Crimson held a slim advantage over the Cadets from the first meeting in 1895 to 1951: 17 wins, 13 losses and 1 tie overall. In the seven most recent meetings from 1980 to 1991, the West Pointers had the better of the competition, with a 5-2 record. On this day in 1980, though, the Harvard defense excelled, as the Crimson, led by defensive linemen Chuck Durst (72) and Dave Otto (94), wreaked considerable havoc and fashioned a memorable 15-10 victory at Army's historic Miche Stadium. Durst, the 1980 captain, was a two-time All-Ivy first-team selection.

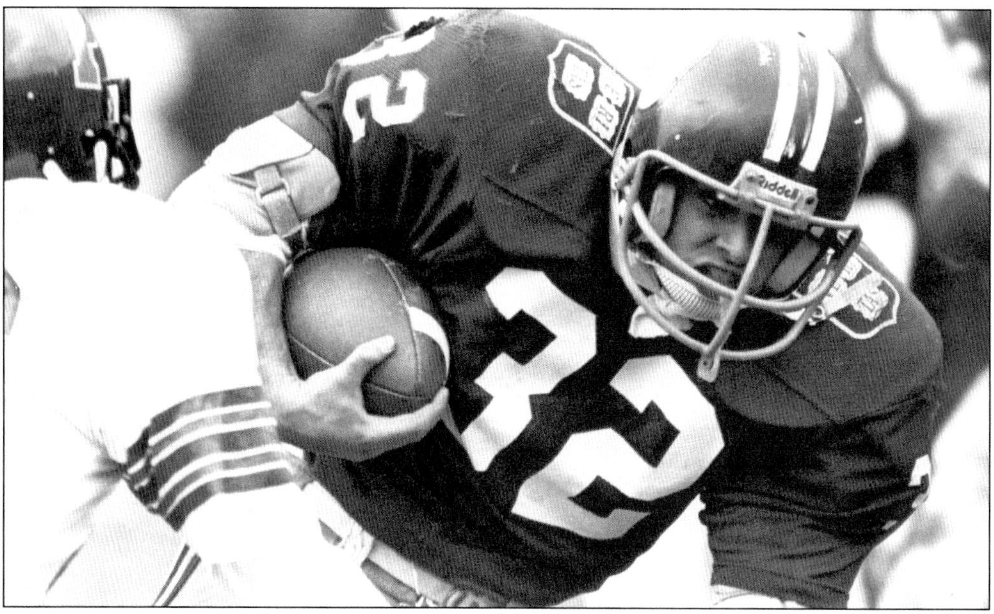

JIM CALLINAN '82. Jim Callinan became Harvard's first 1,000-yard rusher (1,054 yards) with a 60-yard effort in the 1981 Yale game. The durable running back broke a 30-year-old Dick Clasby record of 950 yards rushing in a single season when he made a 66-yard third-quarter touchdown versus Penn. Callinan's single-season total is still good for third all-time.

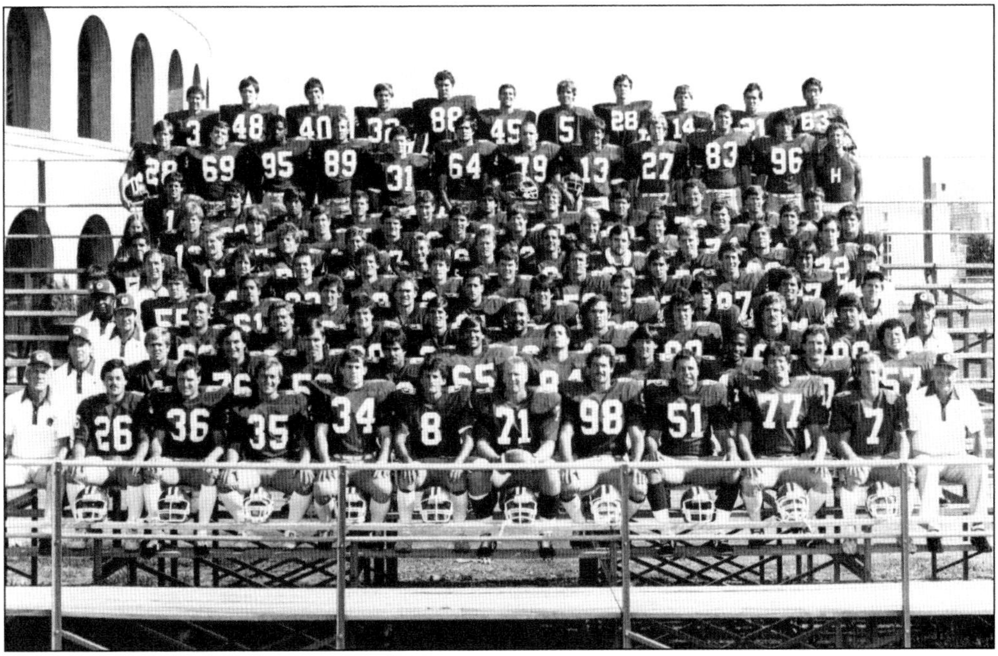

THE 1982 TEAM. The 7-3 Crimson (5-2 Ivy) shared the league title with Dartmouth and Yale.

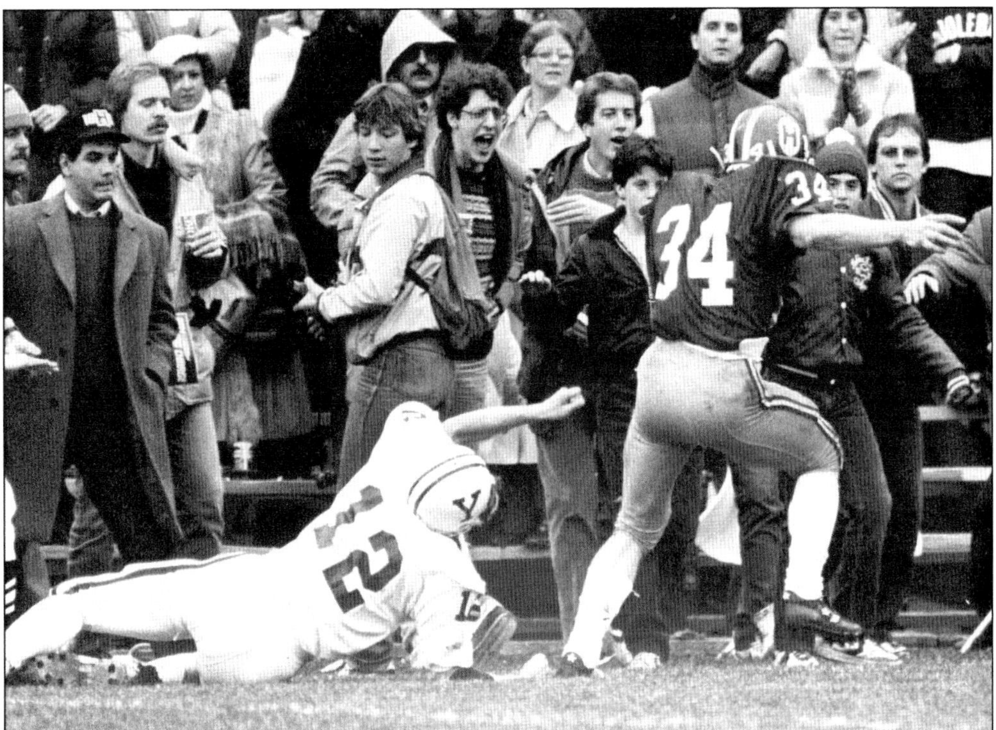

MICHAEL GRANGER '83 VERSUS YALE, 1982. After not scoring for two consecutive years (1980 and 1981), the Crimson exploded, achieving the most points ever for a Harvard team versus Yale: 45. Halfback Michael Granger heads toward the Yale goal line. The Crimson defense held Yale to minus 12 yards rushing and just 116 yards in total offense.

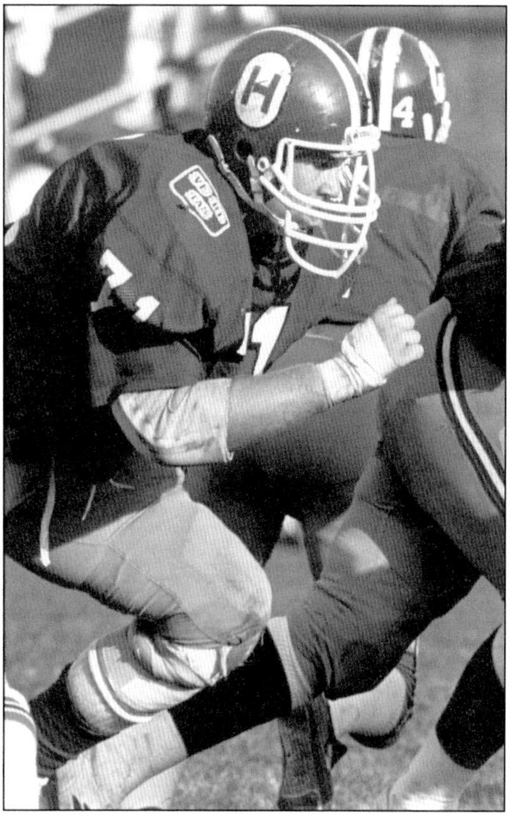

Greg Brown '83. Offensive tackle Greg Brown captained the 1982 team that shared the Ivy League title with Dartmouth and Yale. Brown, along with guard Mike Corbat, anchored a solid Crimson offensive line, earning All-Ivy recognition (along with Corbat) for two consecutive years (1981 and 1982).

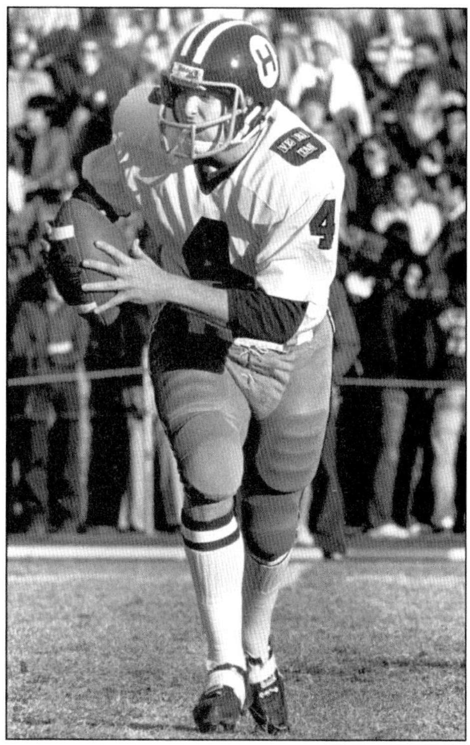

Don Allard '83. Still ranked eighth on the school's all-time passing list some 20 years later, Don Allard, a schoolboy star at nearby Winchester High School, was the co-winner of the 1983 Bingham Award as the school's top athlete. His 358-yard passing (18 of 29, 2 touchdowns) performance in a 31-14 victory over UMass at Harvard Stadium in 1982 set a school record that was not eclipsed until 1999.

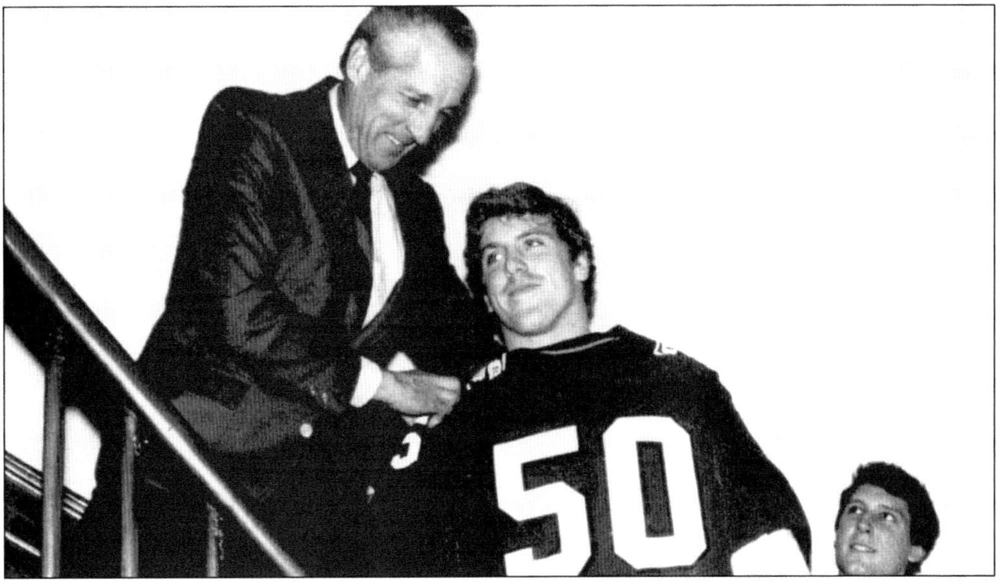

Joe Azelby '84. A beaming coach Joe Restic (left) presents his captain-elect Joe Azelby with his jersey at the 1982 annual Harvard breakup dinner at the Harvard Club of Boston. The event is held annually the Monday evening following the Yale game. Azelby, a native of Dumont, New Jersey, went on to lead the Crimson to an outstanding 6-2-2 overall record and 6-1-1 Ivy League mark, losing only to UMass (21-7) and Dartmouth (28-12). A two-time (1982 and 1983) All-Ivy choice as linebacker, Azelby was joined by fellow defenders Mike Dixon (defensive back) and Mark Mead (defensive end) on the all-star squad his senior year. Azelby, a two-time Eastern Collegiate Athletic Conference (ECAC) first-team all-star, finished with 273 career tackles.

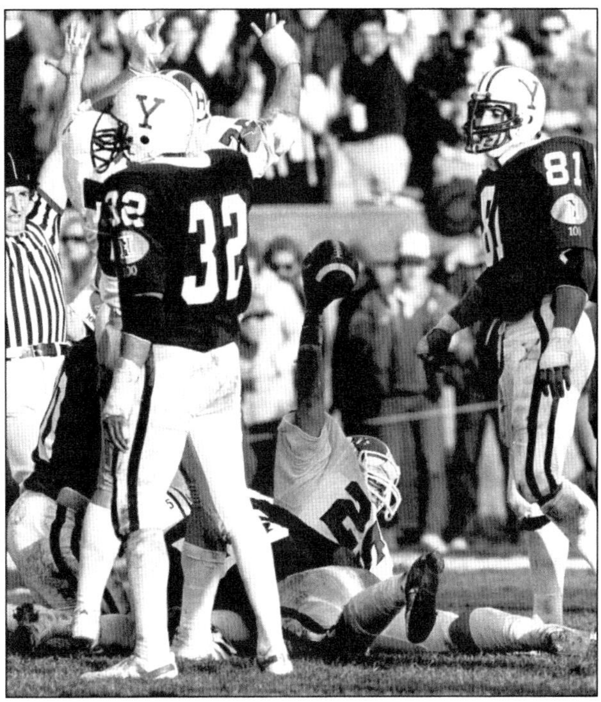

Steve Ernst '84 versus Yale. Steve Ernst (on the ground) celebrates a two-yard touchdown run that put Harvard ahead 13-7 in the 100th playing of the Game in 1983. The 16-7 victory in New Haven gained the Crimson a share of the Ivy League championship with Penn. The senior running back from Clinton, Massachusetts, was a versatile back, contributing to the Crimson attack as a runner, receiver and kickoff-punt returner. He was rewarded by being named first-team All-Ivy in 1983.

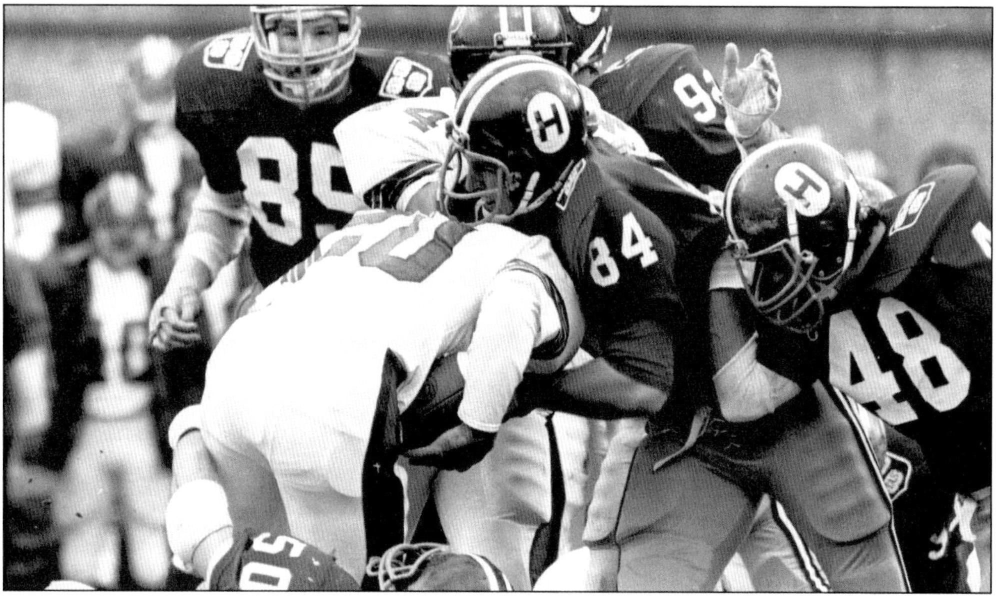

THE HARVARD DEFENSE VERSUS PENN, 1983. The Crimson defense stifled Penn in the final home game of the 1983 season. The resounding 28-0 shutout victory over the Quakers placed Harvard in a position to split the league crown by virtue of a win at Yale the next week. The win was further enhanced by the Crimson gaining revenge for a controversial loss (23-21) at Penn the previous year. A questionable penalty for roughing the kicker on a Quaker field goal attempt had given Penn kicker Dave Shulman a second chance to boot the winning goal on the game's final play.

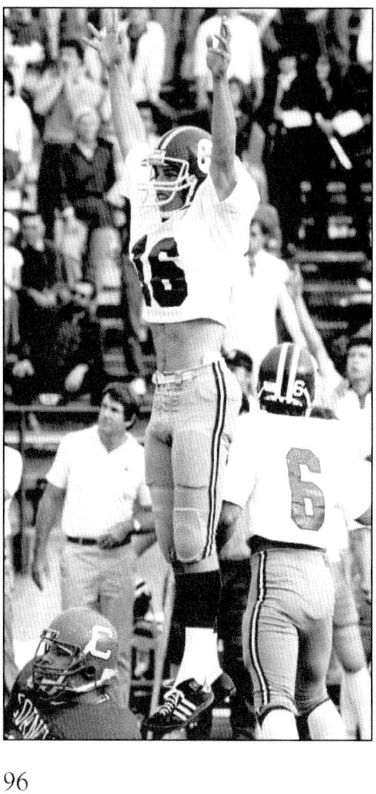

JIM VILLANUEVA '84. Jim Villanueva was the first-team All-Ivy selection as punter-place kicker in 1983. His total of 27 career field goals and a career punting average of 38.7 both remain all-time career marks for the Crimson. His career point total of 139 also currently ranks him as the Crimson's sixth all-time leading scorer. Villanueva's kicking bloodlines were exemplary. A native of Pacific Palisades, California, he represented the Crimson in the 1984 Hula Bowl college all-star contest. His dad, Danny, had kicked for the NFL's Dallas Cowboys.

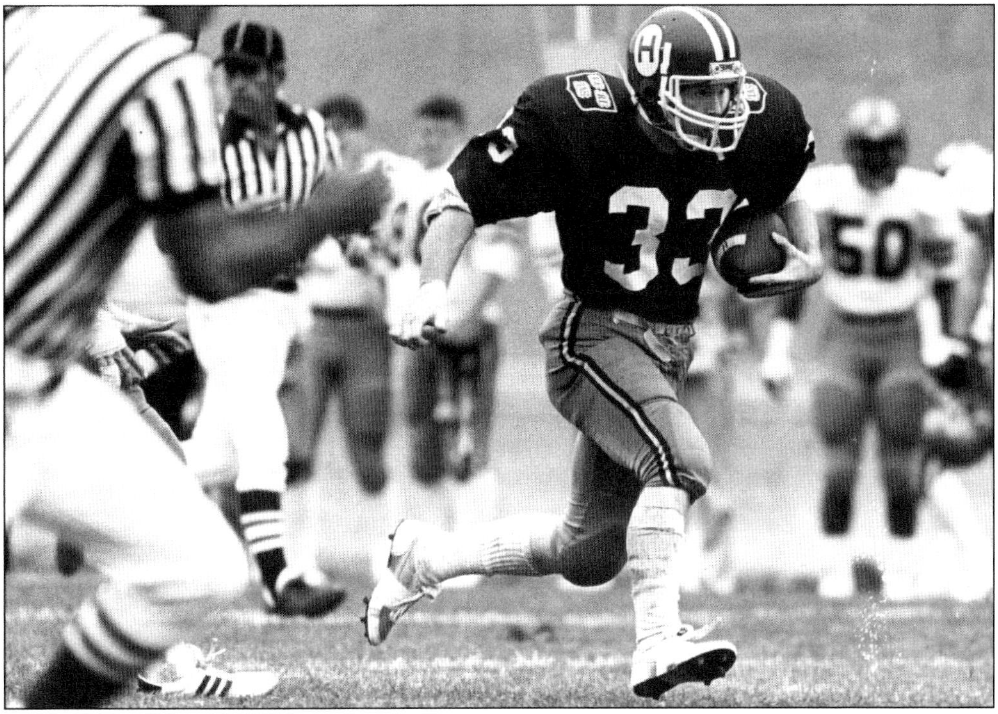

MARK VIGNALI '85. In tandem with running mate Robert Santiago, running back Mark Vignali added speed and excitement to the Crimson ground attack during the 1984 season. The one-two backfield punch bolstered Harvard's run to an impressive 5-0 start.

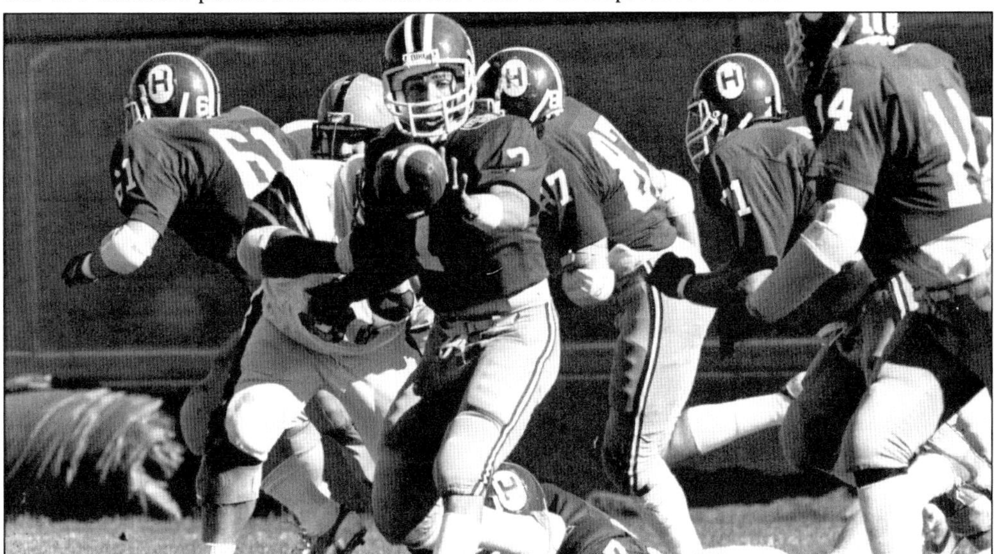

BRIAN WHITE '86. Quarterback Brian White, a native of Groveland, Massachusetts, led the Crimson to a 7-3 record during his senior year. Harvard finished in a second-place tie with Penn after dropping the season finale at Yale (17-6) and defeating Penn by an identical score the previous week. White threw for 2,335 career yards, good for sixth place on the all-time passing list at Harvard. Here, White makes the pitch to Robert Santiago in action versus Princeton at Harvard Stadium.

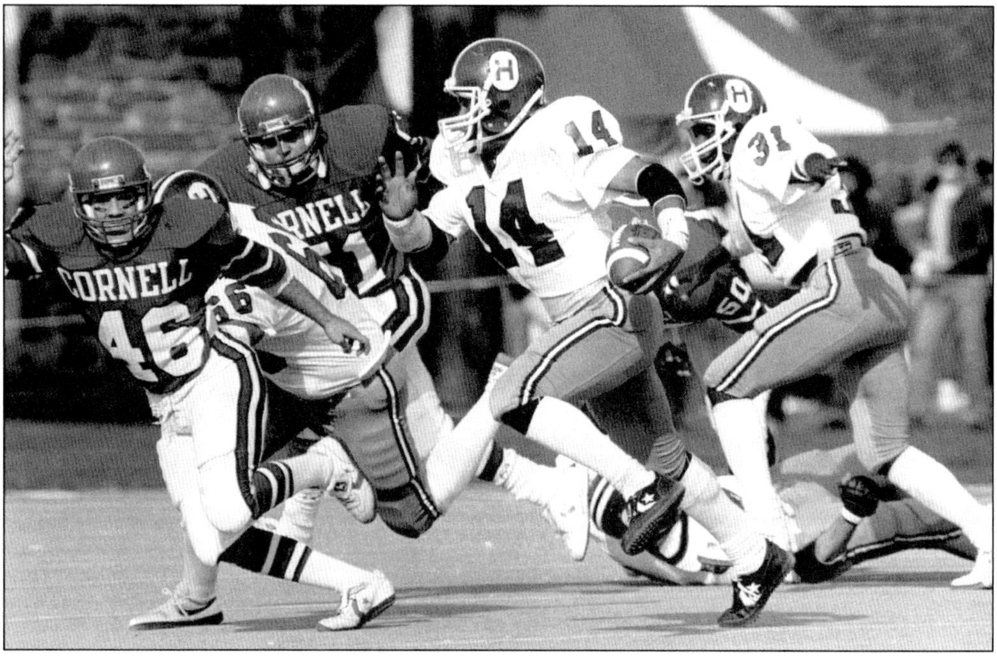

Robert Santiago '86. Speedy Robert Santiago became an impact player for the Crimson. A two-time All-Ivy selection in both 1984 and 1985, the native of San Antonio, Texas, ranks sixth on the Crimson's all-time rushing list, with 1,795 career yards. His 5.1-yards-per-carry average ties him with Ted DeMars '73 for the best in school history.

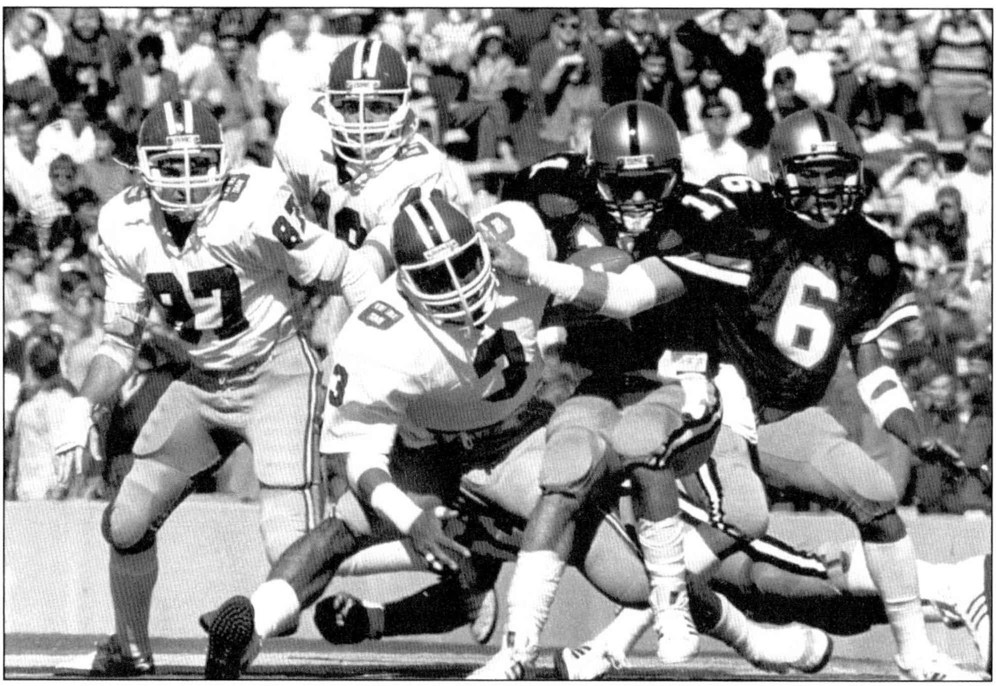

Cecil Cox '86. Hard-hitting cornerback Cecil Cox matched Santiago with back-to-back All-Ivy selections in 1984 and 1985. In a typically aggressive mode, the Dorchester, Massachusetts, native steps up to make the defensive stop.

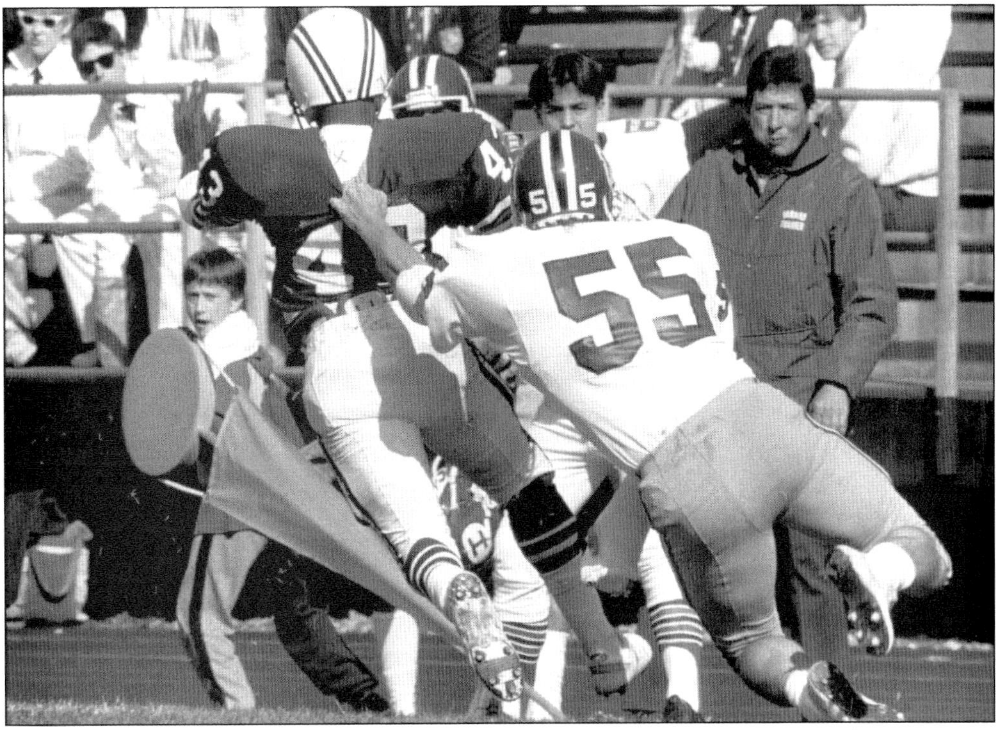

Bob Joyce '87. A hard-nosed linebacker out of Weymouth, Massachusetts, Bob Joyce was a teammate of Bob Glatz and is currently the chairman of the Friends of Harvard Football. On the field, when someone thought he had Joyce beaten, Joyce caught him from behind.

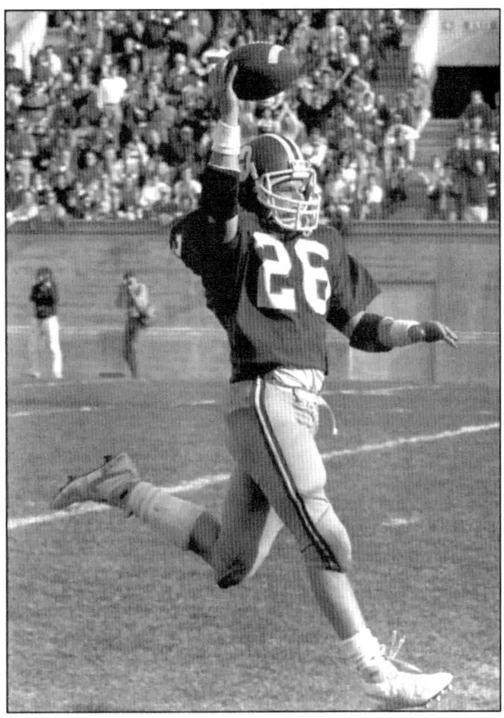

Bob Glatz '88. On the gridiron, Bob Glatz, a high school standout for St. John's Preparatory in Danvers, Massachusetts, was a solid all-around running back. Off the field, Glatz is currently the executive director of the Harvard Varsity Club, the organization that handles the Crimson's 41 active intercollegiate competing teams and alumni support groups.

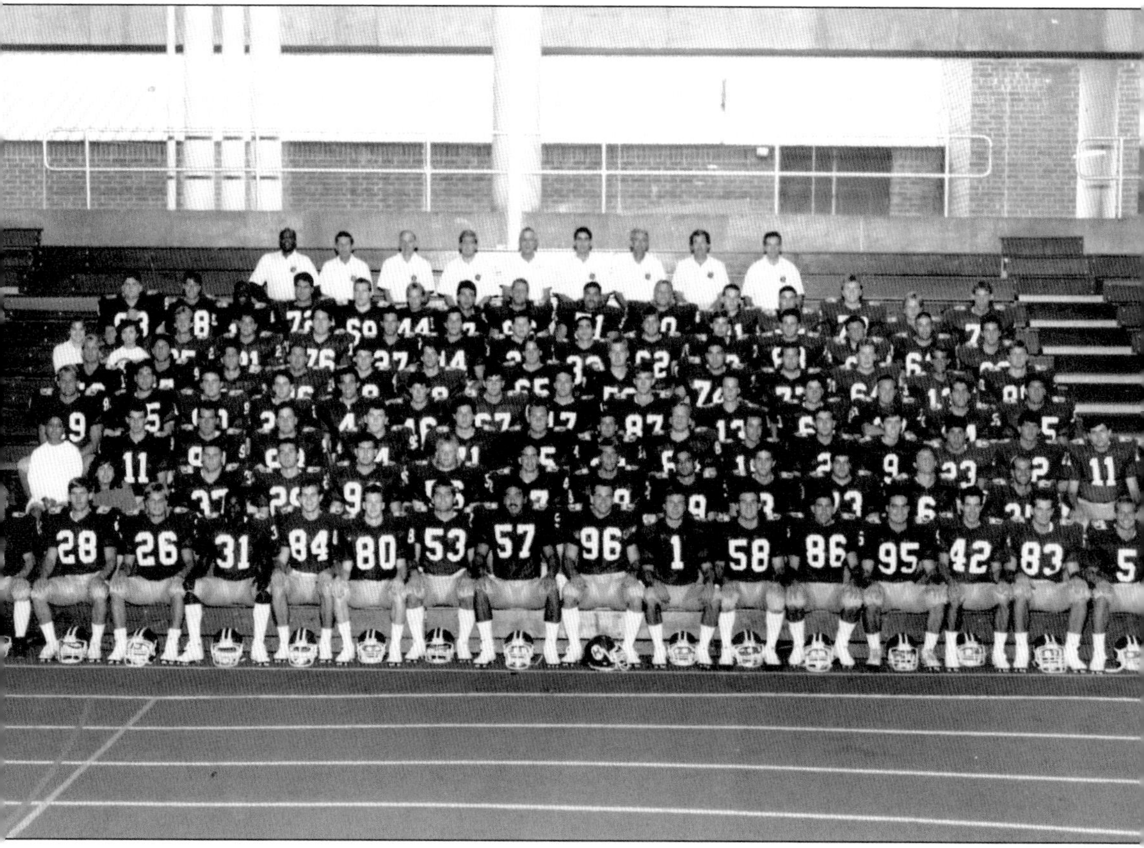

THE 1987 TEAM. The undisputed 1987 Ivy League champion was Joe Restic's most successful team (8-2). The two Harvard losses came on the road at Cornell and Holy Cross. The Crimson capped the banner season with a 14-10 victory over Yale in New Haven.

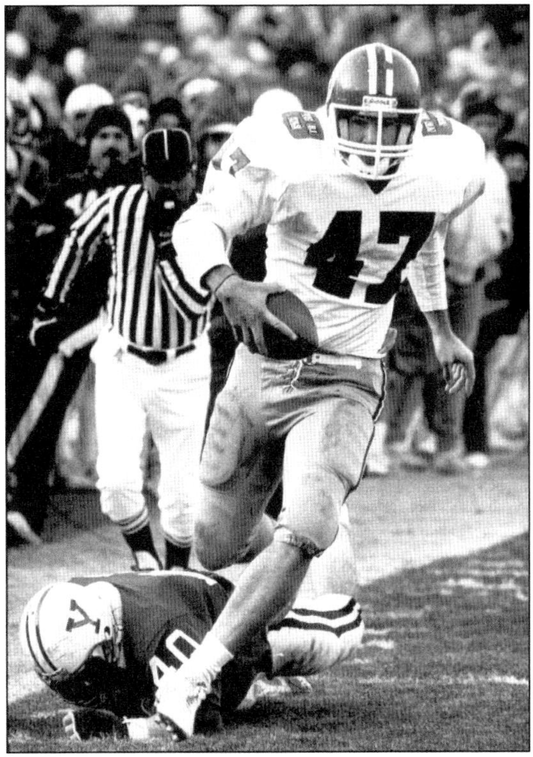

Tony Hinz '89. Tony Hinz was the focal point of the Harvard running attack in 1987. Hinz was named to the All-Ivy team for his considerable junior year accomplishments.

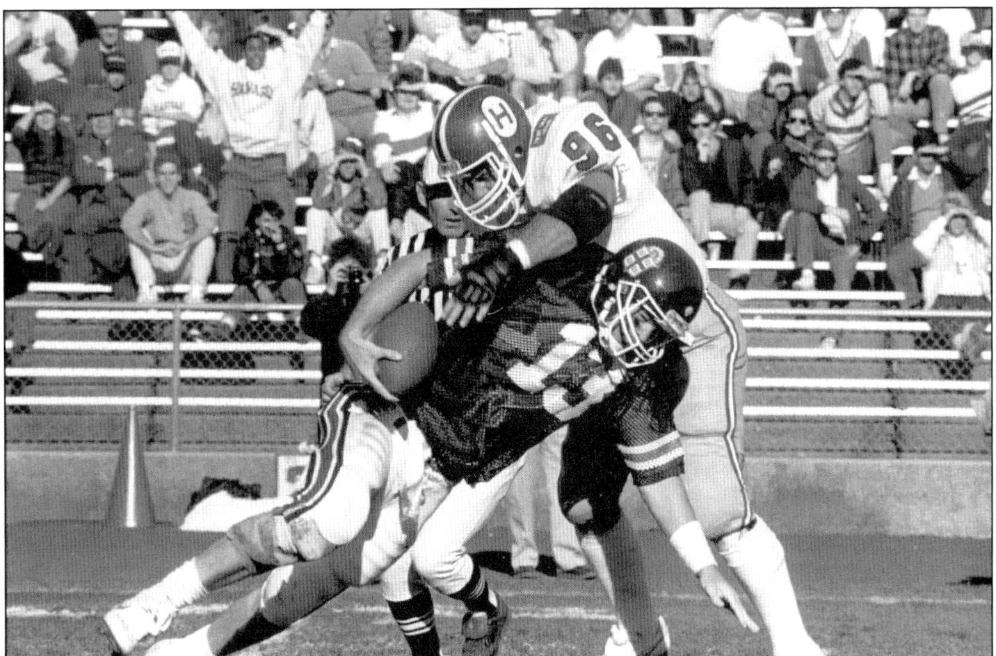

Kevin Dulsky '88 (Captain, 1987). The 1987 Ivy League champions were captained by Kevin Dulsky, the first defensive end to lead a Crimson football squad since John Cramer, in 1969. A native of Woodland Hills, California, Dulsky lettered for three varsity seasons (1985–1987).

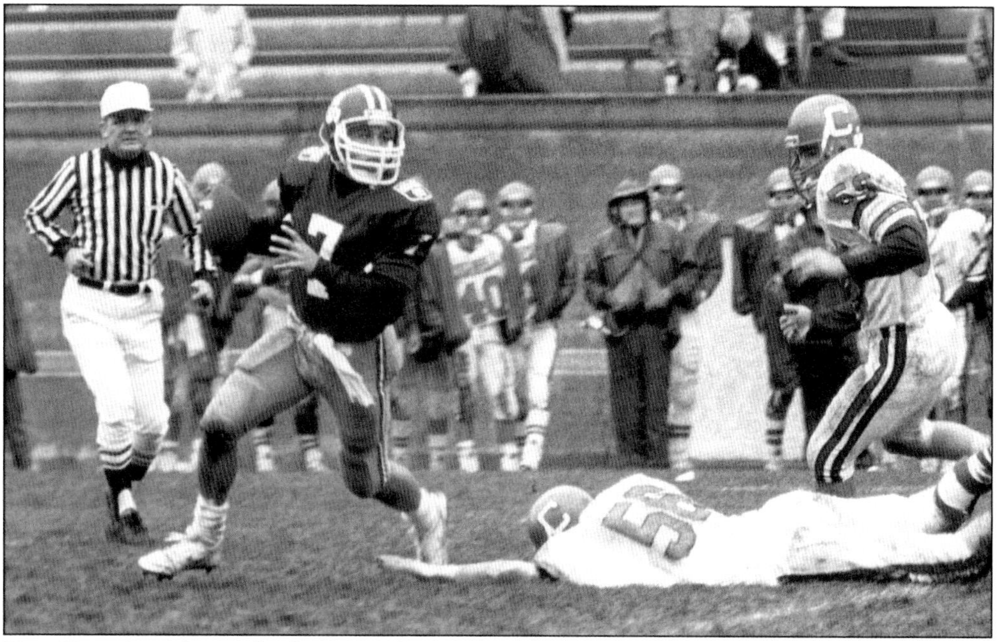

Tom Yohe '89. Quarterback Tom Yohe rewrote the Harvard passing record book. The native of Crown Point. Indiana, remained the Crimson's all-time passing leader until 2001, throwing for 4,407 yards and 30 touchdowns. His 17-touchdown pass mark, established en route to the Ivy title in 1987, remained the school standard until the 2000 season when Neil Rose '02 threw for 18 scores.

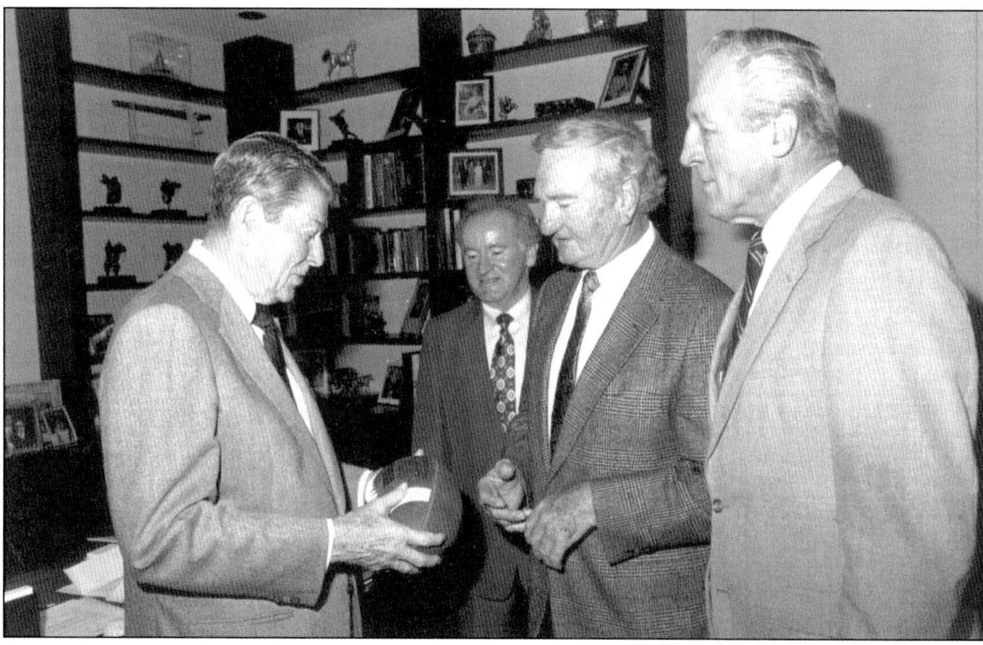

Four Presidents Swap Stories. President Ronald Reagan (left) talks football with three American Football Coaches Association presidents. With Reagan, from left to right, are Don James (1989), University of Washington; Charlie McClendon (1979), Louisiana State University; and Joe Restic (1988), Harvard University.

Eight

1990–1999

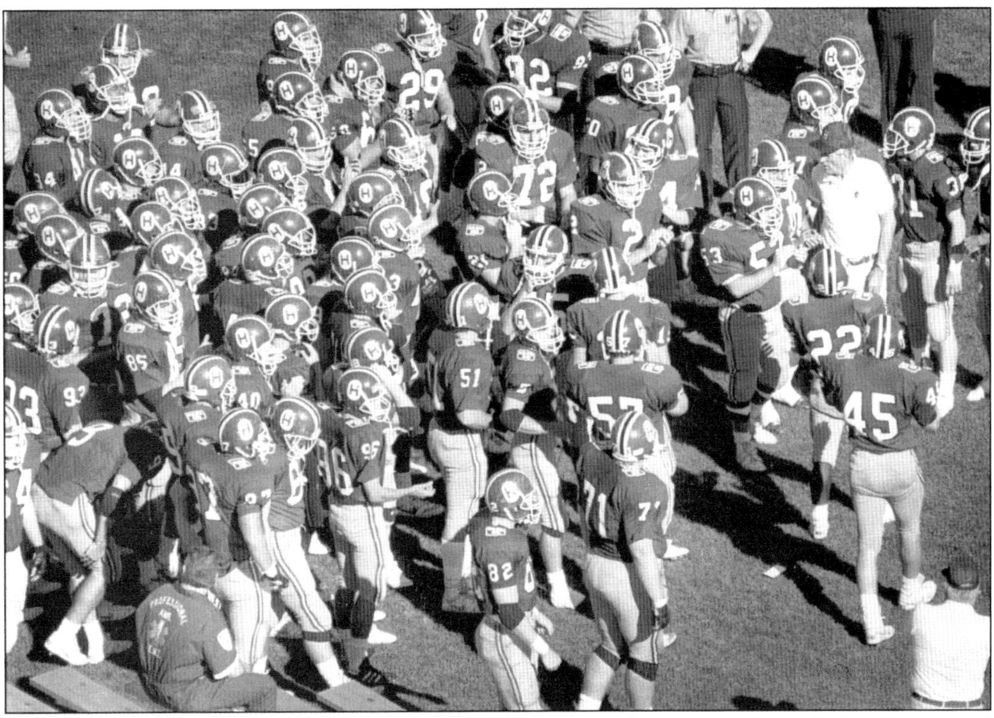

Taking the Field versus Cornell, 1990. The team gathers around coach Joe Restic and prepares to take the field for the Ivy League home opener versus Cornell. The Crimson dropped a close 20-17 decision to the Big Red, a fifth straight loss in the series. The winless streak against the Crimson's Ithaca nemesis did not end until the 1997 Crimson Ivy League champions defeated the Big Red 34-9.

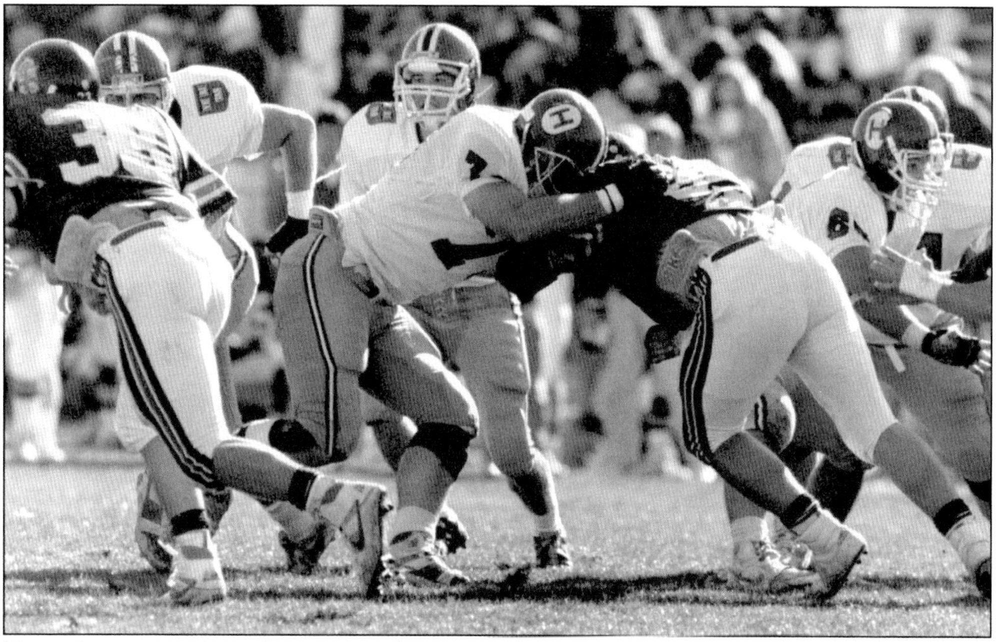

Tom Callahan '91. Protecting the quarterback is a full-time job for any offensive lineman, and Tom Callahan fulfilled his duty well. An offensive tackle, Callahan ushered in the new decade as the Crimson's 1990 captain. The team finished 5-5 overall and 3-4 in Ivy League play.

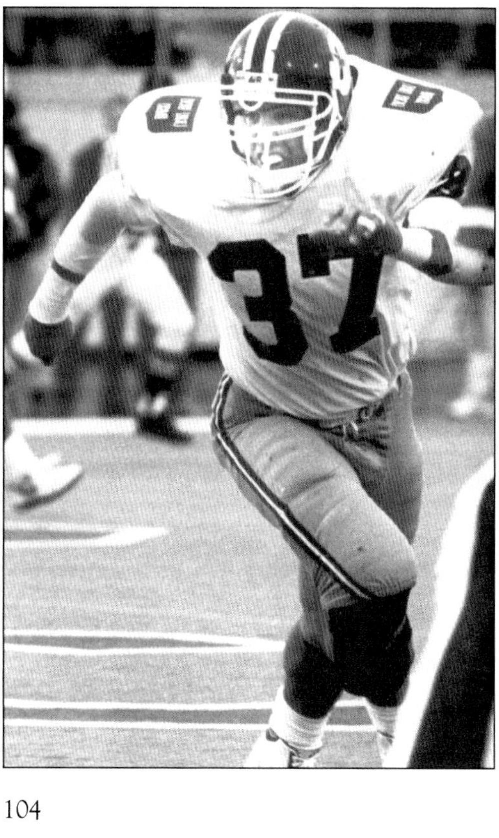

John Lausch '92 (Captain, 1991). A formidable presence from his linebacker position, John Lausch captained a hard-luck 1991 squad. After a season-opening victory (21-16) over Columbia at Harvard Stadium, the Crimson never seemed to fully recover from the disappointment of a heartbreaking 21-20 loss at Army. Harvard did rally in November to defeat Brown (35-29) and Penn (22-18) on successive Saturdays before a loss in the Game at Yale (23-13).

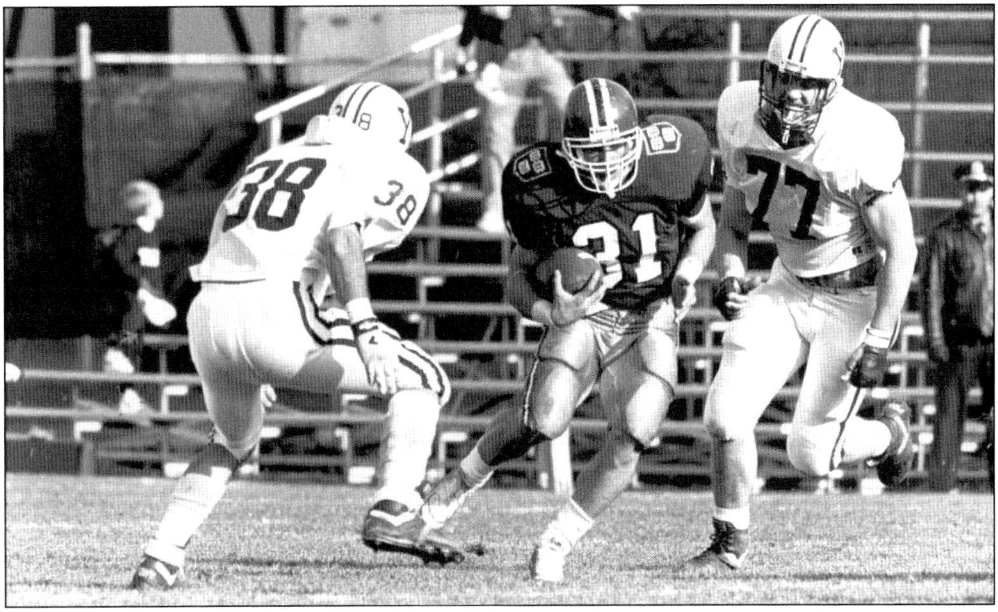

Rob Hirsch '93 (Captain 1992). Rob Hirsch (in action versus Yale at Harvard Stadium) captained the 1992 team his senior year. Despite a disappointing (3-7, 3-4 Ivy) overall season, Hirsch concluded his career by leading the team in rushing and by gaining a victory over Yale in his final game.

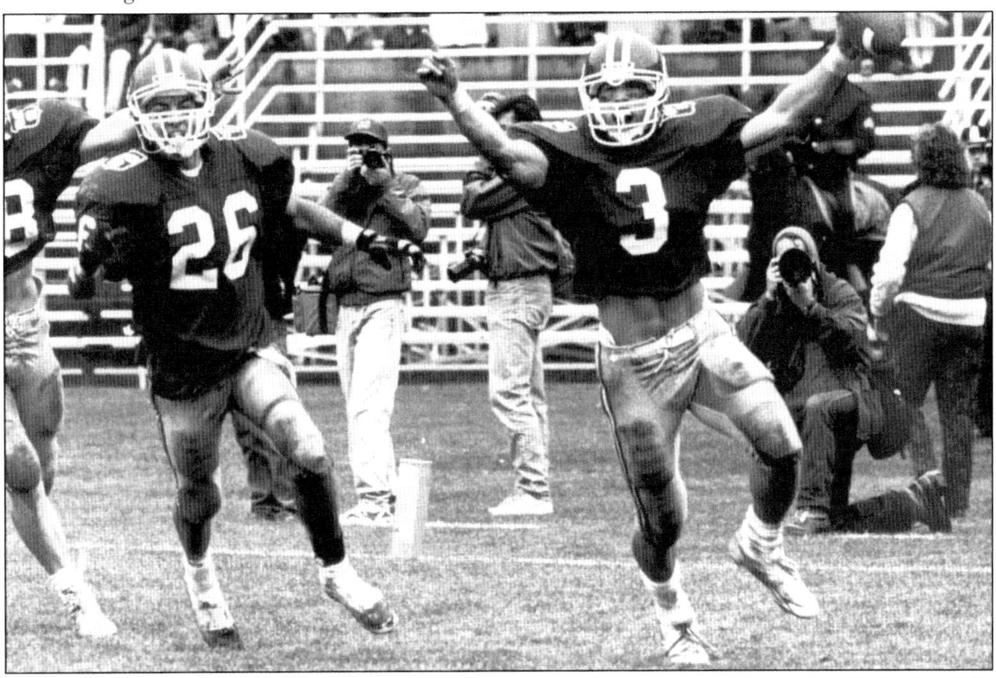

Rob Santos '93. Rob Santos (right) celebrates an end-zone interception that halted a Yale drive in the 1992 renewal of the Game. Escorted to the end zone by teammates Brian Ramer (94) and Robb Sonne (26), Santos's big play was one of many made during the cornerback's senior campaign. He was the lone Harvard player to be named first-team All-Ivy for his overall effort in 1992.

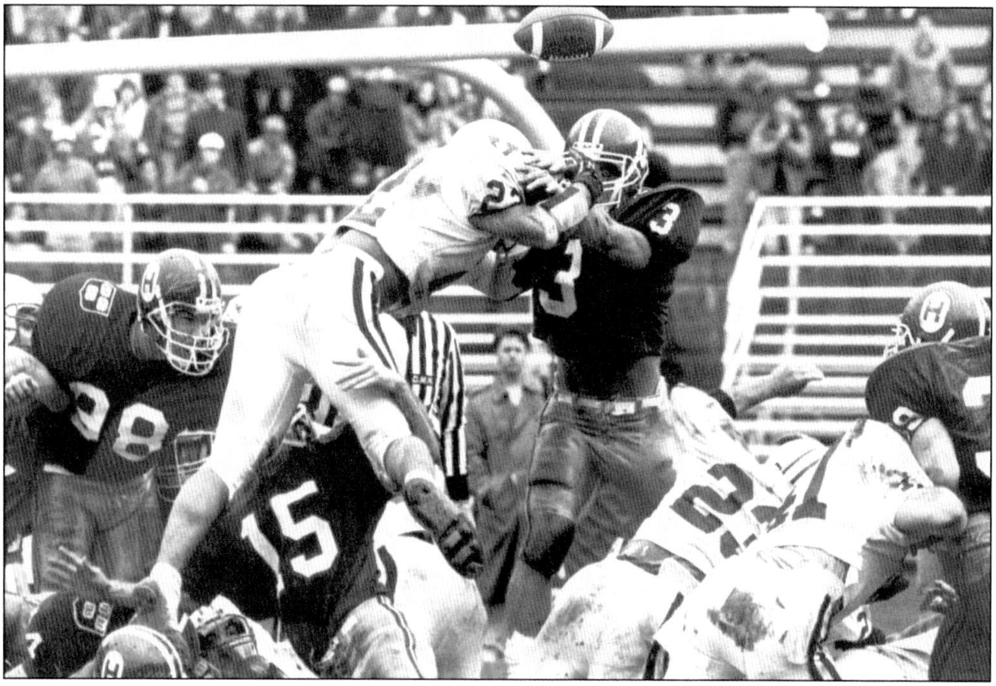

Rob Santos '93, Harvard Defense. Santos plays a little run force from his defensive backfield position. The goal line-stand mid-air hit forced an Eli fumble and helped the Crimson preserve a 14-0 upset victory over Yale.

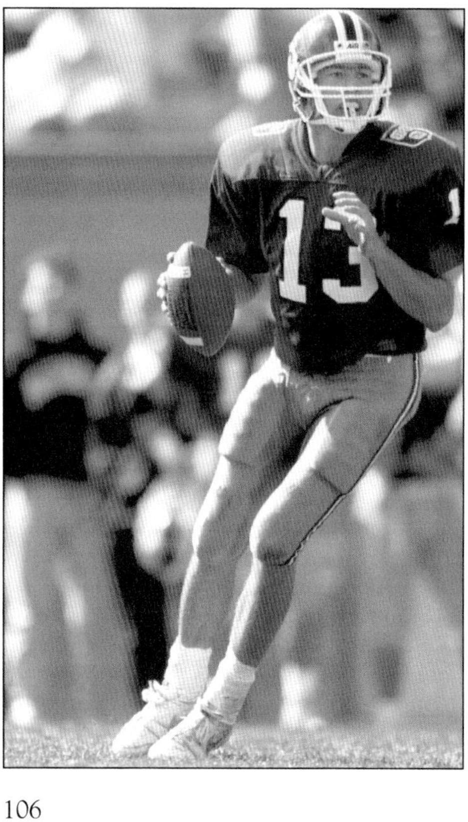

Mike Giardi '94. Mike Giardi still holds a prominent place in the Crimson record book nearly a decade later. The three-sport star from Salem, Massachusetts, High School ranks as the third all-time passer in school history, throwing for 4,198 yards. He is the career leader in most rushing touchdowns all-time, with 29, and also owns the career total offense mark of 5,057 yards for a 5-yard average per touch of the ball. Also an outstanding baseball shortstop, Giardi played baseball in the New York Yankees and Montreal Expos farm systems. He has been the color analyst on the Harvard football radio network for the past seven seasons.

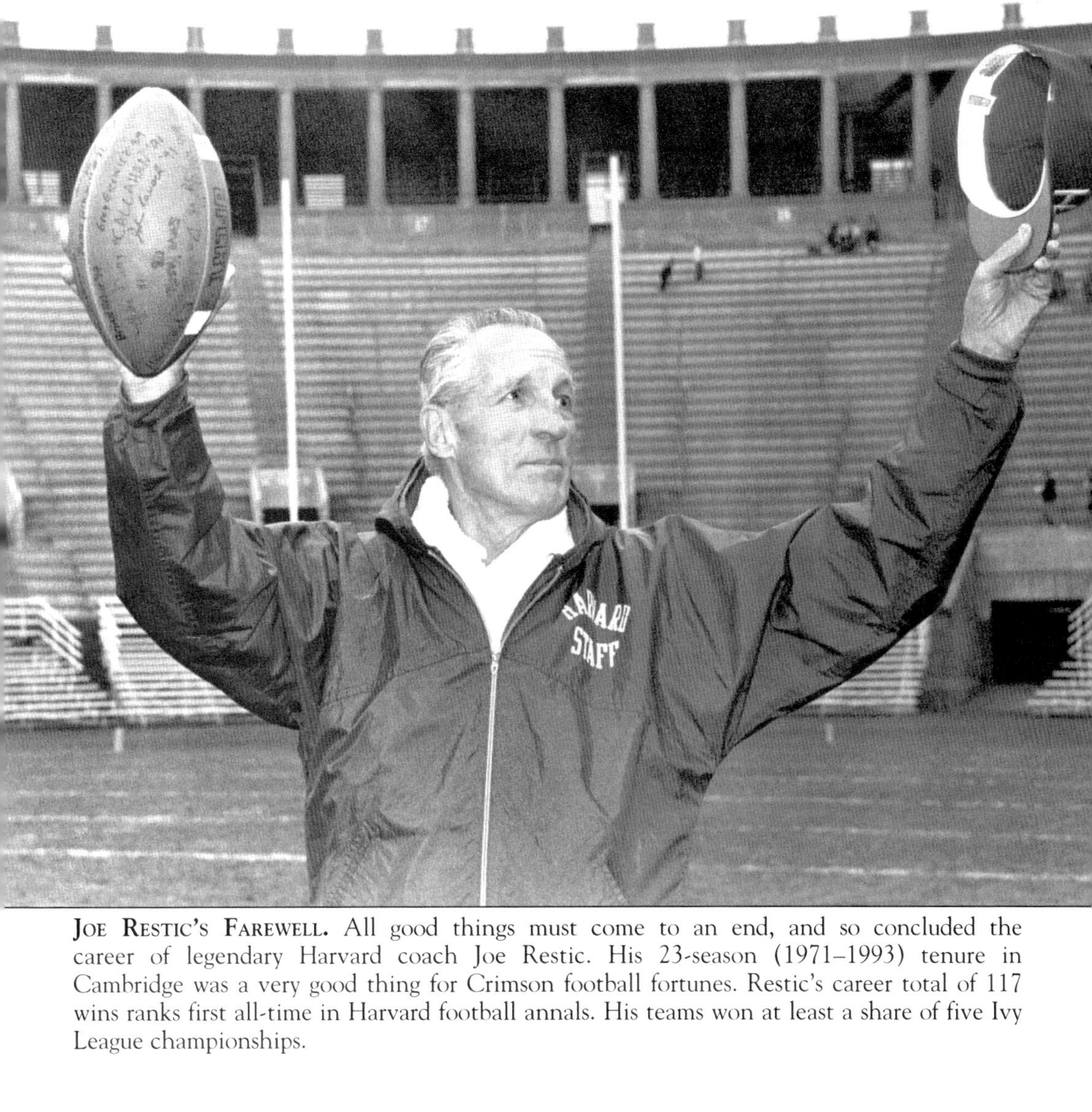

Joe Restic's Farewell. All good things must come to an end, and so concluded the career of legendary Harvard coach Joe Restic. His 23-season (1971–1993) tenure in Cambridge was a very good thing for Crimson football fortunes. Restic's career total of 117 wins ranks first all-time in Harvard football annals. His teams won at least a share of five Ivy League championships.

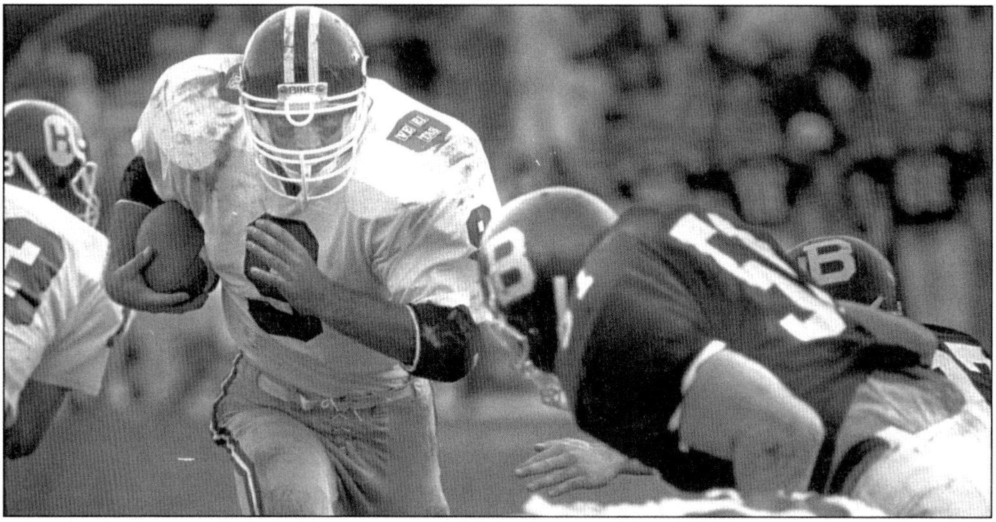

MATT JOHNSON '92. Fullback Matt Johnson had an afternoon for the ages in November 1991. His 323 yards rushing on 33 carries shattered a 54-year-old Harvard single-game rushing record previously held by Vernon Struck (233 yards) in the 1937 Princeton game. Johnson's performance also broke the Ivy League record held by Cornell's Scott Oliara (288 yards) versus Yale in 1990. "It's just the ebb and flow of the season. Different backs get highlighted at different times," observed Johnson from the aptly named hometown of Humble, Texas, regarding his performance.

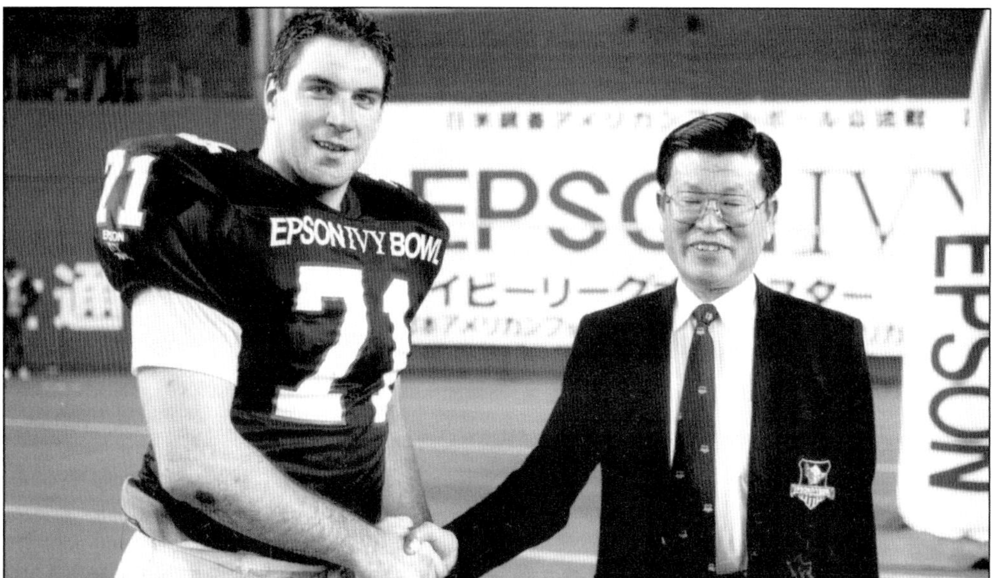

MARTY POPOLOSKI '92 WITH A JAPANESE OFFICIAL. Harvard entered into a unique exchange program with Japan in 1991. On June 22, the Crimson hosted the first Japanese collegiate football game ever played in the United States. Keio University, coached by the Harvard staff, defeated Yale-led Waseda University 21-19. The Crimson then reciprocated in the exchange of goodwill by joining with the seven other Ivy schools, making the trek to Japan, and playing in the Epson Ivy Bowl. Offensive lineman Mary Popoloski exchanges greetings with a bowl official prior to that game.

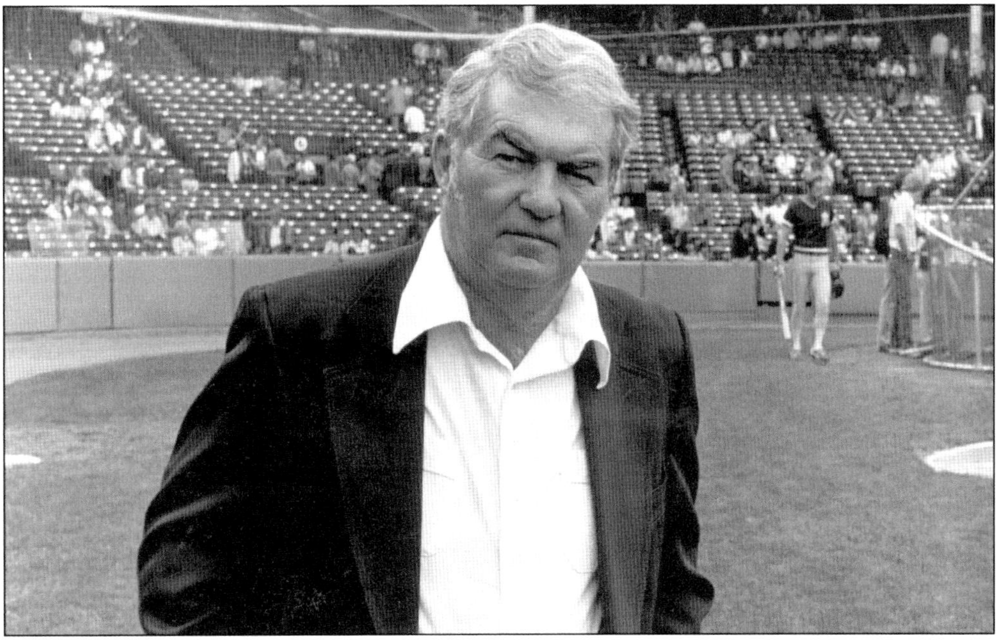

Ken Coleman, Broadcaster. The legendary voice of the Boston Red Sox, the Cincinnati Reds, and the NFL's Cleveland Browns, Ken Coleman was also the longtime voice of the Harvard Crimson. He lent his consummate professionalism and Hall-of-Fame ability to many fall Saturday afternoons at Harvard Stadium.

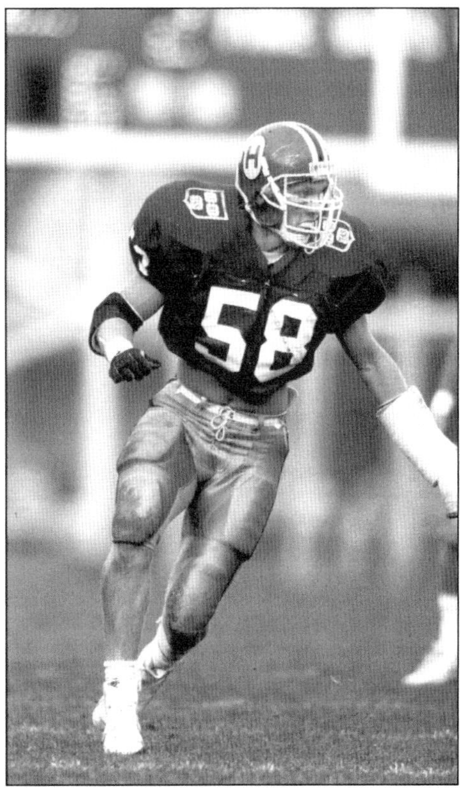

Brian Ramer '94. Brian Ramer captained Joe Restic's final team in 1993. The Crimson began the season in promising fashion, defeating Columbia and Lafayette, sandwiched with a loss at William and Mary. The Crimson tasted victory only once more, however, with a 41-25 win over Holy Cross at Harvard Stadium. Restic's emotional last game as Harvard coach ended in heartbreak—a 33-31 loss to Yale in New Haven.

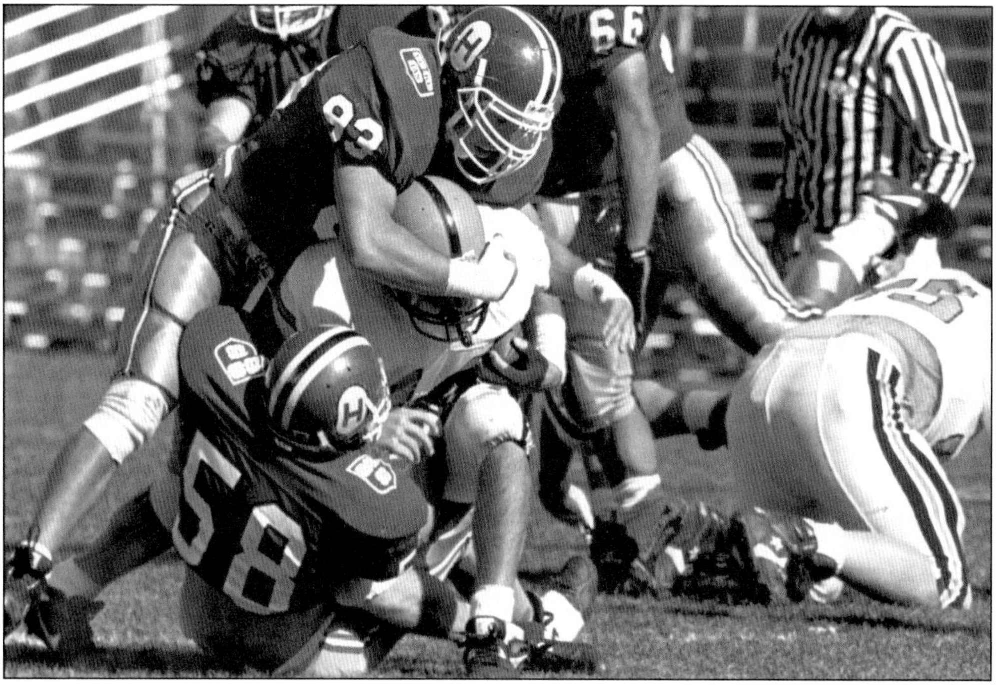

EDWARD KINNEY '95 (CAPTAIN, 1994). Putting the clamps on opposing ball carriers was something that Ed Kinney did on a consistent basis from his defensive tackle position. Kinney was coach Tim Murphy's first captain in 1994, which resulted in a 4-6 record for the Crimson.

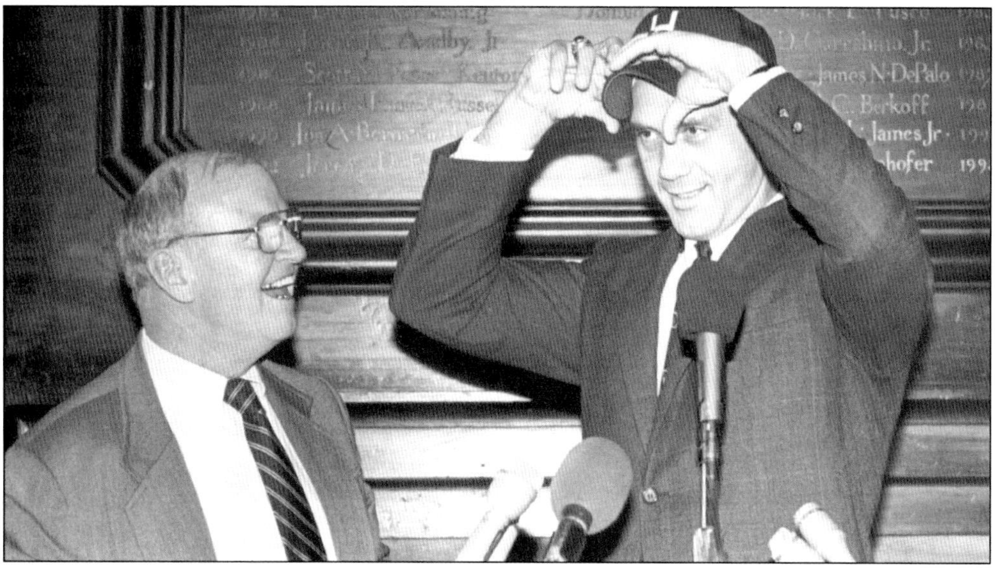

TIM MURPHY (COACH, 1994–PRESENT). Harvard athletic director Bill Cleary (left) announces the hiring of Tim Murphy (right) on December 6, 1993. The 30th coach in Harvard football's long and storied history, Murphy was head coach at both the University of Maine and Division I-A Cincinnati, leading the Bearcats to their best season in 17 years in the fall of 1993. In his first eight seasons with the Crimson, Murphy has compiled a record of 42-37, winning two Ivy League championships (1997, 2001), and he was named the New England Division I-AA Coach of the Year both years.

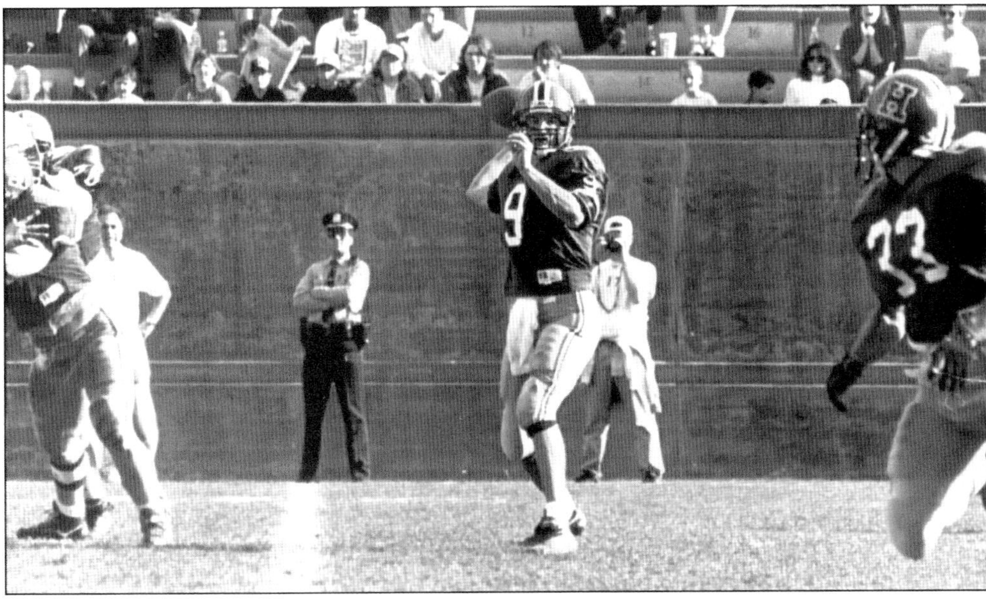

VIN FERRARA '96. A strong-armed quarterback from Florham Park, New Jersey, Vin Ferrara succeeded Mike Giardi as the Crimson starting quarterback in 1994. Ferrara's career total of 3,022 passing yards ranked him fourth on Harvard's all-time list prior to the 2001 season. His .549 completion percentage in 1995 places him third overall. His 3,131 total career yards rank him fifth in total offense.

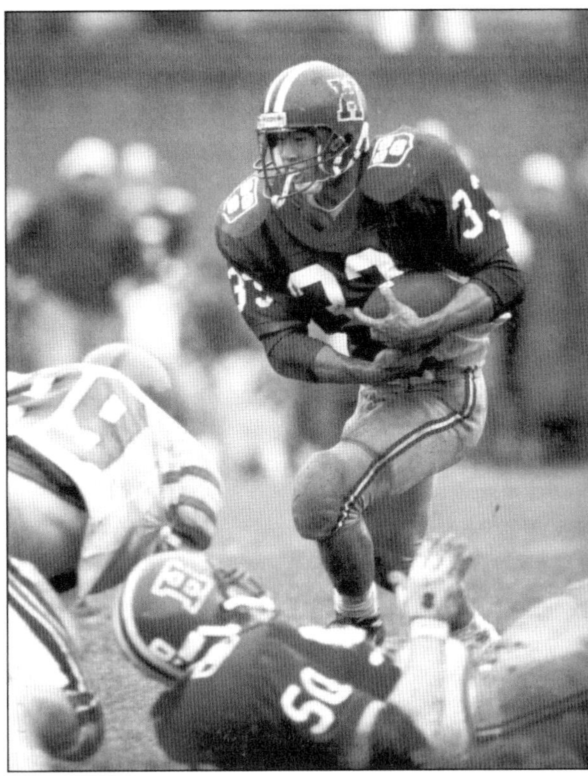

EION HU '97. Running back Eion Hu rewrote the Harvard rushing record book during his brilliant ball-carrying career in Cambridge. Upon his graduation, Hu was established as the Crimson's career rushing leader with 3,073 yards on a record 714 attempts and was deemed single-season champion with 1,101 yards in 1995. Eion had an amazing 16 100-yard games, topped by a 229-yard performance versus Colgate in 1995. The only Crimson running back in history to run for 1,000 yards twice (1994 and 1995), the New England Division I Player of the Year just missed the century record in 1996 with 961 yards on the ground.

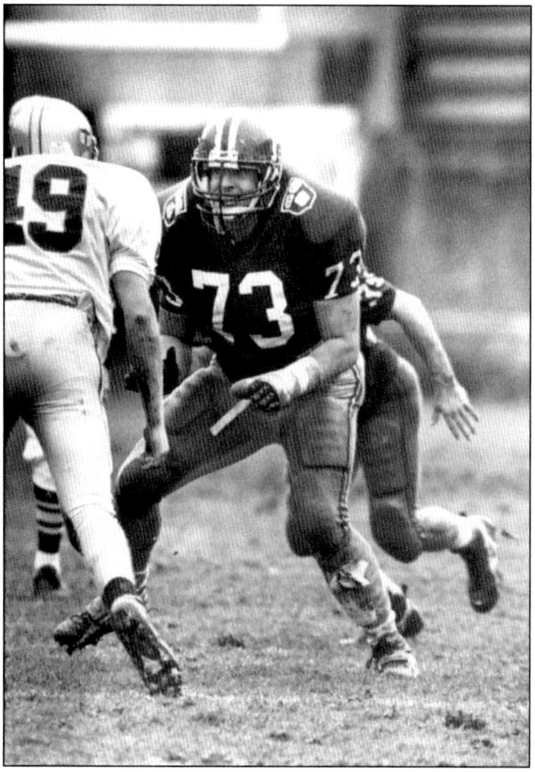

Sean Riley '97 (Captain, 1996). The pride of Greenville, Pennsylvania, Sean Riley ascended to the role of captain of the 1996 Crimson team. A three-year starter as offensive tackle, Riley bounced back from a shoulder injury his freshman year to become an iron man on the Crimson offensive line and an All-Ivy first-team selection in 1996.

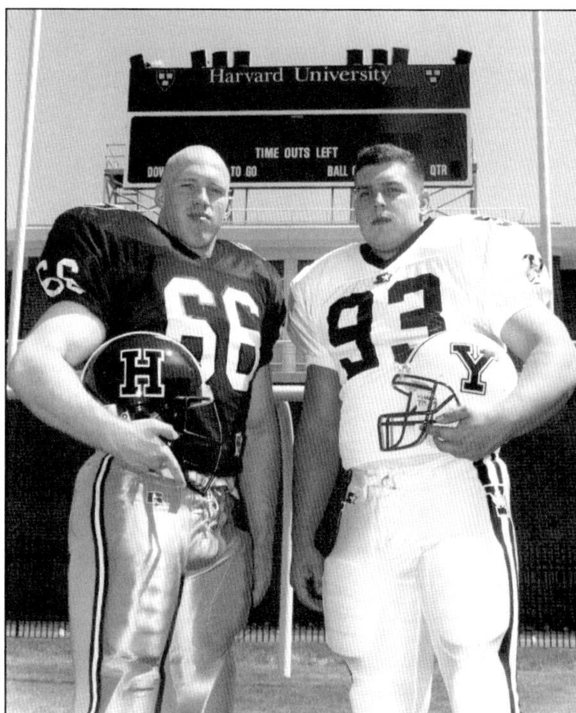

Brendan Bibro '98 (Captain, 1997 and 1998) with Yale Captain Corwynne Caruthers. As the only two-year captain in the 128-year history of Harvard football, Brendan Bibro (left) holds a unique position. A tenacious four-year starter at defensive tackle, the Pittsburgh, Pennsylvania, native was undeterred by a broken foot that forced him to miss half of the 1997 Ivy League championship season. Bibro, particularly adept at stopping the opponent's running game, was the third straight Harvard captain to hail from the traditional football stronghold of western Pennsylvania, following Sean Riley (Greenville) and Justin Frantz (Chalk Hill).

Rich Linden '00. As a sophomore, quarterback Rich Linden led the Crimson to a 9-1 record and an Ivy League championship. A second-team All-Ivy selection, Linden operated an offense that scored more points (301) than any Crimson team in the 20th century. The native of Indianapolis, Indiana, finished his career as the school's number two all-time career passer (4,300 yards), trailing only Tom Yohe, and also as the number two all-time career offense leader (4,657 yards), behind Mike Giardi. A versatile all-around athlete, Linden pitched two years for the Crimson baseball team.

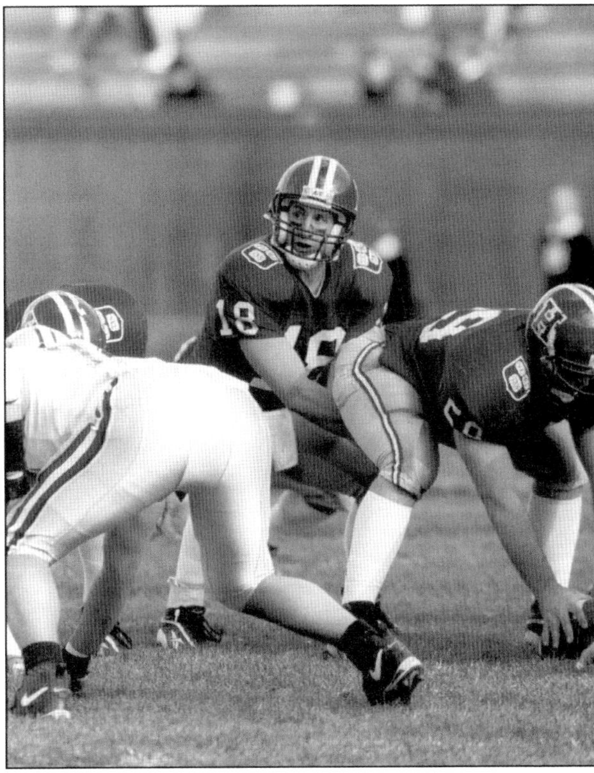

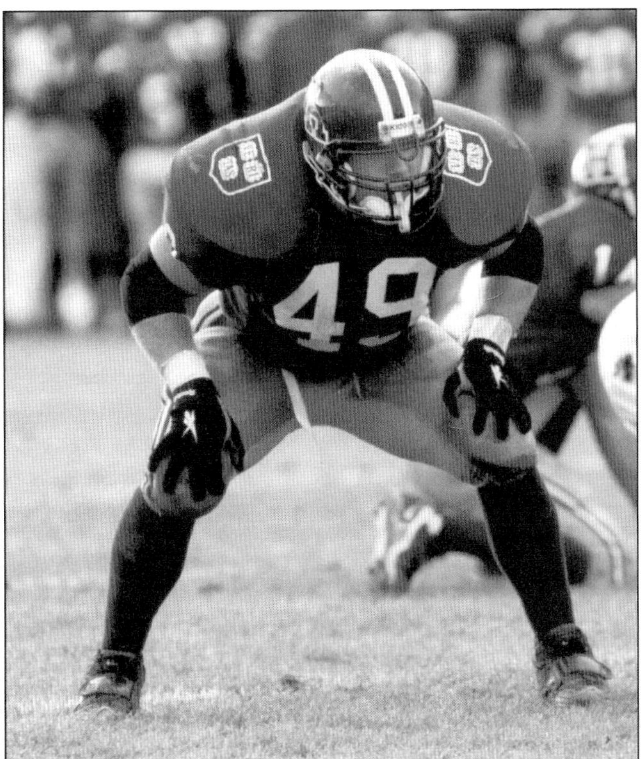

Isaiah Kacyvenski '00. The Crimson's all-time leading tackler, with 395 stops (249 primary, 146 assists), Isaiah Kacyvenski achieved many firsts during his brilliant tenure in Cambridge. The 6-foot 3-inch 240-pound linebacker from Endicott, New York, also set Crimson single-season (135 in 1999) and single-game (20) records for tackles. Named Harvard's first All-American since 1987, Isaiah was the first player in school history to start all 40 games of his collegiate career and was a first-team All-Ivy selection for three straight years. A fourth-round selection in the 2000 NFL draft, Kacyvenski now plays on Sundays for the Seattle Seahawks.

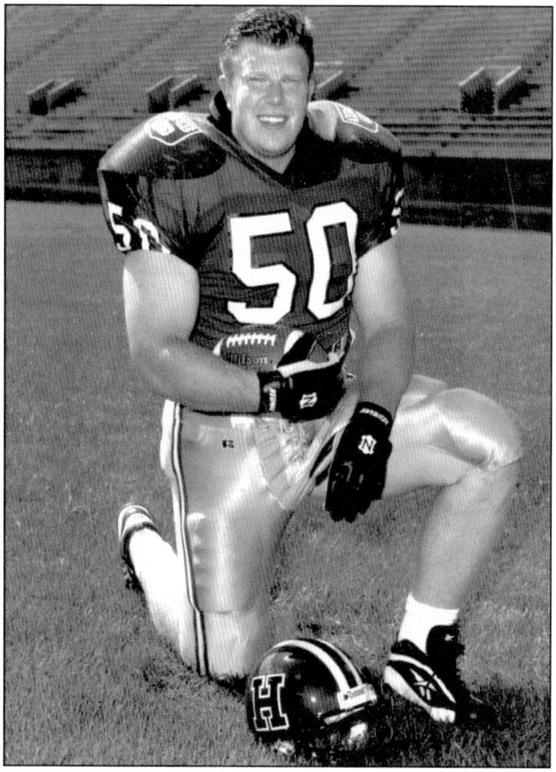

Matt Birk '98. A three-year starter as offensive tackle, Matt Birk, 6 feet 4 inches and 308 pounds, blossomed into perhaps the greatest offensive lineman in Harvard football history. Demonstrating a devastating combination of strength and agility, Birk finished his senior year in 1997 by being named first-team All-ECAC, All-Ivy, and All–New England. The seventh Harvard player named to play in the Kelley Blue-Gray All-Star Classic, Birk (who came to Harvard from St. Paul, Minnesota) had a chance to return home after being selected by his hometown NFL team, the Minnesota Vikings. Matt has become a fixture at center for the Vikings, having been named All-Pro after the 2000 and 2001 seasons.

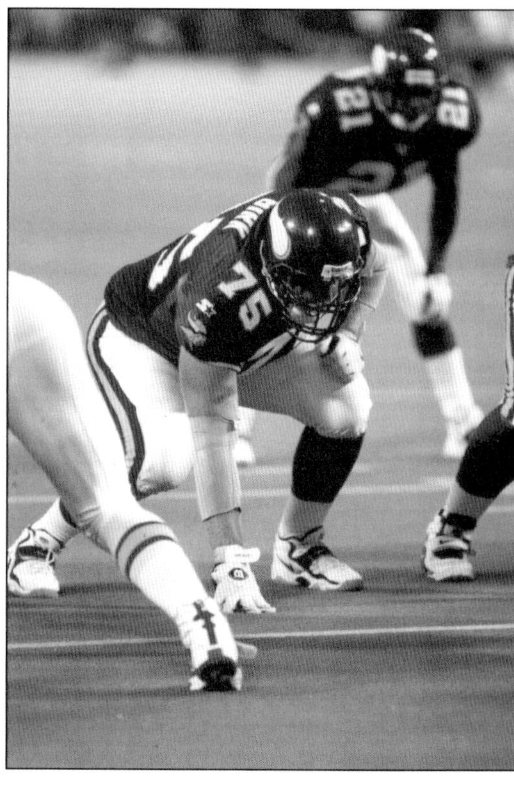

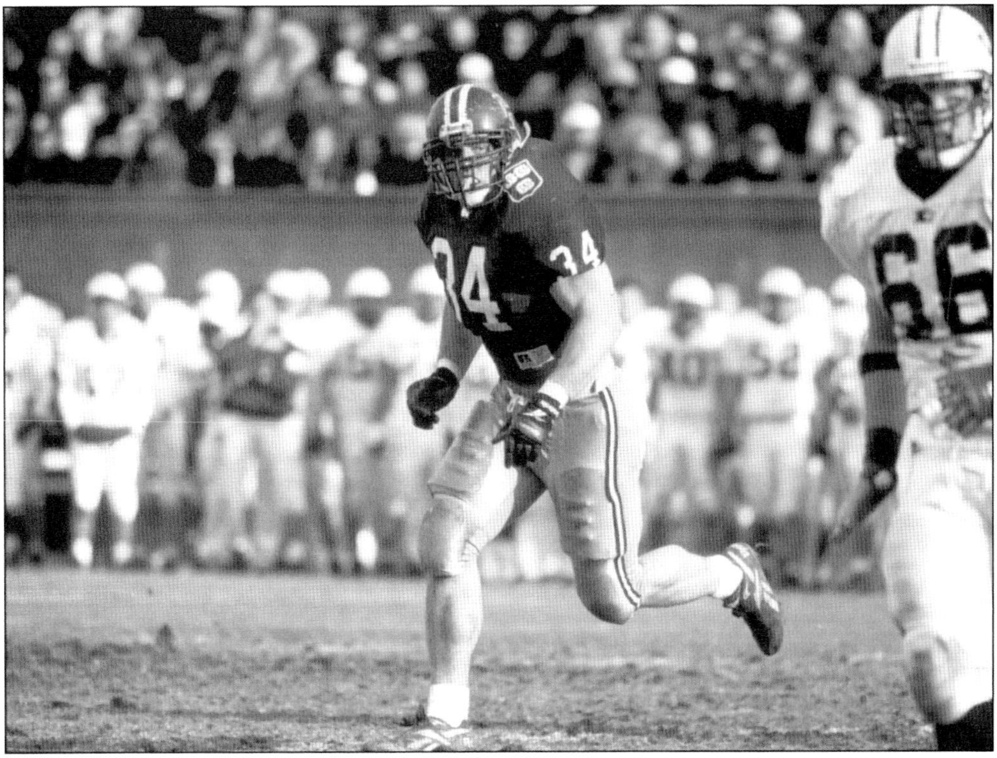

TIM FLEISZER '98. Switched from his original position as fullback, Tim Fleiszer became a dominant defensive end. Named first-team All-Ivy and All–New England for his efforts on the 1997 Ivy championship team, Fleiszer was credited with 33 total tackles and 5 sacks. A strong, quick player, he was a natural pass rusher. A native of Montreal, Quebec, he is fulfilling a lifelong dream playing for his hometown Montreal Alouettes in the Canadian Football League.

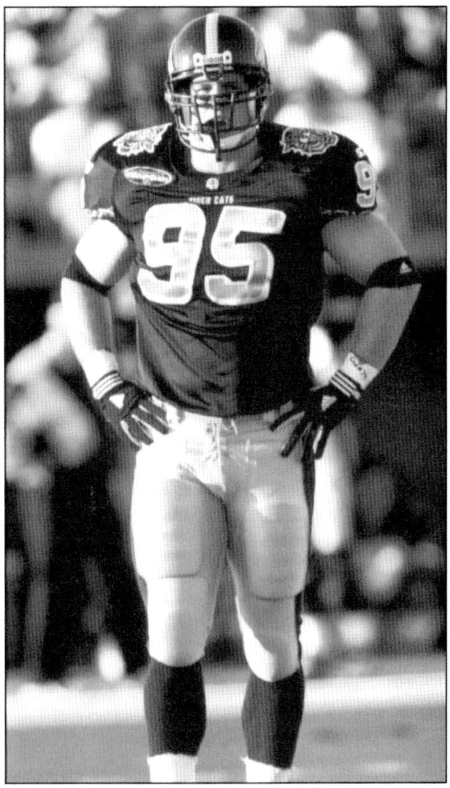

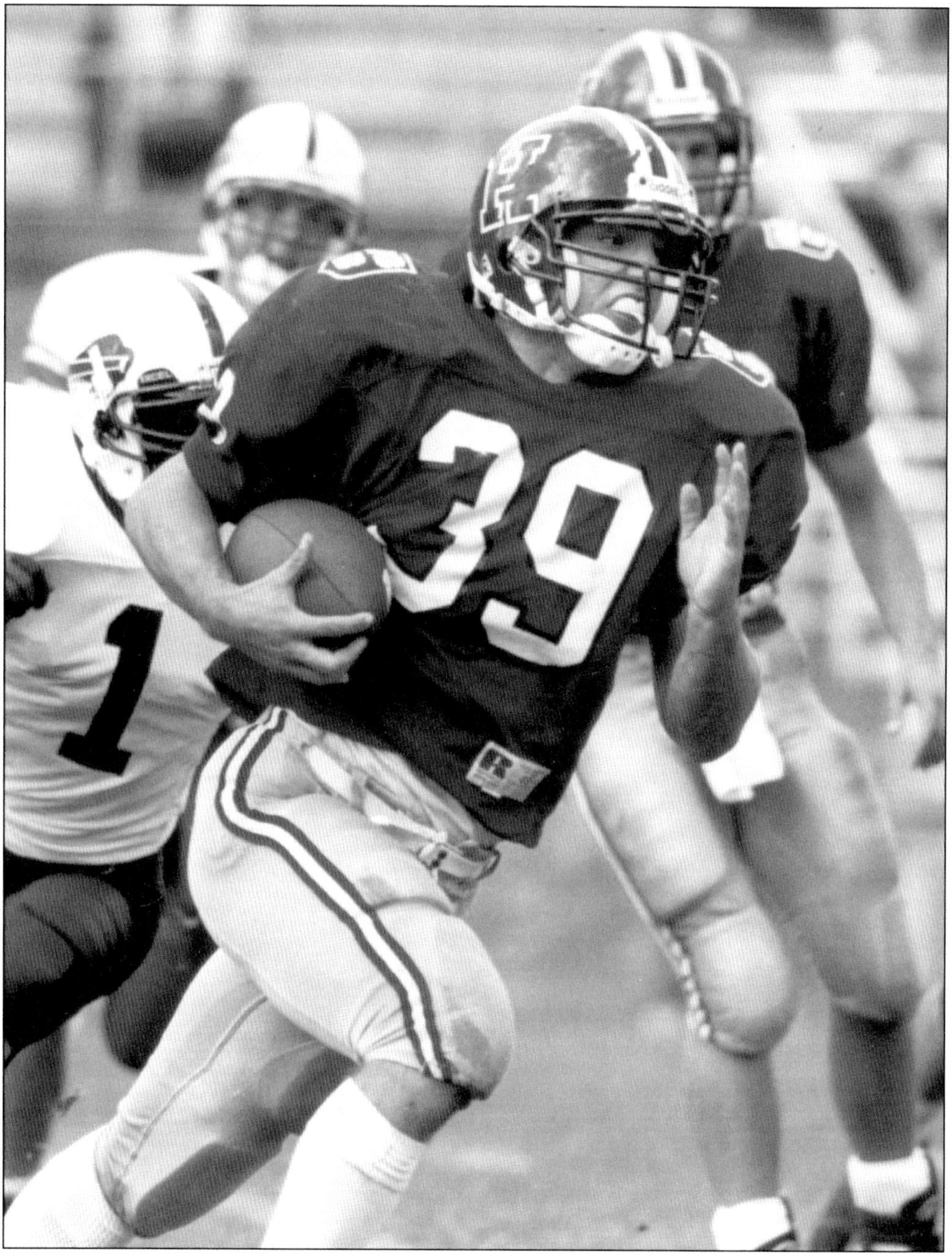

CHRIS MENICK '00. At just 5 feet 10 inches and 185 pounds, Chris Menick personified toughness and durability, finishing his career as the Crimson's all-time leading rusher. His 3,300 yards on 726 attempts are both records, along with his single-season numbers from 1997: 1,267 yards, 247 attempts, 13 touchdowns, and a 5.1 average. Only the single-season touchdown total of 13 is shared with Mike Giardi. A first-team All-Ivy and All–New England selection in 1997, his 84-point total was the most by a Harvard player since 1912 and the second most in school history behind Charlie Brickley's 94. A native of Port Chester, New York, Menick has the second-best single-game effort (34 attempts for 261 yards) in Crimson annals.

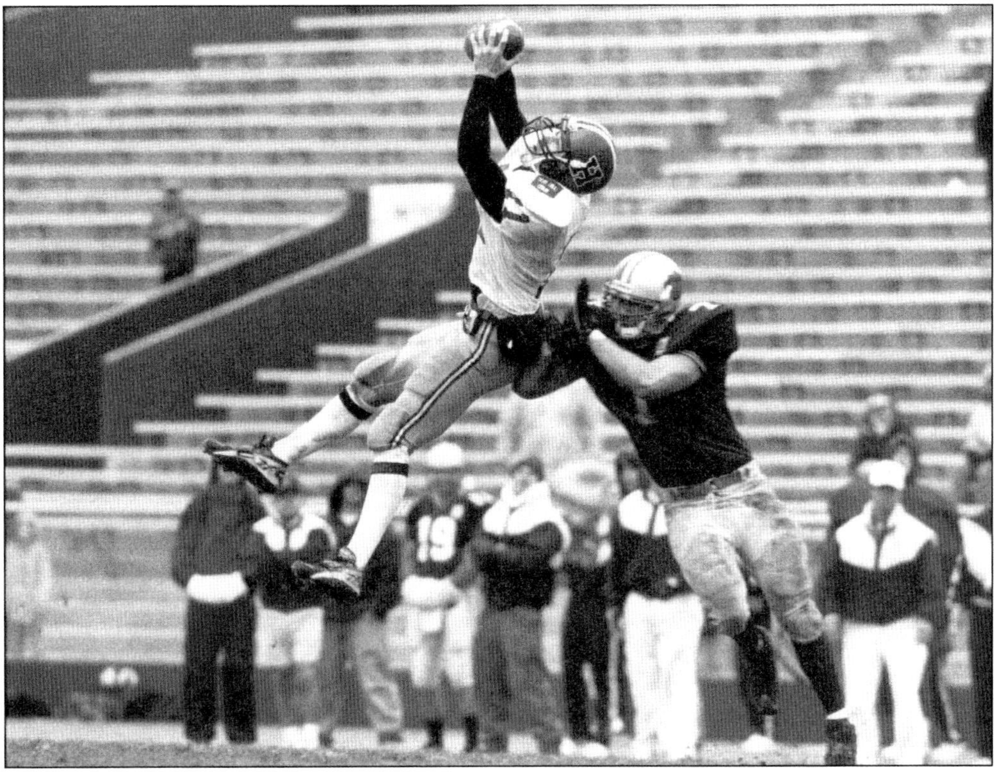

COLBY SKELTON '98 AND JARED CHUPAILA '98. Quarterback Rich Linden was blessed with an array of impressive targets in Harvard's multiple wide-out formations. Seniors Colby Skelton and Jared Chupaila both put together solid, sure-handed efforts, closing out their respective careers as champions. Chupaila's 40 receptions for a 16-yard average per catch placed him second on the team. He was named honorable mention All-Ivy. Meanwhile, Skelton, a consummate possession receiver, finished up as Harvard's all-time career receiving leader, with 127 receptions. An all-purpose player, Skelton established the all-time punt return yardage mark with 825 career yards.

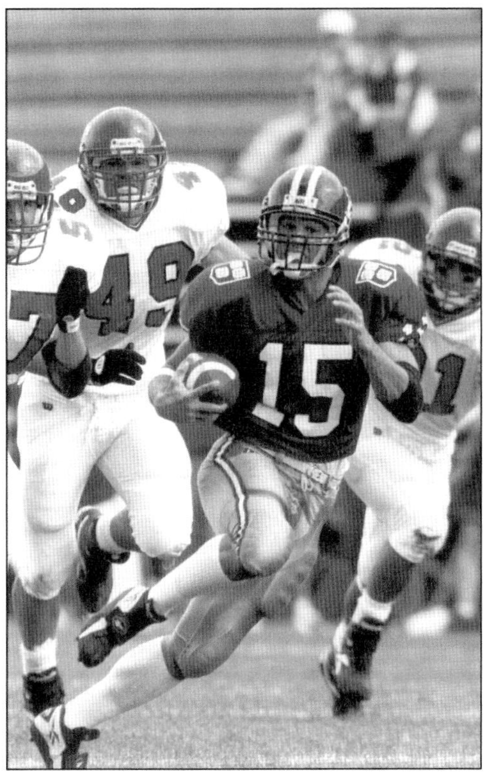

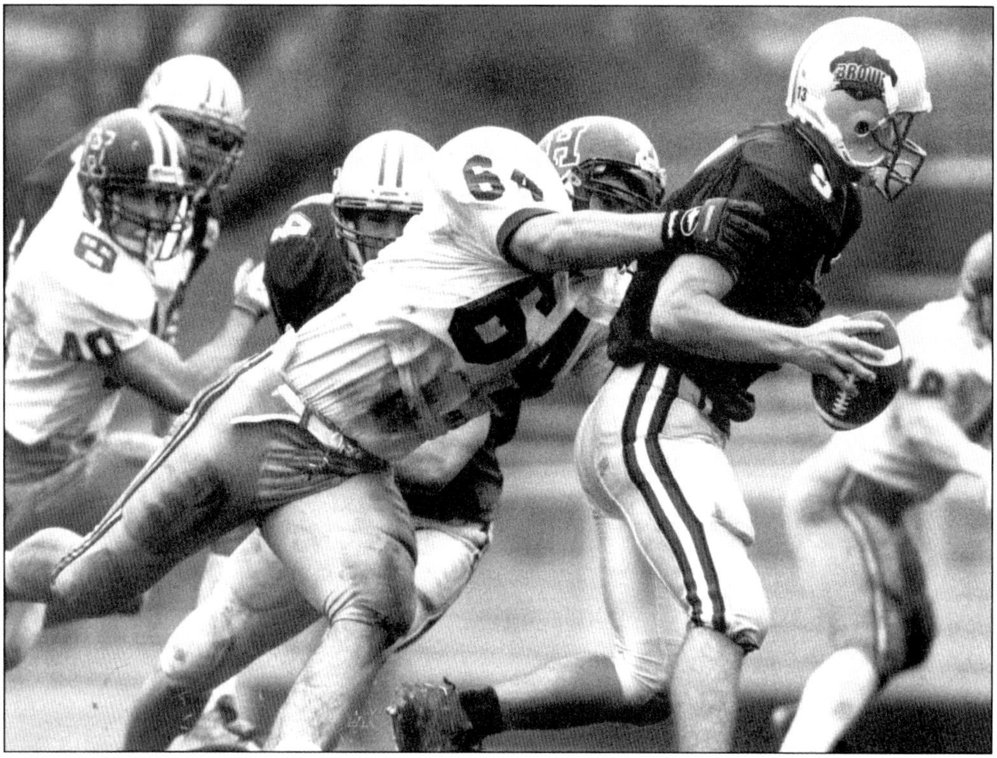

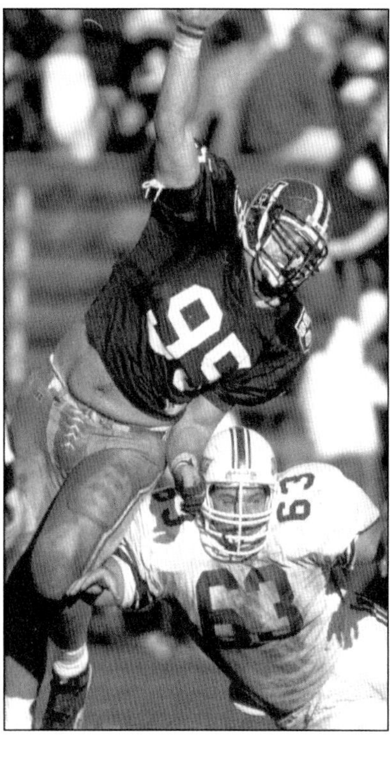

Chris Smith '98 and Jason Hughes '98. Along with Tim Fleszer, Chris Smith (64) and Jason Hughes (95) formed an imposing tandem on the 1997 Harvard Ivy title team's defensive line. Both were named first-team All-Ivy, while Hughes added All–New England honors. Smith was honored for his performance in the classroom by being recognized as a Burger King Scholar Athlete and CoSida Second-Team Academic All-American. He was the team's sack leader with 8.5 and 13 tackles for losses among his 42. Hughes racked up 5.5 sacks and had 10 stops behind the line of scrimmage out of his 44. Smith remains the Harvard all-time sack leader with 20.5.

The Harvard Defense, 1997. The Crimson defense was virtually impenetrable all season in 1997. Statistically, Harvard was the only school in the country at the I-AA level to be ranked in the top five in rushing defense, pass efficiency defense, and scoring defense. Four members of the defense were named first-team All-Ivy. Perhaps the most amazing figure of all was that Harvard allowed just four touchdowns in seven league games and no rushing touchdowns.

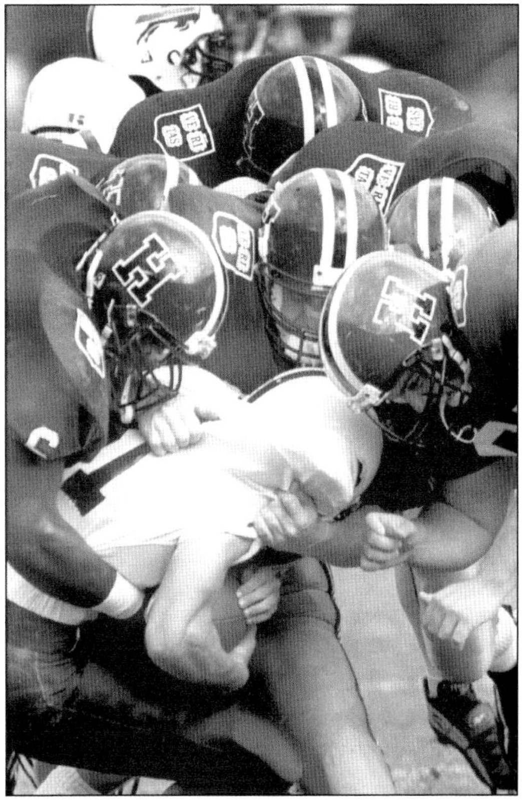

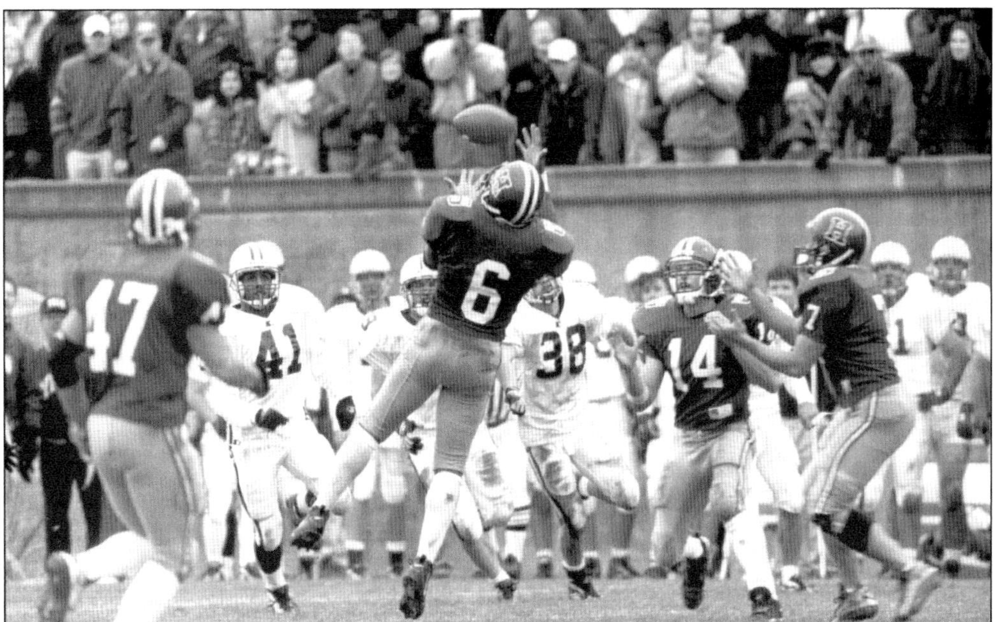

Jeff Compas '98. Not to be overlooked was the play of the Harvard secondary. Jeff Compas, leaping to make one of his 14 career interceptions versus Yale, finished number two all-time in thefts. His 64 tackles, including 49 primary hits, placed him third on the 1997 team as a senior.

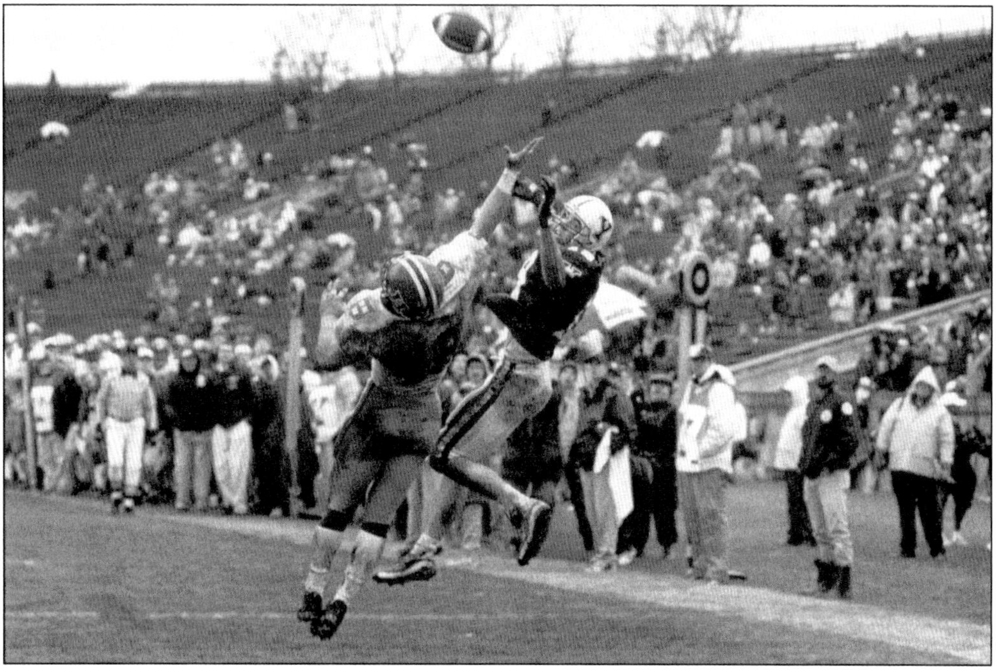

Aron Natale '00. Aron Natale (left) became a big-impact player at the strong safety position in 1997 as a sophomore. His 69 tackles (47 primary) positioned him second behind only Isaiah Kacyvenski. An excellent run force player from the defensive backfield, Natale finished with a total of 276 career tackles, second all-time behind Kacyvenski.

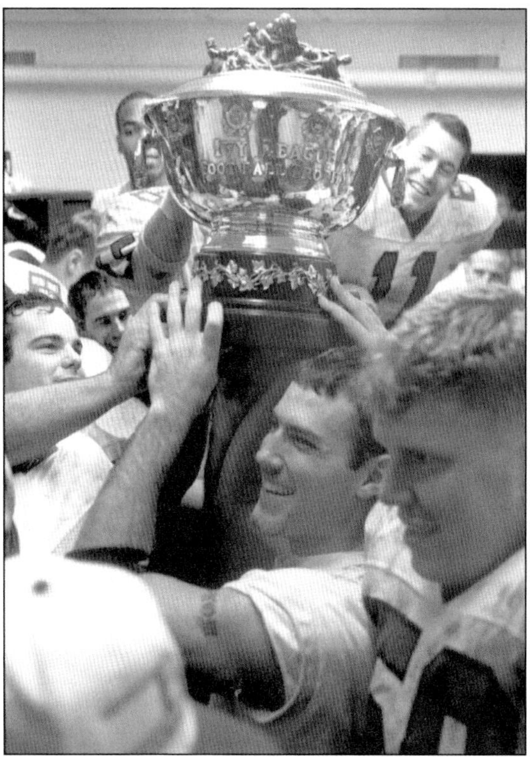

To the Victors. A jubilant group of Harvard players holds the Ivy League football trophy aloft in the locker room at the Yale Bowl after defeating the Eli 17-7. The 1997 title was Harvard's first in a decade. The 7-0 league record marked the first undefeated Ivy season in Crimson history.

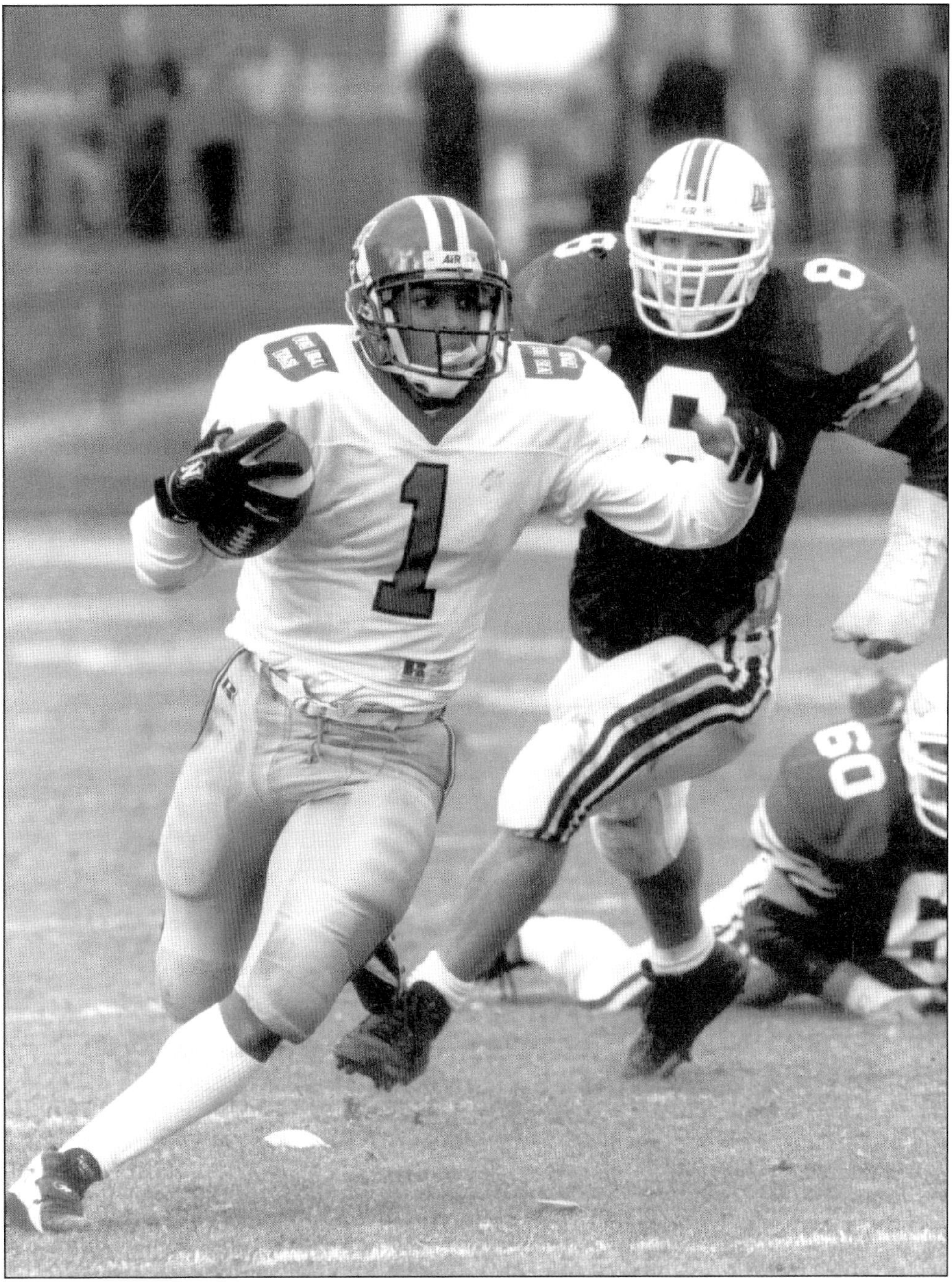

TERENCE PATTERSON '00. A speedy wide receiver from Germantown, Tennessee, Terence Patterson became the Harvard all-time receiving leader with 146 career receptions. Second in school history among punt returners (behind Colby Skelton, the former teammate he overtook on the receiving list), Patterson had the unique distinction of catching, throwing, running, and returning a kick for a touchdown during the first half of his senior year. A two-time All-State quarterback in high school, the leading receiver for the Ivy League champions with 45 receptions made his mark as one of the Crimson's most versatile players.

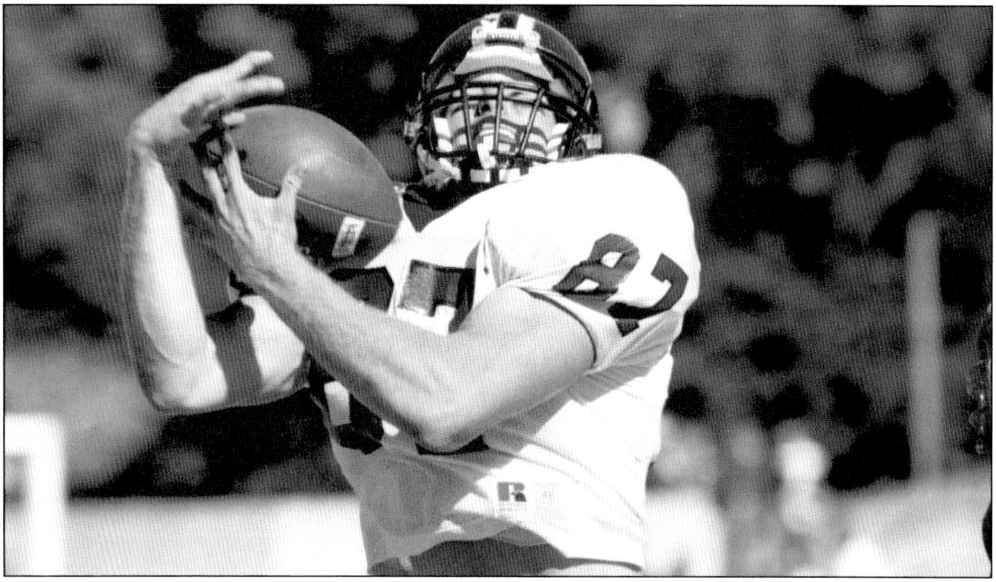

CHRIS EITZMANN '00. A four-year letterman and three-year starter at tight end, Chris Eitzmann had played eight-man football in Nebraska. His high school (Chester-Hubbell-Byron) had a graduating class of just 13. Following his senior year at Harvard (1999), the Crimson captain was named first-team All-Ivy and All–New England. The publication *Successful Farming* named him All–American Farm first team, as an athlete who calls a farm or ranch home. A punishing blocker at 6 feet 5 inches and 250 pounds, Eitzmann caught 45 career passes, which included eight touchdowns. A free-agent signed by the New England Patriots in 2000, Eitzmann saw action with the NFL team in several games during the season.

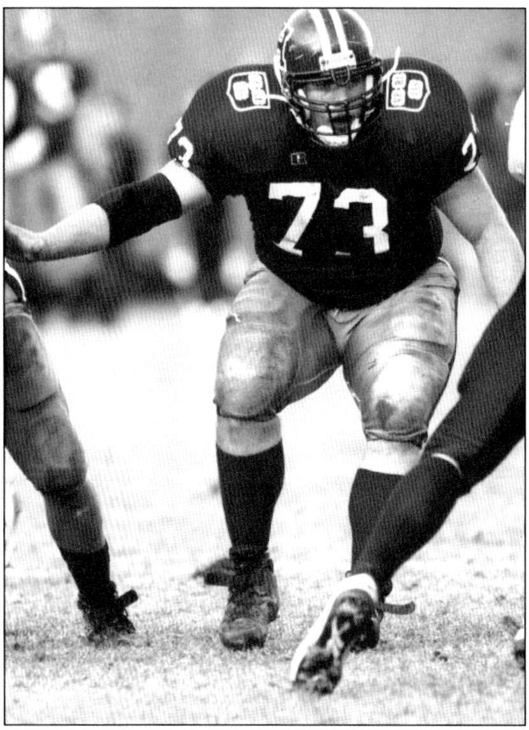

MIKE CLARE '01. A massive specimen at 6 feet 4 inches and 325 pounds, offensive tackle Mike Clare was acknowledged by the American Football Coaches Association as a first-team All-American in 2000. He anchored a Harvard offensive line that set school records for total offense (4,679 yards), first downs (239), and a modern-day record for points (327). Overall, the Crimson offense ranked fifth in the country in yards (467.9 per game) and was established as the number one running attack in the Ivy League (179.4 yards per game). The team captain and MVP from Rutherford, New Jersey, Clare started 30 consecutive games at left tackle.

Chris Nowinski '00. A disruptive force on the defensive line, Chris Nowinski was in on 93 tackles (65 primary) and registered 11 sacks in his final two seasons at Harvard. Quick and athletic, the suburban Chicago (Arlington Heights, Illinois) product attained second-team All-Ivy honors in 1999. He now wrestles for World Wrestling Entertainment.

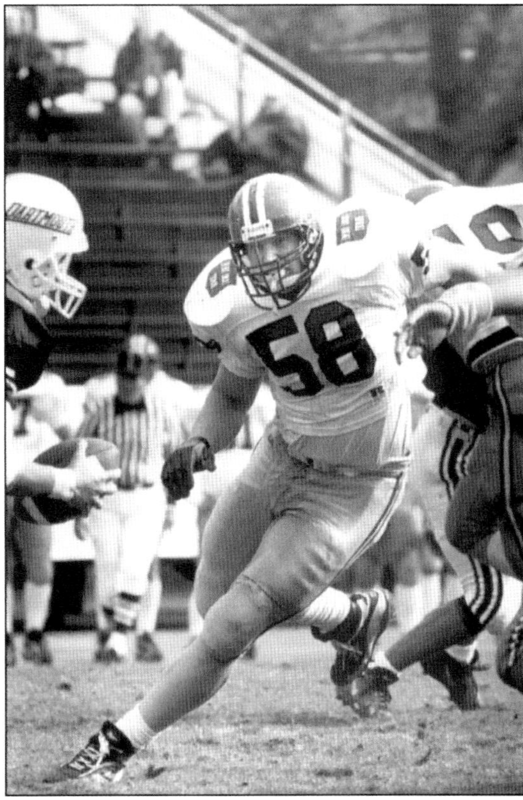

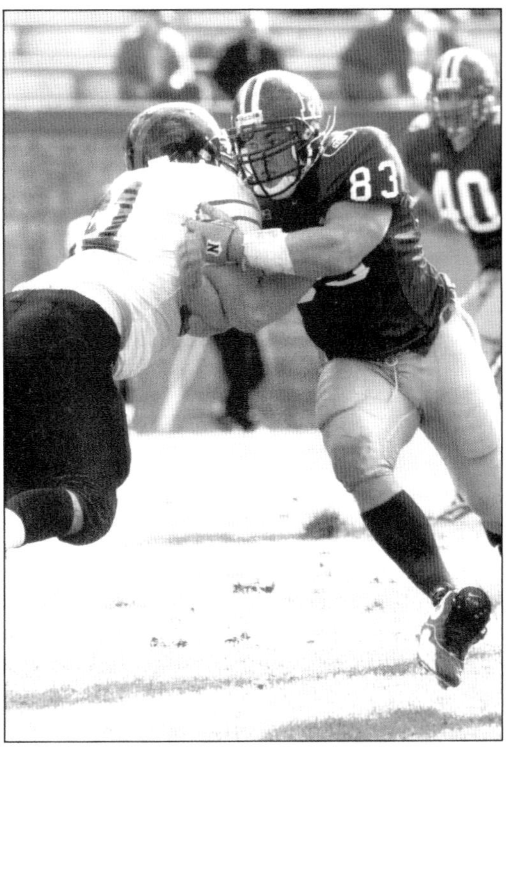

R.D. Kern '01. R.D. Kern saved his best for last as a Crimson player. Playing on a limited basis early in his career at Cambridge, Kern developed into a major impact performer on the defensive line as a senior. The Dallas, Texas, native produced 52 tackles (35 primary), demonstrating his ability as both a run stopper and pass rusher, with four sacks and five tackles for a loss.

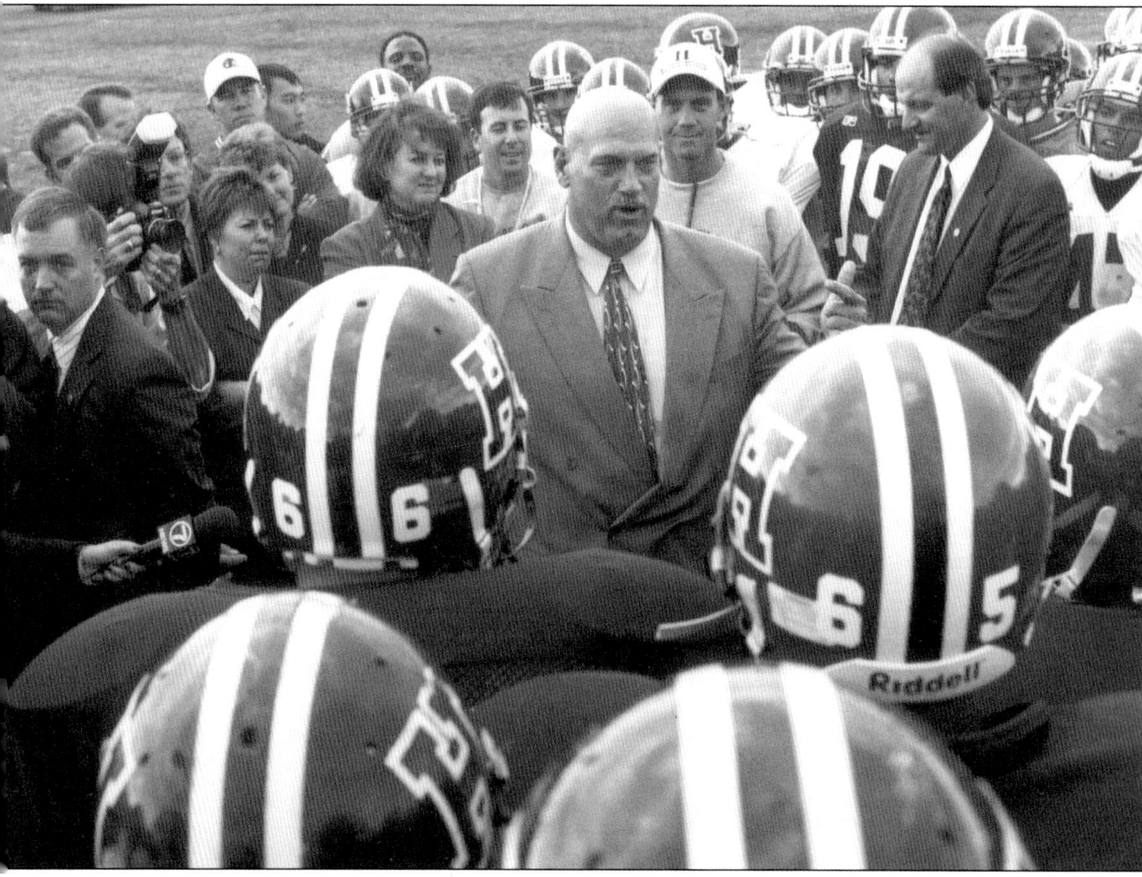

JESSE VENTURA AT HARVARD, 1999. Wrestling legend and current governor of the state of Minnesota, Jesse Ventura took a time-out to address the Harvard football team during a visit to the Cambridge campus in November 1999.

Nine

2000–2001

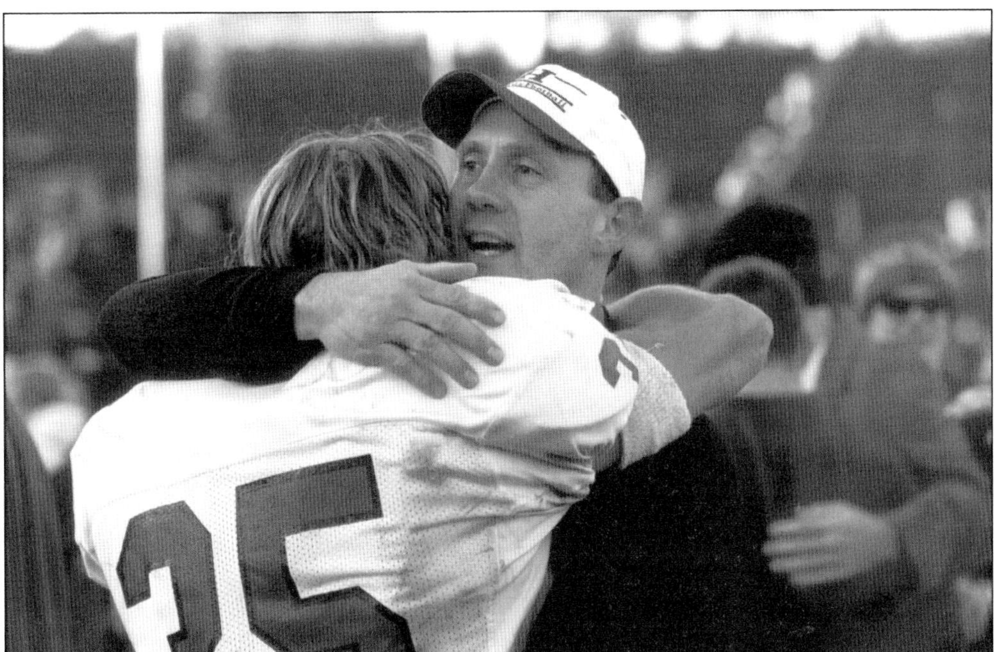

Coach Murphy with Andy Fried (35). Perfection! Coach Tim Murphy embraces senior safety Andy Fried '02 at the conclusion of the 2001 Game. Harvard defeated Yale 35-23 to cap the Crimson's first perfect season in 88 years. Fried made a successful transition from offense (wide receiver) to defense cornerback and was named first-team All-Ivy.

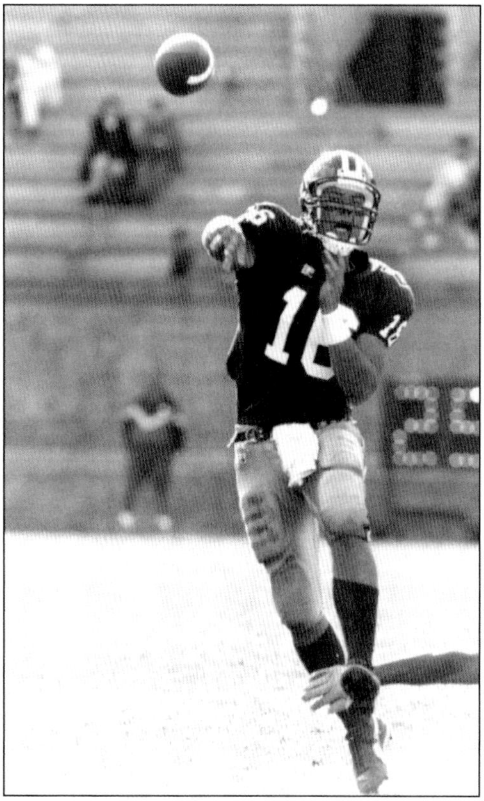

NEIL ROSE '02 AND NICK PALAZZO '03. Quarterback Neil Rose (left) became the Crimson's career leader in yards (4,511), touchdowns (33), and completion percentage (61.1) in 2001. A native Hawaiian in the tradition of Milt "Pineapple" Holt (hero of the Game in 1974), Rose received the Bulger Lowe Award as the Gridiron Club of Boston's New England Player of the Year and garnered first-team All-Ivy and All–New England recognition. Rose's passing and Nick Palazzo's running were a winning combination. The hard-running Palazzo (below) led the Crimson attack with 556 yards, 7 touchdowns, and an impressive 5.1-yards-per-carry average.

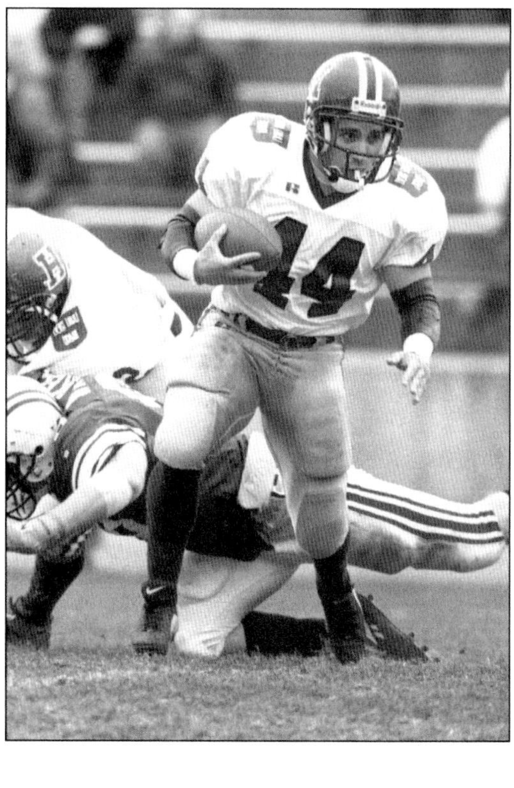

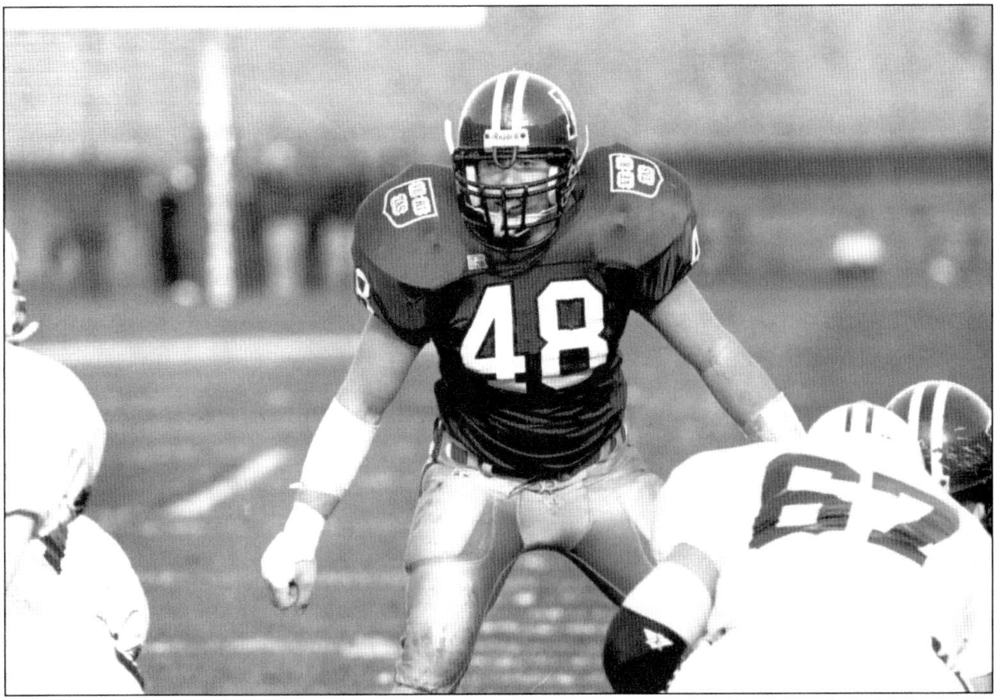

Dante Balestracci '04. Youthful sophomore linebacker Dante Balestracci led the big-play Harvard defense with 58 total tackles, which included 41 primary hits. A unanimous selection as a first-team All-Ivy performer, he also gained first-team All–New England honors.

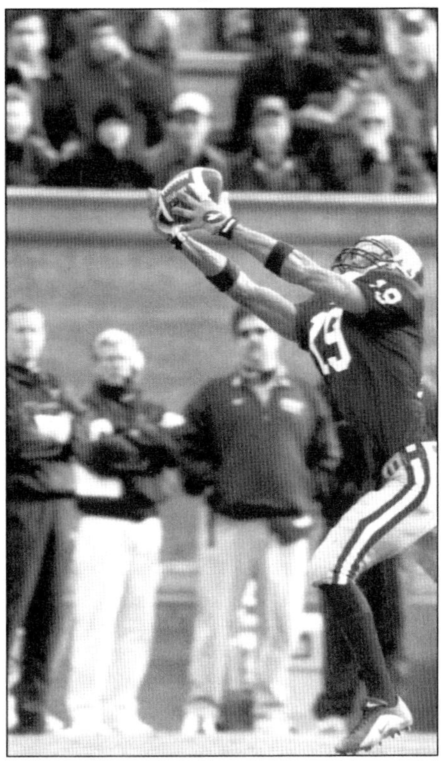

Carl Morris '03. Junior Carl Morris had the greatest season of any wide receiver in the history of Harvard football in 2001. His 71 receptions for 993 yards and 12 touchdowns are now the standards by which all future wide receivers will be judged. The Asa S. Bushnell Trophy winner (as Ivy League Player of the Year) and the New England Sports Writer's Division I-AA Player of the Year, Morris was the offensive question for which no opposing defense seemed to have an answer. A sleek, lethal combination of speed and strength, the 6-foot 3-inch 200-pound native of Sterling, Virginia, was never better than in the Crimson's biggest game. With the Ivy League title on the line and the Crimson trailing 14-7, Morris took the game into his own capable hands. He first scored on a 20-yard pass from Neil Rose to even the game at 14-14. Then Morris completed the season's biggest play with an acrobatic 62-yard catch and dash to the end zone to give the Crimson a lead that was not relinquished. Morris finished the day with 9 catches for 155 yards and two touchdowns.

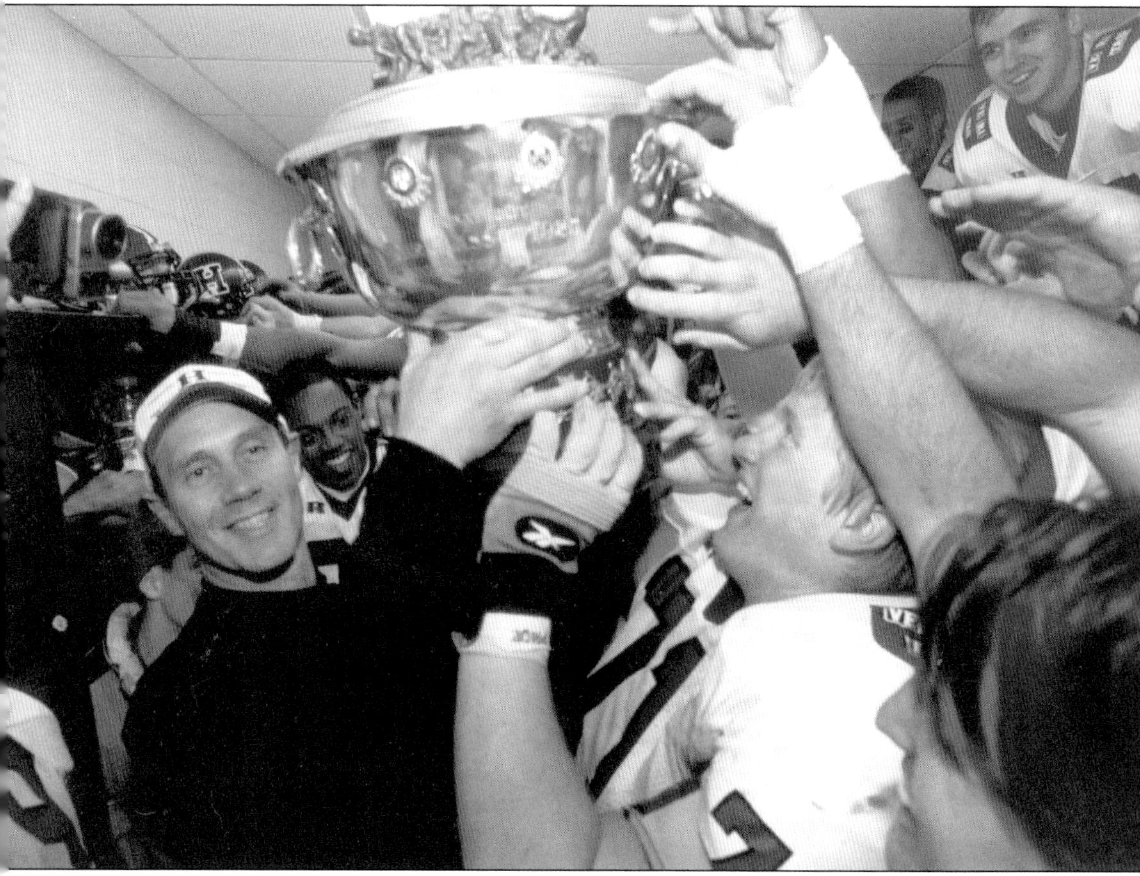

THE CELEBRATION, 2001. Coach Tim Murphy (left) challenged his players one last time prior to their final game at Yale. There was the possibility of sharing the Ivy League title with a loss or tie, but there was the opportunity to make history with victory. The Crimson made history with the victory in New Haven. The 2001 team became the first undefeated, untied team in 88 years. The players will be remembered with all the legends of Harvard's hallowed history.